Selected Papers

of

Benjamin Chapman Browne

Benjamin C. Browne

Selected Papers

on

Social and Economic Questions

BY

Benjamin Chapman Browne, *Knight*

Hon. D.C.L. Durham University
Deputy-Lieutenant for the County of Northumberland

Edited by his Daughters
E. M. B. *and* H. M. B.

Cambridge
At the University Press
1918

CAMBRIDGE
UNIVERSITY PRESS

University Printing House, Cambridge CB2 8BS, United Kingdom

Cambridge University Press is part of the University of Cambridge.

It furthers the University's mission by disseminating knowledge in the pursuit of education, learning and research at the highest international levels of excellence.

www.cambridge.org
Information on this title: www.cambridge.org/9781107536999

First published 1918
First paperback edition 2015

A catalogue record for this publication is available from the British Library

ISBN 978-1-107-53699-9 Paperback

PREFACE

FROM among many papers by Sir Benjamin Browne, the following thirty-two have been selected as the most useful and characteristic. While many existed only in manuscript or in the fugitive form of letters or articles to daily papers, some have already appeared in magazines, and for leave to reprint these, we desire to express our thanks to the Editors of the *National Review*, the *Times* and the *Engineer*, and at the same time to offer our apologies if we have in any instance failed to ask permission.

Sir Benjamin Browne felt strongly that when the great underlying principles of life had once been discerned, they could be applied to politics, industrial questions, and private conduct alike. These were the permanent Form, into which could be moulded the material of each day's events as they arose. This necessarily involved a certain amount of repetition in his writings, because, in discussing different questions before different listeners, or in approaching them from different standpoints, he came back again and again to these underlying principles, and drove them home by reiterated blows. Reading through his scattered writings is like listening to a sonata where three or four leading themes dominate the music, emerging repeatedly in varying keys, and giving coherence to the whole.

The dates when the various papers were written must of course be borne in mind, as some of the statistics, accurate at the time, may have altered. The date of each paper is printed at the head of the page. From the historic point of view, they show the consistent evolution of his opinions.

One good result of this disastrous war may be that all classes of the nation, with conscience aroused, may attack the problems of the industrial world in a better spirit. Sir Benjamin Browne wrote to one of his oldest friends, "I often think, if I had my industrial life to live over again, I would appeal far more to people's hearts, and not trouble so much about their heads"; and these questions were always to him alive with human interest. But he knew that however kindly the heart may be, the *facts that govern* political economy must be known and faced; so he gave continued thought and study to these facts, convinced that schemes of reform must be built on the rock of truth, not on the sands of sentiment.

These papers are published in the hope that the experience embodied in them may help some of those who are turning to study these questions in a new and better mood.

The editors offer their warmest thanks to Professor Edward Browne for his help in seeing the book through the press, and to Mr Benjamin Browne for his advice as to the selection of the papers.

E. M. B.
H. M. B.

WESTACRES,
NEWCASTLE-UPON-TYNE.
April 1918.

TABLE OF CONTENTS

viii   Table of Contents

INTRODUCTION

TO this small volume of selected articles by the late Sir
Benjamin Browne, a short sketch of his life has been prefixed,
in the hope that it may both serve as a key to his writings, and
recall him, in some measure, to his friends, though it cannot hope
to give, to those who never knew him, any adequate idea of the
attraction of his character.

Benjamin Chapman Browne was born on August 26th, 1839,
at Stouts Hill, Uley, Gloucestershire. His father, Colonel Benjamin
Chapman Browne, was colonel first of the 9th Lancers and then
of the Gloucestershire Yeomanry, and his mother was Miss Baker
of Hardwicke Court, Gloucestershire. He was the youngest of
their three sons, and grew up among a large circle of cousins, all
living in the same county. His home, Stouts Hill, was a long
picturesque grey house, situated in one of the loveliest of the
Cotswold valleys, the sides of the hills being covered with beech
and larch woods, carpeted in spring with bluebells. He spent his
early years in the ordinary pastimes of a boy in the country. His
home was in a hunting neighbourhood, and the Duke of Beaufort's
and the Berkeley hounds afforded many a day's sport to himself
and his brothers.

The associations of his boyhood were of the happiest description.
To the end of his life, Gloucestershire was very dear to him, and
even after fifty years of life and work in the north, his heart
always turned to the old county, and anyone with a connection
or introduction from Gloucestershire was sure of a warm welcome.
Once after he had spoken at some public meeting, he related with
delight how a stranger had accosted him afterwards with the
remark, "If I may judge by your speech, Sir, you come from the
West country, as I do myself."

His father died very suddenly, while on a visit to his half-brother, Mr. Orde of Nunnykirk, in Northumberland, when Sir Benjamin was a boy of fourteen; and from then, till the time of his marriage, his widowed mother, a woman of unusual force of character and great personal piety, was the chief influence in his life. He was educated at Westminster, and at King's College, London, but at the age of seventeen, he came to Newcastle-upon-Tyne, to serve his apprenticeship under Sir William Armstrong, at the Elswick works. It was the time of the Crimean War, and his elder brothers were both in the army. His great wish was to enter it too, but at his mother's strongly expressed desire to keep one of her sons at home, he consented to forego it, turned his mind in a different direction, and decided to study engineering.

He was not a born mechanician, like some men. He never aspired to the high technical knowledge of many of his colleagues. What attracted him was the idea of the management of a large number of men, and the co-operation of brain and hand workers for some special end. If he could not be a leader in war, he wished to be one in peace. He seemed born to be what, in the phrase of a later date, is known as a "captain of industry." Neither he nor any of his family had the slightest knowledge of business. He had everything to find out for himself, as to his own training and start. His relations were all either quiet country gentlemen, clergymen, or soldiers. This perhaps gives the key to his whole attitude towards industrial problems. He had in his blood the traditions of the squire, to whom the people dependent on him were the first charge on his income and care, and those of the commanding officer, whose men were as his children, to be trained, led, and kept in the highest possible state of efficiency. The necessity of any antagonism between employer and employed was absolutely foreign to his ideas. I think to the very last it gave him a shock of pained surprise when people spoke as if the interests of the two were opposed to each other. He would as soon have thought of husband and wife, or parent and child, as necessarily in opposition.

At the age of twenty-one, he married Annie, daughter of Mr. Robert Thomas Atkinson, of High Cross House, Benwell, Newcastle-upon-Tyne, and step-daughter of the Rev. William Maughan, the first vicar of Benwell; and they kept their golden wedding together several years before his death. Of his home-life, all that need be said is that it was one of almost unclouded happiness. He had nine children, of whom two died in very early childhood; the others, three sons and four daughters, survive him.

At first he worked as a civil engineer, which he greatly liked. The making of roads, piers, bridges and so on, was to him a very enjoyable and satisfactory branch of engineering. He used to say, "It is a great thing to have your theories tested at once. If your political scheme is a mistaken one, it may take years to prove it so; but if your theory of a bridge is not right, it tumbles down." He worked on the Falmouth harbour works, on the pier at the mouth of the Tyne, and for several happy years in the Isle of Man, at both Castletown and Douglas; but in 1870, the claims of a rapidly increasing family made him anxious for more settled work, and an opening offered itself of taking over the engine works of Messrs. R. and W. Hawthorn, Newcastle-upon-Tyne. It was a very large undertaking for a man of his age to find the capital and the management. He has told the whole story of it in his *History of the new Firm of R. and W. Hawthorn*, and how it was only the loyal support of his bankers and lifelong friends, Dr. Thomas Hodgkin and Mr. John William Pease, that enabled him to carry it through. In the first year of his work as senior partner, before things had got into any sort of shape, he was confronted with the great Nine Hours' Strike. It was a time of terrible strain and anxiety from every point of view, and it put an end to his youth once and for all.

Responsibilities and cares thickened, chiefly responsibility for the capital entrusted to him by relations and friends, and care for the men in his employment, that sufficient orders should be forthcoming to keep them in full work, and it was many years before he felt he had got his head above water.

He did not however confine his energies to his own works. He had inherited what is vaguely described as "philanthropy." His mother's great-uncle was Granville Sharp, the man who, by doggedly carrying the test-case of Jonathan Strong, the escaped negro slave, from one tribunal to another, finally forced the judges to give the historic decision that slavery is illegal on English soil. His own uncle, Mr. Barwick Baker, was one of the original founders of the scheme of reformatories for boys, after their first conviction, and had built one of the earliest on his own estate at Hardwicke Court. Questions connected with the Poor Law always stirred Sir Benjamin's deepest interest. He was one of the original supporters of the Charity Organization Society in Newcastle, and attended regularly for some years the Poor Law Conference at Gilsland. He was on the committee of the Netherton Reformatory, one of the Prison visiting committee, was a magistrate for Newcastle and the counties of Northumberland and Gloucestershire, and worked hard as a Guardian. He interested himself actively in the original founding of the Durham College of Science, Newcastle-upon-Tyne, feeling how important it was that the young men and boys of an industrial district should have within their reach opportunities of high-class scientific education. It was in recognition of this work that the Durham University conferred on him the honorary degree of D.C.L.

He was elected to the Newcastle Town Council in 1879, and threw himself warmly into municipal work. He greatly enjoyed coming into contact with all classes of the community, and the welfare of his adopted town was very dear to him. He was chosen Mayor of Newcastle for 1885–6 and 1886–7, and these two years, though busy and tiring, were years of great interest to him. An exhibition the first year, and the Royal Agricultural Show the second, both held at Newcastle, brought him much extra work but also much pleasure. King Edward VII, then Prince of Wales, visited the Royal Show, and with his keen insight into men, took marked opportunities of learning the views and experiences of his host the Mayor. Shortly afterwards, when all the Mayors were summoned to attend a meeting at St. James' Palace about the foundation of the Imperial Institute, the Prince of Wales singled him out with the special request that he would speak on the subject. Sir Benjamin was greatly pleased at the compliment, but took it as being paid entirely to the town he represented and not to himself.

It was after his strenuous work in connection with the New-castle Exhibition that Sir Benjamin received the honour of knighthood at the hands of Queen Victoria at Osborne, in her jubilee year, June 1887. Some years later, he complied with the wish of the Lord-Lieutenant of Northumberland that he should be one of his Deputy-Lieutenants.

On his retirement from the mayoralty he bought Westacres, a pleasant house in the parish of Benwell, in which he spent the last thirty years of his life. When Hawthorns' was turned into a limited company, he became Chairman, which office he only resigned a few months before his death.

In the course of his various avocations, he necessarily had to give very careful attention to trade and commercial problems, and above all to labour questions, in which he took the most intense interest. Very early in his business career, he saw clearly that if there was any reality at all in political economy, it ought to be applied to practical business life. He gave great study to this subject, and wrote a number of articles, both in British and American magazines, including some notable articles in the *Times*, on various aspects of Capital and Labour. But perhaps his most conspicuous work was in connection with labour disputes. Being associated with the employment of labour not only in engineering and shipbuilding, but also in the Northumberland and Durham coal trades, he had an exceptional experience, and he was always anxious that such disputes should be treated with sympathy in regard to the difficulties of both sides.

In 1905 he was a member of the special committee of the Home
Office to enquire into the working of the Workmen's Compensation
Act, and to make recommendations as to future legislation. He
was frequently called upon to give evidence before various Royal
Commissions on such subjects as the municipalization of various
industries, unemployment, Trades Unionism, recruiting, and
many other matters.

He passed through a period of much work in connection with
the formation of the Engineering Employers' Federation of which
he was for some time Vice-Chairman, and had constant and
exhausting demands on his strength and energy in matters connected with the settlement of strikes. He always maintained that
the day was not far distant when differences would be arranged
by amicable discussion and mutual compromise, and when the
old fighting methods would become as obsolete as duelling.

For working-men as a class, he felt the warmest affection.
There was no trouble he would not take to put their cause on a
permanently better footing; and it was always a singular pleasure
to him to have a talk with one of his workmen, or with some old
foreman under whom he had worked at Elswick, while he was on
terms of warm personal friendship with many of the Trades
Union and Labour leaders. But he deeply deplored the well-
meant but ill-judged interference of theorists, whether politicians,
journalists, or clergymen; and he looked upon those who deliberately tried to stir up class antagonism as madmen, flinging about
firebrands.

But his interests were not limited to the problems connected
with the workers in towns. His early life and friendships had
taught him to understand those who farm and labour on the land,
and had also given him a strong feeling for the small employers
of labour in villages and country towns, whose point of view is
so often overlooked.

His personality was one of exceptional charm. From an Irish
grandmother he inherited his sense of fun, his love of a good

story, his wit and quick repartee. Conversation was his chief recreation. He delighted in the exchange of ideas, and the exploration of other people's point of view. When increasing deafness prevented his joining in general conversation he still enjoyed nothing more than a tête-à-tête with a friend.

Between his busy public life and his happy home circle, he had not much leisure for general society, but he thoroughly appreciated it, and added lustre and interest to any party at which he was present, while his sparkling eyes and gay talk were a proof that he received as much pleasure as he gave.

He was a great reader, as far as the many claims on his time permitted, history being his favourite subject, and had explored various unusual by-ways of archæology and fairy lore, as well as of natural history. It was very characteristic of him that during the two busy years of his mayoralty, he re-read all the Waverley novels, finding his greatest relaxation in the manly and open-air romances of the idol of his boyhood.

His generosity was unbounded. Money was to him, in very truth, only of value in so far as it enabled him to supply the wants of others. What he gave in subscription lists was only a small part. Even those nearest to him were constantly finding out unsuspected instances of help given on a large scale, to tide one over a difficult time in business, to educate the son of another, or to enable a third to take a much-needed holiday. He simply could not refuse money to anyone who asked him for it, and when his family laughed at the obviously undeserving recipients of some of his half-crowns, he would answer, "Cold and hunger are no easier for a bad man to bear than for a good one." His lavishness in giving was the more striking, as his own tastes were simple in the extreme, and to spend money on personal pleasure or luxury never seemed to occur to him. Nor was it that he was vaguely reckless in regard to money. On the contrary, he had a very marked gift for finance, seeming to know by instinct when to venture and when to hold back.

His friendships ranged over an extraordinarily wide social area, and included men and women alike. He was always much interested in the young, and was never happier than when he could help them by talking out their difficulties with them. He liked to hear their youthful theories, though his questions were on the Socratic lines, and would often pierce their cloud-built edifices with some shrewd practical enquiry. He loved original thought, and was always sorry when he found clever young men or women reproducing, as their own, views current in newspapers or magazines, without having assimilated them. On one such, his comment was, "She wants to go out alone into the wilderness and *think*."

Both by nature and tradition he was essentially chivalrous. In reading his writings, it is easy to see how, when discussing any legislative change, he did not heed its effect on the successful and rising young workman, so much as on the elderly or failing man, the struggling small employer, the crippled, one-eyed, infirm, and all those handicapped in the race of life. Though always ready to appreciate efficiency and capability, yet his sympathy was ever with the "lame dogs." It was possible for him, at any rate in earlier life, to be impatient or vehement with his equals, but towards the unfortunate or downtrodden his patience and gentleness were unfailing.

He was a faithful and devoted son of the Church of England, and to the very close of his life held that the Church Catechism was a complete guide to the practice of religion. His mother, who was the great influence of his boyhood, had been a disciple of the Oxford movement, and this was the atmosphere in which he grew up. As a young man, he came under some very strong evangelical influence, which for a time made a great impression on him. As he grew older, however, his deep and true personal religion transcended lesser differences. These things are almost too sacred to write about. The fruits of his faith were visible in his life and conduct. Numerous letters after his death spoke of him as "the ideal of a Christian gentleman," but only those who lived with him could have any idea of the closeness of his walk with God, the earnestness and reality of his prayers, and how, as the years went on, he was increasingly enabled to live more nearly as he prayed.

For the last months of his life, he suffered from growing heart-trouble, and after ten days of acute illness, in the early morning of Thursday, March 1st, 1917, he passed through the valley of the shadow into the fuller light and joy beyond.

When Mr. Valiant-for-Truth understood the summons, he said, "My sword I give to him that shall succeed me in my pilgrimage, and my courage and skill to him that can get it. My marks and scars I carry with me, to be a witness for me that I have fought His battles who will now be my Rewarder." So he passed over, and all the trumpets sounded for him on the other side.

I

Presidential Address to Northern Union of Mechanics' Institutions

[Aug. 10th, 1886]

I FEAR that, in comparing my address with those of my predecessors, it will appear very uneven and disjointed; but I have tried to bring forward a view of the proper position of the working classes which is apt to be overlooked, and from that I shall pass rather abruptly to a few social and legislative questions which may be considered to bear on their welfare and prosperity; and the whole address will, I fear, like everything around us, be in some degree overshadowed by the gloom of the prevailing commercial depression. It is within a few days of thirty years since I first started work as an engineer apprentice at Elswick, and although, since I have been an employer, I have had my attention much and sometimes entirely diverted from constructive engineering by commercial and other matters, still it would have been difficult to spend so large a portion of my life in, or in charge of, the workshop without forming some ideas about the mechanic, his training, his surroundings, and his future.

A MECHANIC DEFINED.

What do we mean by a mechanic? in what does he differ from other men? and how do we propose that he should improve himself? We live in a time when much energy is devoted to the education both of the young and the older. Depressed trade and keen competition have further urged us to endeavour to increase the ability of our producers, and a mechanic's institution is both theoretically and practically a focus of technical, scientific, and literary teaching for the benefit of our mechanics and apprentices, and of a few others. But to consider the ways in which a class is to be improved or developed, or in which the members of it are to improve themselves, we must be sure that first we see clearly what they are like now, what are their essential characteristics, and what we would wish them to be. Now, what is a mechanic? I take it he is not merely a man who has acquired practical information on certain technical subjects, nor merely a man who has learned to perform certain processes with his hands; but he is a man who, having commenced his training in boyhood, has had his whole nature modified and certain faculties very much developed in accordance with the sphere of work to which he has devoted his life and energies. Eye, ear, and hand are quickened, so that he knows and feels more than other men, and can do more than other men. He must have what is really sympathy with the material, such as wood or metal, that he works in; or with the steam, gas, or electricity that works his engine. He knows the feel of every substance that he works on, and the sound that should respond to his blow or touch; and he has the art of using his tools with the greatest ease to himself, and the greatest benefit to the material on which he expends his skill and force. To be a good mechanic is the result of long years of careful training; and almost always of training in youth, while body as well as mind is very susceptible. It is rare for a man who does not learn his art as a boy to become a really good mechanic; we may teach him one or two processes, but he seldom becomes a good all-round man, who knows by instinct in an emergency what ought to be done, and whose hands at once know how to adapt themselves to new conditions. Add to this that a man ought to love his work, and be proud of his calling, and you have a fair specimen of the British mechanic.

EDUCATION FOR MECHANICS.

Now, while in this man there may be, and often is, much room for improvement, there is also much that may be spoiled. In these days we want to give him as much scientific knowledge as we possibly can, but we must take care not to weaken his practical efficiency. Soon after the School Boards came into operation, several of us, enamoured of school training, took to engaging our apprentices two or sometimes three years later than before, but we soon found that this was wrong, and that it was easy to go too far in this direction. An apprentice should begin work as a boy, not as a young man. If my view is correct, we must then chiefly provide such education as may be obtained in an evening after work hours; and I am sorry to say that I think it ought to be considered absolutely necessary for every apprentice to spend a great proportion of his evenings at classes, or in educational work of some sort. The classes that are generally provided by mechanics' institutions are, in my experience, admirable; and the good they do is incalculable. A lad who, during his apprenticeship, attends such classes with diligence, ought, when he becomes a journeyman, to have a sound groundwork of scientific knowledge that should not only be a foundation on which he can go on building all his life, but in itself should be sufficient to keep him from any serious scientific errors. The man may continue to learn either in these classes or elsewhere; for broader culture he can avail himself of the numberless organizations that now exist everywhere, such as the University Extension Movement, Public Libraries, etc. The more education a man can get, the better, provided that his health and spirits do not suffer, and provided always that we never let theoretical training take the place of practical skill. I fear that to keep up the standard we must not look with favour on any schemes that involve the taking of a man for any length of time from his work. Short absences I think are often best utilized as real holidays. Long absences may be sometimes necessary, but I think they are rarely beneficial. Movements have sometimes been set on foot to send working men to our universities, but I never thought them satisfactory, except in those cases where the man was permanently destined for a literary life; and such has nothing to do with the improvement of mechanics. Now a few men will always be found

to attain to brilliant results in the way of self-improvement. Such
should be watched for, and helped forward as much as possible,
but we must also consider carefully how best we can improve the
average man, and even the stupid man. The strength of a chain is
the strength of its weakest link, and though I do not say that the
efficiency of a workshop is to be measured by the efficiency of the
worst workman in it, still it must be remembered that whatever
he contributes to the general output will be below the average,
and will lower the average accordingly. More economical work
means more perfect machinery; and more perfect machinery requires higher-class attendance to keep it in order; *e.g.* a modern
triple expansion marine engine, working at a high speed, requires
far more sustained and intelligent supervision than an old-
fashioned jet-condensing, low-pressure engine of bygone days.

NEED FOR INCREASED EFFICIENCY.

But in case anyone should ask, "Why all this talk about increased efficiency and higher-class work?" I need only remind you
of our depressed trade, and you will agree that we must do all in
our power to increase our efficiency and to satisfy our customers.
For this, two things are essential: first, to find out what people
want to buy; and then, to supply them as well and as cheaply as
possible. It is often thought that Englishmen, both manufacturers
and workmen, are too apt to make what they think people ought
to buy instead of what the customer himself prefers. They say,
"This would really be far best for him if he only had the sense to
see it"; but it is an old proverb that "the man who pays the piper
has a right to call for the tune," and both our sense of justice and
our self-interest ought to overcome our prejudice and make us
acknowledge that the purchaser must be the absolute judge of
what he requires. Some time, not long ago, many engineers, myself among the number, took opportunities publicly to deplore the
fact that we were compelled, by price and efficiency combined, to
use foreign instead of British steel-castings in our engines, etc.

We could not get English makers to supply them at a reasonable price free from honeycombs. The Englishmen declared that their steel was far stronger and better, even with the honeycombs, than the foreign castings without. Perhaps this was true, but our customers would not accept the honeycombed castings from us, so we could not take them from the makers. But after a great deal of fuss and trouble our steelmakers took up the question in earnest, and I believe that to-day the average of English steel-castings are as sound as foreign castings, not more expensive, and decidedly stronger. Again, the manufacture of light iron girders for building was, practically, for many years a monopoly of Belgium. Now, I understand, girders can be bought on the Tees at the same price and of better quality. So with nearly all the articles of manufacture in which we have been surpassed by foreigners. We must carefully and most earnestly study and spend time and money to find out what people want to buy and give them that, and not something else; and we must never abandon the attempt to produce something always better than before, and at a diminishing price. But I must again remind you that the highest science and the most artistic taste will not make your manufactures good unless you have the trained skill of the high-class mechanic to carry them into effect.

TRADES UNIONS.

I would now pass on, and ask you to consider with me how good trade, bad trade, prosperity, or adversity will affect the mechanic himself, and also how he can affect them. Has he, by his ability and energy, made our trade? or has he, by greed and ignorance, ruined it? This brings us face to face with some of the gravest social problems of the day; may we be given wisdom to study them in a courageous, unprejudiced, and unselfish manner! And now we rise more to the tone of the addresses of my predecessors; we no longer take our tone from the ledger and workshop, but from the highest light of benevolence and Christianity. Not that I would disparage the tone of the workshop if we adopt it honestly and loyally. St Augustine truly says, "Little things are little things; but to be faithful in little things is great." The first general question that we must touch on, and without which the position of the mechanic can hardly be properly considered, is the trades union question. While mechanics themselves are proud of the position and influence of their unions, many people look on them as most mischievous and as having contributed not a little to the depression of our trade. My own impression, after many years' experience, is that workmen's unions are not only beneficial to the men, but are also an advantage to employers. No doubt unions are sometimes well and sometimes badly managed; sometimes union leaders make great mistakes, but on the other hand their constant attention keeps the working men out of many errors, and gives them both more information and wider views than they could get otherwise. Their faults probably amount to neither more nor less than those of railway companies or other public bodies and organizations; and if they sometimes keep up wages when they had better not, they sometimes make an important reduction with a speed and reliability that would be impossible if men had to be dealt with singly or in undefined groups.

WAGES.

As to what wages may be in the future it is hard to say. If the productive power of each man be very much increased, wages might remain where they are, but it must be remembered that the greatly reduced price of all the necessaries of life makes it possible for the rate of wages to be reduced without the standard of comfort being lowered. We cannot now investigate the abstract principles or the practical considerations that should govern a body of men in asking for an advance of wages or accepting a reduction; but I believe the question is capable of being reduced to a few broad principles which are not difficult of application, assuming always that workmen want to get as much for their labour as they fairly can, and do not, of course, wish to destroy or injure the trade by which they live.

But there are other social, and especially legislative questions which may affect the well-being of the mechanic; and those that interest us most are those that are likely to affect the present depression of trade. Some people advocate fair trade as a remedy for our evils. I cannot see my way to approve of it. For the moment it might alleviate, but only to produce a worse state of things afterwards. It would draw too much capital and labour into certain trades, and when they became as unremunerative as they are now, every way out of the condition of things then existing would be very disastrous indeed. We have our share of the trade of the world, but we want more than our share—except, of course, in that greatest of industries, agriculture. Some recent legislation connected with the working classes has, however, influenced seriously our position in the trading world. The Employers' Liability Bill brought about a distinct improvement on the old state of things, but further legislation in that direction would require much careful thought. No Act was more important to this district than the Mines Regulation Act; but, though in many ways beneficial, I fear there is no doubt that it very materially increased the cost of working coal. What the actual increase may be, I cannot of my own knowledge say; it is frequently stated that the working of this Act increased the cost of coal 1s. per ton; but if it increased the cost 9d., or even 6d., it is evident that it materially cripples the sale of British coal as against foreign. If our Northumberland coalowners could reduce their selling price 6d. per ton, they would bring to this country an enormous increase of orders which would enable thousands of men to work regularly who are now only partially employed or altogether idle. I have had the privilege of examining and verifying the accounts and working cost of steamers trading under foreign flags as compared with precisely identical work done under the British flag. I am sorry to say the results are not gratifying. Comparing the two, I find the wages for men and officers per month to work out thus:— English crew, £130 per month; foreign crew, £90. The foreigners are steady, sober, skilful men; and though perhaps they have hardly the dash and energy of Englishmen, yet they are not deficient in these points, and the foreign officers have the reputation of being very able men of business. In insurance and other matters I do not observe much difference. One point in our regulations I do think unfair, which is that while a British ship has a fixed load line weighted below which she may not go to sea, a foreign ship may jeopardize the lives and safety of the crew by leaving the port with an amount of cargo very much in excess of what is allowed to the English vessel. I think a vessel sailing from an English port should only carry what English law declares to be safe. I don't at all complain of our laws for the safety of miners and sailors, but nothing can be got for nothing, and in expressing satisfaction at this legislation, it is just as well to see what the cost of it really is.

GENERAL PRINCIPLES.

As to the state of trade. I will take the liberty of making a few remarks which I would impress, not on account of their novelty, but of their importance. The prosperity of a country does not depend only on its natural advantages. Many of the most fertile regions of the earth are in a very miserable condition. More depends on good government and security for life and property; and probably most of all depends on the industry, energy, and adaptability of the inhabitants. Now a revival of trade cannot be arbitrarily brought about either by a government or by a union of capitalists. Trade consists in enabling somebody to get something he wants; and we should remember that, as in a battle, not only the strategy of the general is necessary to victory, but the courage and self-sacrifice of each private soldier. Every man and every boy should use his utmost skill in production, and keep all his wits about him to see where one additional sale can be made or one order secured. First get us all to work again; after that, profits will follow. Let us each strive to bring a return of prosperity to the country, as if the whole matter depended on ourselves. I don't believe that England need consider that her time has gone by, and that other countries have superseded us. We may be handicapped in the race, but not, I think, beyond our strength, if we really exert ourselves. We can make our country essential to the commercial prosperity of the world yet; and, whether I were advising an individual or a nation, I could not do better than quote the advice Sir William Armstrong gave me when my apprenticeship ended: "Never mind what pay you get; get work and make yourself useful; and when people find they can't do without you they will *have* to pay you." I hope the world cannot do without England, and that England cannot do without her North-country mechanics.

II

The Unequal Distribution of Wealth, and its Responsibilities

[Newcastle Diocesan Conference, Oct. 29th, 1890]

PROBABLY, though few will urge the possibility, and fewer still the desirability, of all incomes being equal, no one will say that the present distribution of wealth is all that can be desired. We may look on an income from two points of view: 1st, how much is necessary or desirable for our comfort; 2nd, how much can we usefully spend or distribute. As regards the first, I often question whether a man really adds to his comfort after he has sufficient money to supply his wants according to his bringing up, and a trifle over. No doubt he may easily learn new ones, and, having supplied those, his wants will grow and grow without limit. But no one in these days will tell us that we may look on wealth simply as a means of gratifying our fancies. It is trite to enlarge on how simple our needs may be. A rich man often finds that his greatest luxury is to sit over the fire with a pipe and a book or a daily paper, his drink either a cup of tea or a glass of whisky and water, all of which delights are within the reach of any of his workmen. There is no doubt that the most refined ladies and gentlemen can live on wonderfully small incomes, where there are plenty of others in the same position to keep them in countenance, and, generally speaking, I think we shall all agree that our feeling comfortably off depends very much on what our income is compared with that of our neighbours. But while we may take very philosophical views of what it is worth while for people to spend on their own enjoyment, when we have got rid of that question, we have hardly begun to consider the uses of an income. Even in the expenditure of rich men, the size of house, number of servants, etc., etc., are not governed by their own wants so much as by what they require for their friends and acquaintances; and the difficulty of deciding how far each man has acted well and wisely in the selection, treatment, and number of his friends and associates, and the object for which he has gathered them together, makes it very difficult indeed, if not (providentially) impossible, to decide for others whether they are doing what is right or not, and using their incomes well and wisely. For the owner of the income, the question, if he will look at it rightly, is a much more simple one. The wealth, great or small, is a trust from God for which he is answerable; or, in other words, all property carries corresponding duties, and every extra pound added to a man's income brings additional responsibility. We may therefore imagine that a wise man gradually finds what scale of living, both as to quantity and quality, enables him to perform his duties according to his station in life in the most effective manner, giving little thought to his own indulgence and much to his duty to his fellow-men. For, as I have before said, all property is a trust; or really, all income of whatever sort is salary for implied duty. Take as an illustration a clergyman. He is placed in possession of a parsonage house and an income, in order that he may devote himself to a certain work. Of the proceeds of his living, as long as he performs certain duties, which may legally be reduced to an infinitesimal amount, he is absolute owner. For his lifetime he is as much master of his house and income as his neighbour the squire. But he feels that he is morally and spiritually bound to work zealously, and a clergyman who only works to the extreme minimum that will save him from losing his position is so rare as to be almost a phenomenon. In fact, most clergymen whose incomes are fixed, work just about as hard as professional men who are entirely paid by results. The clergyman knows that his position brings duties, and he tries to live up to them, not for fear of losing his income, but because his conscience tells him he ought. Now, if we take the case of the squire or landowner, I believe that we shall decide that his hereditary income equally is meant to be payment to enable him to perform certain duties. Formerly his ancestors held their estates by military service. This is now commuted into special or general taxes. He always had a duty towards the support of the poor, which is now partly crystallized into rates, though most is left to his conscience. Some of his old duties have vanished. But enough remain to remind him that, by the law of man, as well as God, and clearly by the Constitution of England, property has its duties as well as its privileges. The whole system of English law and administration is based on the principle that among men of means and leisure a large proportion will always be found continually to devote both time and money to the public service. But what the law compels is very far less than what society expects, or duty demands. As owner of land, it is the squire's duty to use his utmost efforts to see the land properly cultivated, the farmers encouraged, and the labourers supported. He should be the responsible head of the community dwelling on and around his estate, devoting his life and energy to the temporal well-being of his district, as the clergyman does to the spiritual. To do this is simply his duty. The old baron measured himself not by his income, but by the number of followers that would fight or die for him, and had he rack-rented his farmers or ground down his labourers, I fancy our ancestors would hardly have held their own so valiantly in civil and foreign warfare as they did. Even so discreditable a nobleman as Reginald Front de Bœuf, though he might murder Jews and pillage Saxons, could always depend on his own people fighting for him; and comparing the history of England with that of other countries, we see that very nearly all our civil wars were either Baron against Crown, or Baron against Baron, not rich against poor. The influence of an aristocracy, whether landed or commercial, really depends on how much they are beloved and leaned on by their neighbours and followers; and the chief who will freely give life and fortune for these will never lack a devoted and loving following. I only take the landowner past or present as a type of wealthy men, because his position is more tangible and more capable of legal definition. But morally the same principle applies to every man, whether merchant, banker, manufacturer, shopkeeper, or any other who has more than his share of the world's wealth. All have duties according to their means, whether we look on the question from a legal, moral, or religious standpoint. I imagine that much modern confusion of thought has arisen from owners taking a very exaggerated idea of their rights. Lord Douglas recognized his true position when he said:

> "My castle is my king's alone,
> From turret to foundation-stone;
> The hand of Douglas is his own,"—

looking on the king as representing the executive government of the country. He knew that his castle and possessions were given him because it was good for Scotland to have a strong man who could both keep order in the country and defend it from its enemies. But he was responsible to his own conscience for being ever ready to risk or give life and property freely for the service of his country. Again, there is no constitutional limit to the amount that either Imperial or Local Government can take from us if they believe the public need really requires it. When France was being invaded in November, 1813, Napoleon, in raising taxation, said, "According to the urgency of events there is no reason why the contribution should not rise from one-fifth (where it had been) to one-fourth, one-third, or one-half of the whole income. Indeed," he concluded, "there is no limit." I dwell on these facts to show that, after all, property of all kinds exists for the good of the State; and to turn from the view of the political economist to the view of the Churchman, nothing so counteracts that desire for riches, which is generally considered to be so universal, as to keep constantly before the mind of all, and especially of the young, the doctrine that wealth means duties; more wealth, severe duties; and great wealth a burden almost too great for an ordinary man to bear with happiness. Wages are payment for *work done*. Inherited wealth is payment for *work to be done*, and a strict conscience ought to see that this return is paid to the uttermost. However, both as to responsibility and wealth, the division is certainly most unequal, and I should like to touch very hastily on a few points as to the possibility of arriving at greater equality. I believe one great cause of disparity is to pretend an equality which does not exist, as in the United States. The average income per head of population is higher in England than in the States (16 per cent. a few years ago), but there are far more men of enormous wealth in the States than in England, and far greater inequalities, and I think something of this is due to the fact that there is much less recognised obligation for men of wealth to devote part of their time and energy to public business; and also the absence of all honours and titles makes wealth almost the only mark of professional or commercial distinction. A soldier who has led a forlorn hope is not only satisfied with, but proud of his Victoria Cross. If he had to be bribed to risk his life by a mere money payment, it would need to be a very large one indeed, and the same principle applies to all walks of life. Many who wish to see wealth more equally divided fall into the mistake, so common among Socialists, of speaking as if they thought the existing wealth of men ought to be redivided. Now for one person who would listen to this, hundreds can be found who wish the wealth that will be created in future years to be more evenly divided. The first would simply make all property insecure, and all history, in every age and every country, shows that where property is insecure the first to suffer are the weak and the poor. The possession of riches is the greatest force for getting more, and, in the general upheaval, what was not destroyed would more and more accumulate in a few hands. The annual increase of wealth is of course very great, but this mainly represents the saving out of the enormous returns of trade which are divided between capital and labour. Capital will take very low interest indeed if the security is perfect; whatever arises in the way of risk perforce raises the rate of interest. To show how certainly labour might, by even in a slight degree sharing the risks of capital, add to its own wealth, and surely (but not necessarily slowly) improve its position, is rather the work of the economist than the Churchman. I have often thought that one of the quickest ways of further improving the position of the working classes would be by their going further in the direction of contracting for the amount of work that is to be done. If there are 100 workmen to one employer, the brains of all the 100 would be as much devoted to increased efficiency and economy as that of the one employer is now, and whatever reduces the risk and anxiety of the capitalist must, in the long run, proportionately increase the amount that goes to the workman. If time had allowed, I would have enlarged further on this topic. I wish I had had time to speak also of our unemployed, our poorest, and our vicious classes. A book has just been published by General Booth, called *In Darkest England*. I will only say that while all that he says is deserving of our most respectful attention, and while the work to be done to relieve darkest England is very great, I think everything goes to prove that these classes are gradually diminishing, and that Christian work and humanizing influences are producing an appreciable effect, certainly in reducing their numbers. What one would like to hope is that in dealing with ignorance and crime the age of experiment is passing away, and that with the knowledge and experience that the Church and the State possess, we may feel that we are drawing rapidly to the time when we shall have the knowledge and power, as well as the will, to deal far more successfully with these blots on our civilization. Of course, we all agree with Mr. Booth in the principle that the man's nature must be changed by Christianity at the same time that his circumstances are improved by philanthropy. Beyond this the book must speak for itself. He is only one of our many great workers. I believe that though there is still much vice and much misery, especially in our large cities, yet there never was a time when what is good in the world was in so favourable a position for overcoming that which is evil.

III

The House of Lords

AN INDEPENDENT VIEW

[Newcastle Daily Leader, July 23rd, 1894]

THERE is no question more prominently before the country than the question of the House of Lords, its position and powers. Many people, crying out that it thwarts the work of the House of Commons and obstructs the will of the people, say that it ought to be abolished. Others, and even many who applaud its action in throwing out the Home Rule Bill and the Employers' Liability Bill, still say that it is logically indefensible, and that it would be better if it were reformed and brought more into accordance with modern thought and modern ways. It seems to me that few ask themselves what really are the duties of the Second Chamber, what power the Lords actually claim and practise, or what sort of men would make the best Court of Appeal from the House of Commons.

"To be mended or ended." The second alternative makes us ask whether we want a Second Chamber; the first makes us ask whether, assuming that a Second Chamber is necessary, we can suggest any important improvements in the present House of Lords.

Before we discuss the necessity of a Second Chamber we had better consider the uses and nature of the First. What is the use of the House of Commons? What are its more or less important duties? and how far is it fitted for the performance of them?

In the compass of a short paper it is impossible to do more than sketch the broad features of the case, and much that is important must be passed over very superficially. Both houses have equally the power of originating legislation, and in the majority of cases it is both convenient and customary for this initiative to be taken by the House of Commons.

But the great use above all others of the House of Commons has always been to preserve the liberties of the people, and to see that the executive does not use the powers entrusted to it otherwise than in the interests of the nation as a whole. The machinery for carrying this into effect is of the simplest possible description. It is the power possessed only by the House of Commons of voting money. The people of England cannot be taxed at all without their own consent as expressed by their elected representatives.

Should the Sovereign or executive declare an unpopular war, let the Commons refuse to vote supplies; should the executive adopt any objectionable practices, or persecute or unjustly annoy any individual, let the Commons refuse to vote supplies; should the people want anything done which the Government refuses to do, or should the House of Commons think the King ought alto-gether to change his advisers, let them refuse to vote supplies. A proceeding beautifully simple and absolutely efficient. "Grievance before supply" is the old political watchword. No money will we vote till our grievances are redressed. Obviously, as long as the Commons are true to the electors and do not vote money for more than a reasonable period (practically one year), their control over the Executive Government is supreme. In the theory of the British constitution everything centres on securing the liberty of the people, both as regards their persons and goods.

In recent times there has been so little attempt to encroach on the rights of the people that the question of liberty has, perhaps unwisely, become a very secondary one in the eyes of many people, and the nation looks more to the House of Commons to legislate on all sorts of subjects, some very complicated and delicate, and gives little heed to the question of strength and simplicity.

The central idea of the House of Commons is that it shall be strong, firm; and that it shall be able, simply and quickly, where necessary, to support or check the action of the Executive Government, and guard us from danger.

Being, as everyone knows, composed of individuals generally of no special training, commonly called away from other avocations to which they still have to devote much of their time and more of their thoughts, and each member being liable to lose his seat at very short notice, the House of Commons can in no sense be looked upon as an assembly of expert legislators.

Entirely changed or re-elected at each general election, they represent, as to the majority, the popular feeling of the country at the moment of election. That this may not be a permanent feeling is obvious from the fact that, with one exception, every general election for long past has taken power from those in office and given this power to their opponents. Thus, since 1868 to 1894, our Prime Ministers have been Disraeli, Gladstone, Disraeli, Gladstone, Salisbury, Gladstone, Salisbury, Gladstone, now succeeded without an election by Lord Rosebery.

The tendency, when party feeling runs high, is for the Ministerial majority more and more to vote what it likes, utterly ignoring the wishes of the minority. Some people say this is right, but this view is a very superficial one; if in one Parliament one set of measures is carried, the wishes of the Opposition being utterly ignored, it would be quite possible—if party feeling ran high enough—for these measures to be reversed in the next Parliament when what was the Opposition becomes the Ministry.

The reasons why this does not actually happen are simply two; first, because in most cases proposed legislation is discussed with more or less thoroughness, so that the Opposition, though still an Opposition, feel that the case is against them, and that the feeling in favour of the proposed change is too strong and deep to be safely reversed even after a return to office; or else, if the majority of the House of Commons, refusing full and fair discussion, forces extreme measures through the Lower House, there stands the Upper House, the House of Lords, as a safeguard.

Is the House of Lords to oppose the will of the people? If the will of the people is, after due deliberation, clearly and fully expressed, the Lords do not and cannot oppose it. Practically the powers claimed by the Lords are two; first, to reject any Bill till it can be clearly ascertained, without doubt, that the will of the nation, after full consideration, is in favour of it; second, to amend Bills with a view to their greater efficiency.

The general principle may be seen in the case of the disestablishment of the Irish Church. When Mr. Gladstone first raised the question, it was near the end of a Parliament, and the Lords declined to treat the matter as a foregone conclusion till the nation had been consulted. When, after a dissolution, a Parliament was re-elected distinctly favourable to the disestablishment, the Lords, though with a strong protest, let the Bill pass.

Now, considering that the nation has, for long past, alternately given the preference to the two great parties, it does seem both natural and wise that the Second Chamber should be able to check any violent change till such times as, by dissolution or otherwise, the country has obviously made up its mind finally on the question. Were there no Second Chamber we might see each Parliament rescinding the measures of its predecessor.

It may be well to consider what would happen if the Lords set themselves hopelessly against the well-considered wishes of the nation. For example, let us take the case of the Home Rule Bill. The majority of the House of Commons might now, if they were confident they had the support of the people, in voting the supplies for this year, give notice that they would vote no more supplies at all till Home Rule was passed. This would obviously force a dissolution, and if the same party came back to power the threat would stand, and as the Lords cannot tax the country, and the Government cannot go on without money, the Lords must then inevitably give way. In fact, therefore, the Lords have the power once to ask the country to reconsider, and if the country confirms the action of the House of Commons, the Lords must and do give way.

2—2

As regards the second purpose—the amendment of Bills—it can hardly be seriously denied that the experience of the Lords makes their revision often very valuable; on many of the usual subjects for legislation the Lords have a training and experience far superior to an average House of Commons.

For, having recognized the fact that the primary use and duty of the House of Commons is to secure the liberty of the subject and guard against unlawful interference, we must bear in mind that, while the members are probably good representatives of the various classes of the community, yet certainly the method by which they are selected is not calculated to gather together a body of men with the judgement and experience necessary for making the best possible legislators. To legislate well a man ought to have a mind trained from his youth (or a very special aptitude), and permanently to watch and study the art of legislation and the working of Governments, both imperial and local. No doubt there are a few men in the House of Commons who come fully up to this ideal, but as a rule they are men taken suddenly from other and generally very absorbing careers, commercial or otherwise; very often till late in life they never have thought about either the making or administration of laws, and while in Parliament their attention to their old avocations must continue, the more so as none of them can feel sure how long they may occupy their position as members of Parliament. An admirable body for defensive purposes; by no means an ideal body for the almost professional work of legislating.

A Peer, on the other hand, is either a man specially selected and raised to the Upper House, or else he is born and brought up to the business. It is not necessary here to claim that there is anything in heredity, but there certainly is a great deal in training, in association, and experience. Experience shows that most boys and men take a special interest in what they know will be their sphere of work in future, and in all times a very large proportion of heirs to peerages have sought seats in the House of Commons. Besides this, magistrates' and other local work, and even the management of a large estate and the many questions connected therewith, are in themselves valuable training, and as a Peer knows that he holds his position for life, he feels it is worth while to qualify himself for it. Every man ought to have some special sphere in which he is an authority, and the sphere of a lord ought to be Government. No doubt there are some idle, stupid, or bad ones, but so there are bad specimens in every calling, and practically such men take very little part in the working of the Upper House.

Any lawyer or engineer will tell us how much more ably, as a rule, a Railway Bill or Local Government Bill is handled by a Committee of the Lords than by a Committee of the Commons; and certainly, for business purposes, the concise, practical debates in the House of Lords compare very favourably with the interminable and so often unprofitable torrent of words with which the Commons waste so much time.

And as regards the hereditary principle in the abstract; the custom, that is, of sons being expected to follow their fathers' occupations, and succeed to their duties, as well as inherit their properties, surely this has been common in almost all times and in almost all countries. Probably no class of men are universally allowed to understand their business better than the bankers of London, the chief financial city of the world, and a very large proportion of them owe their position to their fathers and grandfathers having been bankers before them. In our own North of England coal trade most of our distinguished mining engineers and coalowners have had the great advantage of succeeding to fathers whose positions they inherited. In our manufacturing and mercantile houses the principle of the son inheriting his father's influence and responsibilities, as well as his property, is as common as possible. Even on boards of directors, such as that of the North Eastern Railway, it can hardly be denied that many directors, and some of the ablest of them, have been selected in the first instance simply because they were their fathers' sons. Among skilled mechanics and in all professions it is very common to prefer a son who is to follow in his father's trade, and a lord, looked at apart from all feeling, is simply a professional legislator, neither more nor less.

Besides, to a very great extent, the Lords are landowners, and a little reflection must show anyone that landowners not only have, from the nature of their property, a close connection with the traditions of the past, but they have, which is more important, the most real interest possible in the prosperity of the country, even into the far future. If the general interests of the country suffer, the land suffers accordingly, and a man whose wealth is invested in land is obliged, of necessity, to look very much further ahead than a business man, and still more so than a professional man or a working man.

It may be interesting to note that five Northumbrian Peers have, among them, sat for over 100 years in the House of Commons, *i.e.* for 27, 25, 19, 17, and 13 years respectively.

This indicates not only that they took pains to qualify themselves for their position as legislators, but also that the electors chose them over and over again as the best representatives they could get.

Two other points may be noted. First, that a purely popular Government almost always ends sooner or later in a despotism of some sort; against this a House of Lords is the best practicable safeguard, and makes impossible the immense amount of corruption that appears to be almost inseparable from a republic. And, secondly, if the Upper House were abolished, it is not easy to see how Peers could be kept out of the House of Commons; where, judging from all experience, they would exercise as great an influence as they do now; for they would, though having rather less power on each subject, have the power of interfering in taxation and matters which they are not now allowed to touch, and each Peer, being a representative member, would have more power if he went into Parliament than he has at present. If anyone doubts the probability of a very large majority of Peers being elected, let him consider, first, that a substantial number of the people of England are Conservative; and, second, that both parties are even now much disposed to elect sons of Peers, and would not be less likely to elect them after they had inherited their estates and titles.

Some of those who clamour for the abolition of the House of Lords are fond of alluding to the time when not only the House of Lords was annihilated but the King was executed. They seem to forget that a dominant House of Commons not only refused to be dissolved, but became so intolerable that they had to be expelled by Cromwell's soldiers. All history teaches us how often and how quickly a too-democratic Government merges into a military despotism; but it is well, further, to remember how, after a short experience of these two forms of Government, England not only restored, with almost unanimous enthusiasm, the Monarchy and the Upper House, but it was nearly two hundred years before any Englishman could be found with a short enough memory to ask seriously "What is the use of the House of Lords?"

IV

Land compared with other Property

[Read before the Economic Society, Newcastle-upon-Tyne, Dec. 11th, 1895]

I HAVE undertaken this evening to discuss the nature and character of landed property as compared with other property. Is it altogether the same, or is it in the nature of things slightly or wholly different? Some see no difference whatever. On the other hand, some even of those who fully acknowledge the rights of other kinds of property deny the right of any man to be the absolute owner of land. They say no man made the land and no man can own it, or give it to another to own. In our country, which is a fair type of most of the civilized world, ownership in land is recognized, but not on the exact footing of other property. We call landed property real property, and other sorts personal property, and, if the owner dies without a will, the two sorts are passed on under different rules to his next heirs. I think before we go further we had better try to define what we mean by property, and what ideas are connected with it. That such a thing as property, or ownership of wealth, exists is in some degree admitted by everybody. No one will question a free man's right to his clothes, but they may nevertheless wholly deny any man's right to claim as his own a piece of land, which existed from all time, and on which he has bestowed, possibly, no labour. I shall proceed at once to give the result of my investigations, giving at the same time, as far as I can, the evidence in favour of what I say.

In regard to ownership, certain rules have been recognized ages before anyone tried to study the question philosophically, so what

Land and other Property 25

we want is to trace the lines of thought that gradually shaped themselves in the minds of our ancestors, and on which our present laws and customs are based. On this subject I think that three ideas have been more or less clearly seen at all times, and the divergence in men's views lies in the practical application of them:

(1) That such wealth as could be enjoyed by the whole human race, irrespective of any man's thought or labour, is public property (*e.g.* deep-sea fishing). Some of this, to wit land, has practically been conceded by the State to individuals, but it has been, or ought to have been, sold or exchanged, not given. If this is true, we must remember presently to try and see what price landowners have paid for their land.

(2) That all property or wealth carries with it certain duties. This idea is usually very undefined, but it is recognized, not only as a Christian principle, but as a matter of State policy.

(3) That whatever wealth a man could call into existence by his own ingenuity, industry, or other talents, was his own, to use as he pleased, and to give away, either during his life, or at his death. This last is the obvious form of private property; but even then the State only allows the accumulation of property and the disposal of it under certain stringent conditions:

(*a*) The first of these in England was formerly that one-tenth had to go to the support of religion, education, and other Church purposes. This was the tithe; it was probably originally based entirely on the idea of a religious duty. If a man, by draining, fertilizing, building, fencing, or otherwise, improved the productive power of the land, he used to pay the tithe on the improved value, not on the original value only.

(*b*) The second condition was that the State could always claim as much of a man's property (and his person also) as it really needed. It was never lawful for the State to invent wants for the sake of confiscating property or imposing taxes; but, in its extremity, there was no limit to what it could claim; just as now, if England were invaded, Parliament might raise taxation to an unlimited extent, and, of course, it might call on all men to give personal service also.

(*c*) The third condition was that the rich must provide the poor with at least the bare necessaries of life; or, in other words, property was rated for the support of the poor. The remarks that apply to taxation apply to rates. There is no limit as to the amount that may be claimed as rates, except that it is the duty of the Government to expend the money raised as economically as possible, and only on the supply of the bare necessaries of life. If there had been absolutely no capital accumulated by anybody, no one could have had much more than this. We find here, of course, the principle of poor rates, and upon property there is no limit as to the amount of poor rate that may be levied. In the writer's knowledge, in one parish in Gloucestershire, the annual poor rate was for many years actually 18*s*. on the net value in the £, and this is not an isolated case.

(*d*) A man must provide properly for his family. In some countries, therefore, his power of disposal after death is limited.

I will note a few points in connection with the propositions I have suggested, and I would ask you to bear in mind that I shall base my illustrations as far as possible on England and English laws and customs. I must take one complete system, and of course we know our own practice better than other people's; and what I say about English land would require much modification if applied to even Scotland or Ireland, and still more to other countries.

I have said that such wealth as could be enjoyed by the whole human race, irrespective of any man's thought or labour, is public property. The Government, who act for the public, may sell or exchange such, but should only do so to secure a greater benefit to the public. Now, at first sight it might be suggested that the fact of property in land was a direct contradiction to this, but I don't think it is. If the country was all open, and had very few inhabitants, probably everyone could wander about, and pasture their flocks and herds where they liked. Abraham and Lot appear

to have done this; but even then the people who took the trouble
to find water and sink wells were allowed to keep them for their
own, and sell or give them away as they liked. When once men
begin to plant, and practise agriculture, a man must be able to
call the land he cultivates his own, either permanently, or for a
time; and, without this much ownership of land, no food except
meat could be raised. Temporary ownership is sufficient for temporary improvement; a farmer cannot raise anything unless he has
secure possession till he has gathered in his crop. If the land has to
be drained—and millions of acres would be of no use without it—
he must hold the land long enough to recover in profit the money
he spent in making the drains. But if he is to build a stone farm-
house, with elaborate outbuildings, nothing except ownership, or
a very long lease indeed, will compensate him. It must be remembered that a ninety-nine year lease is practically as valuable
as a freehold, and yet a tenant leaving at the end of a ninety-nine
year lease might, if he had built a good house, have a formidable
claim for tenant-right, or unexhausted improvement.

I believe, in the interests of the whole community, it is necessary
that the land should be divided among owners or perpetual tenants
under the Crown. Justice, however, demands that these owners
should have bought or else annually return to the public either
money or money's worth equal to the annual value of the land as
it was bestowed on them or their predecessors. The nation will
then get this value, and enjoy it, instead of the land. Now, the
question is, do the landowners pay this? And here is a question
on which a great deal has been thought and written lately.

Originally, land involved military service; but this was, from
early ages, sometimes commuted for money payments. The king
perhaps preferred their money to their presence. This we find,
even in Henry the First's reign. As barons, franklins, or yeomen
continued to hold land from father to son, and expected to do so,
they built houses, made roads—either singly, or in combination of
parishes or townships (as ratepayers)—fenced, made watercourses,

and, in endless ways, employed their spare labour and money in making the land more productive. As the land was increased in value it required closer attention to cultivate it, and parts were divided off, and sub-let to others, who paid rent. Ultimately, what had been a forest, a moor, or at best a sheep-walk, became a number of farms, and the owner found it both to his interest and pleasure to supervise the whole property, rather than to be a farmer himself. All this time he paid tithes, military service, and, informally or formally, had to support the poor of the district.

We now come to the settlement of the land tax instead of military service. What were the Crown's rights as against the landowners? The Crown had a right to what is called the "quit-rent," or interest on the prairie value of the land at that time. What the Crown tenants had a right to was fair rent, free sale, and fixity of tenure. The first was settled at a given time at one-fifth of the then total value of the land and improvements, tithes and rates being paid out of the other four-fifths. I don't fancy that the Crown, which was a greater power then than it is now, would think it had made a bad bargain; but, having fixity of tenure, the owners poured out their capital and labour upon it freely, and increased the value, which, constantly rolling up at compound interest, has brought the land of England to its present value—indeed, had the same money and labour been expended in any other way (and, of course, accumulated to the same degree), I believe the result would have averaged far more to the present owners. Mr. Smith, M.P. for Liverpool, writing many years ago, considered that land improvement hardly paid three per cent.; I don't think anybody estimates it much more highly, and lately it has paid much worse.

Of course, I have gone over this question in the baldest manner, but I wish to give you an idea why some of us consider that landed property is just as sacred as any other property, and that the two, in fact, must be placed on the same footing exactly. As a matter of fact, land (with its improvements) is taxed to nearly one-third of its net value—*Encyclopædia Britannica* (date 1882, article

"Land") says thirty per cent., and since then the value of land has fallen and the taxes have not. The nation, as a whole, does not pay quite one-tenth of its gross income in taxes, and I think that the extra twenty per cent. that land pays is probably far more than a sufficient quit-rent for the prairie value of the soil of England.

There are two other points in connection with land which, though I have not space to discuss, I must just touch upon—unearned increment and mineral royalties.

As regards the unearned increment: If the State confiscated a rise in value, caused by an action over which the owner had no control, it ought in justice to compensate an owner for a decrease in value similarly brought about. I have seen land rise in value because a shipyard was started in the neighbourhood, and the ground was wanted for workmen's houses. I have seen land fall in value from free trade. American competition has ruined many farms. In this country much land has gone out of cultivation. In many cases the apparently unearned increment is really the result of owners' self-denial and enterprise. To take a different but parallel case. If new industries open, wages may rise from a cause beyond the control of the workmen, but nobody thinks of confiscating these workmen's rise of wages by calling it an unearned increment. All property is liable to vary in value from outside causes: and land is on the same footing as steamers, pig iron, or cotton.

I have passed rather quickly over the question of unearned increment, or the extent to which the value of land may be increased by what is neither the work nor wisdom of the owner. But most of those who have advocated the confiscation of land base their views on land as a producing agent, *i.e.* on its agricultural value. Into this view unearned increment hardly enters; it is chiefly connected with town land or manufacturing and mining premises; but though the increment of value is in certain cases simply enormous, as in the city of London, still it only applies to a very small fraction of all the land in England. It would be difficult, if not impossible, to estimate the value of the unearned increment in

England; but probably land has not gained more in this way than other kinds of wealth. A man may have a large stock of anything in hand; if it rises in value he gets the good, if it falls in value he suffers the loss. If the State claimed the gain, the State should compensate for the loss. The Franco-German War was followed by a great rise of wages in England; it would have been very extraordinary if the State had proposed to confiscate this advance on the ground that the British workmen had not caused the Franco-German War.

Besides, there are two points about unearned increment that are often overlooked. If we take the case of building land near a town, you will see that an energetic owner will get his land into the market and built upon, while an indolent or inexperienced man, though perhaps in a better position, will not sell a site. Here the unearned increment is reward for talent and industry. Then it is often forgotten how long this unearned increment has to be waited for; an estate that is now coming in for building was very likely sold at an enhanced price on account of its prospective value sixty years ago, and this extra price, calculated for sixty years at compound interest, would quite make up the new selling price. Here the increased increment is really self-denial. But above all, if Government claim a right to an unearned rise in value, they ought, in justice, to compensate any landowner whose land falls in value through no fault of his own. This would be simply ruinous to the Government, and they will be much better off by leaving things where they are.

The estate that I know better than any other doubled in value (purely for agricultural purposes) between 1776 and 1800. The great Berkeley Vale property let all last century at £1 per acre for grass, and 10s. for plough. By 1810 it had doubled in value. It has now sunk to 30s. and 12s., and is likely to go lower. Mr. Gladstone told us only last 3rd of October that the landed property of Guy's Hospital in London had fallen from £40,000 a year to one-half that amount.

The value of land is then made up of three things: the prairie value, the improvements thereof, and unearned increment (if any). Of this last I have spoken. The two first really represent the agricultural land sometimes said to be the source of all wealth, and which is also considered to have been wrongfully come by. Some politicians and writers, like Henry George, have even said that this ought to be confiscated, and that then the country would be so rich that there need be no more taxes. Now if we look at the Parliamentary return of the rateable value of land in England and Wales (April 5th, 1895), we find that land, including farm-houses, farm-buildings, and all improvements of every sort for agricultural purposes, is only worth $33\frac{1}{2}$ millions per annum, in 1870 it was 39·8 millions, and as a large part of that is due to improvements distinctly made by owner or occupier (not by the State), the prairie value of England and Wales is not so very great a sum after all. The return in the *Chronicle*, November 19th, 1895, makes out that all the land in England, exclusive of London and fifteen miles round it, is worth less than half what it was in 1875. Nor did the present owners get this for nothing.

It is not correct in England to say that any landowner got his land by right of conquest. The nation may have conquered; the individual, whether high or low, had it assigned to him by the State on certain definite terms that I have already mentioned. First service, then service commuted into money payment, with secure tenure, which encouraged the owners to spend the necessary money. Then about 200 years ago, as I have said, the Crown settled its rights by the land tax, which put an end to military service in return for land, though there was, and still is, a feeling that ownership in land involves certain undefined duties, such as serving as high sheriff or magistrate, the officering of the militia and yeomanry, etc. The traces of these last are much fainter since the tolerably large standing army became a permanent institution.

So I would say that of the three possible elements in the value of land, the prairie value was disposed of by the nation to the individual for what it considered at the time a sufficiently good bargain. The improvements have been entirely executed by private money. The unearned increment cannot be touched by the Government except on such terms as would make it worth less than nothing. But the agricultural value of the land of England is, as I have said, far less than is generally imagined. I have given the annual rateable value as only £33,654,000, and it is estimated that the value of this property had fallen 22¾ per cent. since 1879, and is still falling. There has been a great fall in land since 1879.

It may be interesting to consider when the land first got the high value that it had prior to 1879, and I believe if we take rather a comprehensive view of this, we shall come to some conclusions that have not been generally noticed. Many of you will remember a very interesting chapter in Macaulay's *History of England*, where he describes the state of England a little over two hundred years ago (end of Charles II's reign). "In the year 1685 the value of the produce of the soil far exceeded the value of all the other fruits of human industry, yet agriculture was in what would now be considered as a very rude and imperfect state. The arable land and pasture land were not supposed by the best political arithmeticians of that age to amount to much more than half the area of the kingdom. The remainder was believed to consist of moor, forest, and fen. These computations are strongly confirmed by the road books and maps of the seventeenth century. From those books and maps it is clear that many routes which now pass through an endless succession of orchards, cornfields, hayfields, and beanfields, then ran through nothing but heath, swamp, and warren. In the drawings of English landscapes made in that age for the Grand Duke Cosmo, scarce a hedgerow is to be seen, and numerous tracts, now rich with cultivation, appear as bare as Salisbury Plain. At Enfield, hardly out of sight of the smoke of the capital, was a region of five and twenty miles in circumference, which contained only three houses and scarcely any enclosed fields. Deer, as free as in an American forest, wandered there by thousands."

This condition of things lasted without serious change well on into the next century, but during George II's reign the cultivation of waste land was seriously taken in hand, and by the end of last century about 10,000 square miles were enclosed by Act of Parliament and an immense additional amount by private ownership. Prosperity, trade, and even war, all combined to benefit agriculture, and not only all the good land in England was fully cultivated, but much bad land was laid under cultivation, and enormous amounts of capital were spent in improving it by fencing, draining, and building. This state of things reached its climax during the French War, after which agricultural prosperity languished and the prices went down. But the development of steam power, of railways, and manufacturing greatly brought about a second revival, and land still maintained its high value. This lasted to about 1875, when we had a bad year or two. The world thought it was only temporary, but since then the fall in the value of land has been very great; as I have already pointed out, from 1879 to 1894 it has fallen nearly 23 per cent. But while some of the best land keeps its full value, other land has become practically valueless, and the care and capital that had been spent on it are utterly lost. Of course corn lands have suffered most. As railways increased the value of land in England, by bringing the produce easily to the towns, who were the customers, so now steamers have brought the produce of other countries to our markets in competition with our home supplies. The truth is that carriage adds hardly anything to cost in these days, and it is hard to see how England can ever again hope to be a wheat-growing country. My opinion is that the value of land in England from about 1775 to 1875 was utterly abnormal. On account of the rapid growth of population, the produce of land, and hence the land itself, had, generally speaking, a purely artificial value. No doubt the best land in England can hold its own against the best in any other country, but the best in this sense is a very small portion of the whole.

At the time I first mentioned, say two hundred years ago, the value of unreclaimed land, not specially well situated, was very small indeed—even in England there was more land than anybody wished to cultivate. This is, of course, the case now in the colonies; for example, in West Australia they recently passed a Homestead Act giving any poor man a fair-sized piece of land on condition that he should cultivate it, and very few emigrants seem to care to get the land even at that price. As an interesting example of home colonization, I may mention that the present owner of Exmoor used, as a young man, to allow young married couples to occupy as much land as they could cultivate, giving them a lease for both their lives at 6d. per acre. The land was good. When both died, of course, the estate inherited the improvements, and this arrangement worked well, and was, I understand, satisfactory to all parties.

And, indeed, to consider the merits of land ownership, let us look at the position of such a colony as I have mentioned, viz., West Australia, and ask ourselves if we were among the legislators to-day how we should deal with the land question. They have unlimited land, limited population, no traditions, no aristocracy, and all the experience of all ages. The country is nearly nine times as large as Great Britain and Ireland, the population about one-half that of Newcastle. In this case the value of even the best land utterly unreclaimed, and difficult of access, is infinitesimal. The first necessaries to utilize the land are roads to get there, shelter for man and beast, wells where there is no water, and drainage where there is too much. We will borrow the money to make the roads, and repay ourselves by a charge on the land that is thereby increased in value. But the occupier must build his own house and farmstead, and to do that we must give him undisturbed possession for a long time. To put up good stone buildings he ought to have at least 100 years, and the buildings might still be of good value. That is a lease practically equal to, and as valuable as a freehold. Then even by the time the young couple who took it have got old they will hesitate about further improvements unless they get further security, and by the time the whole thing is worked out, it will be found that if the Government can get a small payment in cash down or a small perpetual rent charge, it would be much the best for the community as a whole.

Such as West Australia is, such every country was. Of all the Queen's dominions probably England is practically the only one where all the land is taken up, and here much that was taken up was not worth it. Here is a specimen of the colonies' recent legislation. They want a railway costing about a million, to open out a large tract of country. The railway will not pay probably for some time, the colony has not got the money and does not like to borrow it, so they find a company to make it on these terms. If they make a railway as long as from Newcastle to London they may, out of an area half the size of England, select a piece of land nearly as large as Yorkshire. Of course, at present, this land brings in next to nothing, but if the railway company make roads, import settlers, and spend money, it may presently become valuable. But somebody must not then get up and say that land cannot be alienated and try to confiscate it; yet that is exactly what the land nationalization people say they want to do in England.

To sum up, it seems to me that for the nation to take over the land without compensating for money spent on improvement would be simple robbery; to take it over, paying such compensation, would be simple ruin. Our ancestors were neither knaves, fools, nor slaves; they have left us a magnificent heritage based on a system which, though not of course perfect, is, at any rate, so good that people opening out new countries cannot devise anything better. Even in England agriculture is our most important industry, and yet few, if any, industries give so poor a return on the expenditure either of labour or of capital.

V

Education from an Employer's Point of View

[DELIVERED TO THE TEACHERS' ASSOCIATION AT THE COLLEGE OF PHYSICAL SCIENCE, NEWCASTLE, APRIL 25TH, 1896]

IN most cases a lecture is given by one who has made a special study of a certain subject to the general public who wish to avail themselves of his knowledge and experience; but in this case the position is reversed, and it is with considerable diffidence that I realize the fact that whereas the subject on which I have to speak is one which you have all studied as the work of your lives, I am only able to speak upon it as one of the ordinary public. I acceded however to your president's wish that I should address you, in the belief that you would be glad to hear from me, as representing one special section of the public, their views as to the results of the great educational work now going forward in this country. The modern education movement is generally considered to have begun with the Act of 1870, which covered the country with School Boards, and placed education within the reach of every boy and girl in the Kingdom, by providing schools and also by making attendance compulsory; but the way had been paved for the satisfactory working of this Act not only by the grants which had been given, with corresponding supervision, from the Imperial Treasury, but also by the whole system of National and other schools in the movement that was inaugurated by the Rev. Andrew Bell and Joseph Lancaster about 100 years ago. If I mistake not, the special work of these two great men was to create a system whereby those taught were also to take part in the teaching, and the present system of pupil-teachers is, I believe, a direct outcome of this. In one other respect the teaching provided by the National Schools or by the modern denominational and Board Schools stands in striking contrast to the education which has been provided for generations past, and which is still provided, in our large Public Schools, in our costly private boarding schools, and in the Universities, for the wealthier classes; and that is, that it is only among teachers for popular schools that the art of teaching has been properly recognized as essential to a schoolmaster's success. Especially at Universities, and also at our Public Schools, there are often found men in the position of teachers who, though they know their subject thoroughly, have never given any serious attention to the science of imparting knowledge to their pupils. Some men and most women have this gift naturally, but in any case it is very much improved by training on sound principles, and many people are so deficient in it that their powers as instructors are very much less useful than they ought to be.

Let us now ask ourselves what the state may hope to do in the way of education and what it cannot do. The first thing it can do, and has done, is to place a good education within reach of every boy and girl in the country. Our schools, though of course not perfect, are for the most part exceedingly good; the enormous army of teachers (male and female) that are engaged in the work are inspired by great enthusiasm, love of their work, and probably almost universally with a deep sense of the responsibility of their position; but though you may lead a horse to the water you cannot make it drink, and it must never be forgotten that far more than the power of the state is the will of the child. You may do what you can to make learning attractive; you may do what you can to work on the sense of duty of both child and parent or even on their ambition; parents and teachers may combine to point out to the child to what an enormous extent the happiness of its whole life depends on the use that is made of the years spent at school— but after all we cannot shut our eyes to the fact that it is within the power of the child, if it is stupid or obstinate, almost to waste its advantages, and though it may be uncommon for them to be wasted altogether, still, on the other hand, probably few children, if any, realize to the full extent the advantages which are put before them. Really the value of education very largely depends upon the amount of trouble and pains spent over it by the child. The boy or girl who has prospered most is the one who has made the most self-denying efforts; but where the state and the teacher can supremely help is in seeing that these efforts are so invested as to give the child the greatest practicable return for what it does. Of course education does not so much mean cramming the child with learning as training the child's mind, and perhaps I might here say a word or two by way of illustration upon the art of learning.

Old fashioned education consisted to a great extent of what appears to be the comparatively useless study of Greek and Latin, but I believe that the reason these held their own was because, though of no great practical use in themselves, they were as a discipline some of the best possible subjects for training the mind. If we had for them substituted French and German these might have been picked up superficially by contact with natives of those countries; but Greek and Latin, especially in the scientific and anatomical way in which they were taught, had to be thoroughly reasoned out and learnt by heart, and there was no royal road to acquiring the Greek irregular verbs or to rendering a paragraph of an English book into graceful Latin prose. Still our utilitarian minds cannot but think in these days that some subjects might be found, almost if not quite as good as mental exercises; which would also be of real use in after life. But besides there being an art of teaching there is an art of learning, and I have certainly known cases where a few minutes' explanation to an apparently stupid child would make it see the right way of learning a lesson which before had been beset with insuperable difficulties. When I was a boy we had to learn by heart a great deal of Latin verse, and the science of doing this easily was to have it explained to a boy that he must first of all thoroughly master the sense in English

and then he would find it very easy to commit the Latin to memory.
Here, in Newcastle, business men sometimes have to learn a language with which they were not previously acquainted. I know
men who do this quickly and successfully by taking four or five
pages of prose, working out the translation by brute force with
grammar and dictionary, then committing these pages to memory,
and they say that after that to get a fair knowledge of the language
is very easy indeed. No doubt they have then arrived at the first
useful point in a language, which is the translation of ordinary
prose into English, and they are not far removed from the next
stage, which is being able to carry on some sort of ordinary conversation. These two points once arrived at, improvement is of
course rapid.

There is one other point which also should never be lost sight
of in a child's education. Having acquired the art of learning, it
should also acquire the art of thinking, the art of reasoning when
facts are put before it and of being able to discriminate in regard to
conflicting evidence. In the case of history, of course it is obvious
that no one can make much progress in the useful study of it unless
he is prepared to spend time and trouble in trying to reconcile
apparently inconsistent statements, and in being able to form some
idea from any given authority on what points he is likely to be
correct and on what points he is likely to be misinformed.

A more difficult object of attainment, but a most desirable and
attractive one, is to try and impart to the pupils some of the
enthusiasm for learning which exists among their teachers. This
is possible even in young children, and I believe that modern
teachers have succeeded very much better in this way than was
the case with their predecessors—partly I believe because corporal
punishment, or government by fear, is the exception not the rule.
The very fact of a boy associating the cane with his lessons necessarily takes away the charm and pleasure from them. It was not
merely the suffering but the humiliation and the feeling of disgrace
and the antagonism to his master which it created. Whether we

shall arrive at the point when corporal punishment can be altogether abolished I do not know, but there is no doubt that it is a
point towards which we ought all to strive most ardently. In
encouraging this enthusiasm we recognize the fact that we want
not only to train the boy's intellect but also his character, for his
future success in life depends probably very much more on his
character than on his intellectual powers. Such qualities as per-
severance, energy, the power of deliberately doing that which is
distasteful and disagreeable, unselfishness, and many others, have
more to do with a man's success in life than any store of learning
that may be put into his brain. But again, when we talk of a boy's
success, it does not necessarily mean that he is to succeed in what
is called rising in the world. Many of the men and women who
lead the best and most useful lives remain in the same position as
their parents and grandparents were in before them, and I believe
it is quite a fallacy to suppose that by raising a man's social status
you add either to his usefulness or his happiness. "Man does not
live by bread alone" even as regards this world, and it is a great
thing for a man to feel strong in the position that he occupies, and
to have a life full of interest both as regards usefulness and intellectual occupation, and not to be simply straining and striving to
add shilling to shilling or to be always sacrificing his health and
strength to try and raise himself a degree or two higher in the
social scale. When a lad first starts work he probably does not
himself know what he is fit for, nor does anybody else know, but,
though I have not even heard it suggested, I fancy that most young
men by the time they are at any rate thirty ought to be able to
gauge themselves in some degree against other people, and form
some idea of whether they are likely or not to rise very high in the
world. I believe that if a man sees that he is not remarkably
superior to his neighbours, he will do wisely to try and become a
first-rate man on his existing level rather than break his heart in
trying to rise to positions which he would not be qualified to fulfil
even if he attained them. It is of course on this principle that so

many men are found willing to accept a permanent situation at a moderate salary when there is often no prospect of its ever leading to anything better, and probably they are wise. A man feels himself to be conscientious, careful and steady, but he realizes also that he has not the gift of governing his fellow-men, and that he is not prepared to make the sacrifices which are necessary for scaling those giddy heights to which ambition might otherwise lead him.

Again as regards a boy's training. I believe the system is right that up to a certain age a boy's special talents and gifts ought not to be considered; so far he ought to be expected to adapt himself to that uniform training which is marked out for all boys of his age. When he has sacrificed something towards the conventional course of learning he may then gradually devote himself more to those subjects or branches for which he has a special talent, but I think all history of human progress shows that no man ought to be encouraged to become a specialist until he has some considerable measure of general knowledge and information. For example—in the medical profession every man has to qualify as a good all-round doctor before he can begin to devote himself to any one special subject. We see this principle carried out in almost all examinations for honours. In the lower examinations you have to take up a variety of subjects, in the higher examinations you may take up fewer and fewer, and possibly at the last end in taking honours in only one or two.

I have spoken about the boys and girls who are really in your hands. Now comes a point at which I think there is a serious blot in our educational system. Many boys leave school at thirteen or fourteen years of age and after a time begin to look out for work. Perhaps they put their names down to be apprenticed in some factory, but it may be a year before there is a vacancy for them. During this time I regret to say they are often allowed to stay at home doing nothing. This is simply detestable, and no words of condemnation can be too strong to express our disapproval. To begin with, while I do not at all object to pay taxes to educate my neighbours' children, I think it a burning shame and a scandal that after having received the education which I have paid for, they should be allowed deliberately to throw it away and to lower themselves to what would have been their natural state of ignorance, merely through idleness. This is a matter which of course is very much beyond the control of you as teachers, but I think it well that you should recognize the evil, so that, if any opportunities arise, you may lift up your voices against it and perhaps do something to mitigate it. I sometimes wonder whether the same law which enables us to compel children to attend school up to fourteen years of age could not be extended so as to enable us to compel attendance for two or three years more, provided always that the boy could not show that he was either at work or in some way improving himself for his future life. I also think that our system of technical education might make a special effort to meet this time, and to have classes for boys and girls of from fourteen to sixteen, to sit all day and every day—but perhaps I may here digress to say a few words on technical education.

The idea of technical education is not to supersede the apprenticeship which in some shape or form is the only way of learning either trade or profession, but rather to give boys and girls such learning as may enable them to acquire knowledge in the field or the workshop more thoroughly and quickly than they would otherwise do. Of course some trades may be perfectly taught at a school or college. An artist or a sculptor may work in a school of art until he is qualified to take his position as a finished artist. A watchmaker or a plumber might learn a very great part of his trade in the same way. So equally might a dressmaker, a cook or a laundress; in fact any trade which can be carried on in what may be called a solitary manner, or which does not require more appliances than can be collected in a school, can of course be completely taught, and some things beyond this. For example, I have known a professor of surveying teach his pupil partly in school and partly in the field, so that he can at once go out into the world and earn a full salary as a land surveyor. But more often the object of technical education is to throw some light on the principles of a trade that will be ultimately learned elsewhere. For example, it is a great thing for the young miner to learn something of geology. In many trades it is a great advantage to learn some branch of chemistry, which in technical education will be specially applied to the trade in question, such as to the art of dyeing clothes, manuring the soil, the treatment of ores and metals, or the preparation of food; and if the year or two that I speak of as being so often wasted was spent in this way, a boy would come to his trade immeasurably better qualified to do good both to himself and his work than he commonly does at present. Of course gregarious trades, or those where a number of people combine together, cannot be taught except where they are carried on. A miner or a quarryman can only learn his trade in the coal-pit or at the face of the rock. A farmer or an agricultural labourer, although he may often acquire valuable technical information as to the use of manure and as to the natural history of animals and vegetables, must really learn his work on the farm in the open air. Shipbuilding and engineering can only be learnt by the actual construction of ships and engines, and our large workshops in such a town as Newcastle are none too large for the work that has to be done in them. I wish to emphasize this point by saying that much harm has been done at some of the Universities and Public Schools, by persuading unsuspecting parents that the boys can be taught to be engineers by playing with a few small lathes and the vice and chisel of what is called the "College Workshop." They neither learn how to deal economically or effectively with masses of material, nor do they learn the great difficulties of combining these large pieces in one uniform whole; they do not realize what it is for a score of men to be working, with no apparent co-ordination, in such a manner that their work should all come together as though it were the work of one man; and above all they cannot in any degree realize what is required for the organization of a large body of men. What applies to engineering applies still more to shipbuilding, though here again a year or two spent by a lad in the theoretical and scientific study of the principles that underlie ships and engines would be clearly of the most incalculable value to him, and would make him spend his after years in the workshop to far greater advantage. The same applies to the soldier and sailor, who ought to have their experience in the field or on the water supplemented and strengthened by scientific training such as can be admirably supplied at a school or a college.

There is one future for which provision is often made for a poor boy, the advantages of which I think are exceedingly problematical. I allude to a University career. It seems to me that to make a great effort to send a poor boy to a University is a very doubtful kindness; indeed, unless he obtains a fellowship (and the chance is enormously against this) he is turned out at two and twenty not really fitted for any walk in life and with almost everything to begin. The only exception to this is if he wishes to be a clergyman, and this exception I am perhaps prepared to admit, but otherwise he has simply had a very enjoyable three years with nothing like an adequate return in the way of power to earn his living or make himself useful hereafter. Then, if he gains a fellowship, this very probably only lasts for six years, and though it may be worth two or three hundred a year, he will find that if he stays at the University, he is almost obliged to live on a scale proportionate to his income, so that he can save very little; or on the other hand, if he leaves the University, there is practically no prospect of his fellowship being renewed.

Of course it is easy for those who have never had to manage a school to make suggestions to those who have been working in schools all their lives; but it always seems to me well in managing any large number of people to individualize as much, and to generalize as little, as possible. I have had something to do with Eton, which is the largest of our Public Schools, and I have been astonished to find there how much they can individualize, bearing in mind the special features of every boy in the school. In one or two cases I found them most ready to consider a peculiarity in a boy's character or future prospects, and they never told me that out of so many they could not take the trouble to make exceptions, which I may say I have often been told in places where there were not one-tenth of the number. I always so much admire the manner of a London physician towards his patients. He may see you only for four or five minutes, but for those four or five minutes you are to him the only person in the world; he thinks only of you; his whole energy is centred upon you, and for that time you can rely upon getting the best attention and the best opinion which it is possible for his enormous experience to give you. So I believe if, even at very long intervals, a master could speak alone to each of his pupils, and let him feel that for that minute or two the master really cared for him and was taking an interest in him, the effect of it would be very great. It is disheartening for children, and even for grown-up people, to feel that their individuality is not recognized, that they are lost in a multitude, and that nobody thinks of their special trials and troubles. Whatever a master or mistress can do in this way is of incalculable value, and I believe this is the way interest is not only made but used to the best advantage afterwards.

Finally, shall we say that the education movement has been on the whole a great success or a great disappointment? Paradoxical though it may sound, I believe it has been both. The effects it has had in civilizing, in improving, and adding to the opportunities and advantages of the young generation have been great indeed, and I believe have far more than repaid the country for all the trouble and expense which it has involved. But there is no doubt that many people expected from it something much more than this, in fact they expected impossibilities, and therefore to a great extent they have been disappointed. I have heard politicians and leading workmen assume that when the young generation got all the advantages of education they could, it would eradicate every distinction between them and the wealthier class. This has not turned out to be the case. It was impossible that by taking a boy and training him, you could rely upon infusing into him qualities of which he had no trace before.

It is a practice among a certain class of politicians to speak of the wealthy class as the idle class; other people in a milder way speak of them as the leisured class. It does not follow because people have money that they are idle, or even that they have leisure. Many of the wealthiest men that we know are among the very busiest, and there is no doubt that if rich people give way to idleness, they have taken a very long stride towards providing that their children, or at any rate their grandchildren, shall not be rich people any more. It is about as hard to keep money as it is to make it, and those who have it, unless they exercise great force and vigilance, are very likely to find the time rapidly coming when they will have it no longer, and if their want of industry is on a par with their want of vigilance, they will sink down in the world. But this is perhaps rather beyond the scope of school education.

Be it yours to make the best of every boy and of every girl that is placed in your charge, and if you cannot show them how to raise their position, at all events you can brighten their lives, making them good, useful, and happy men and women in every relation of life, whether it be as children, parents, citizens, or workers; and it must be remembered that the value of a school career is not to be measured by the amount of information that the boy or girl has got during the years that were spent at school, but rather by the amount of desire and power that they have acquired to accumulate knowledge by their own efforts in after life.

VI

The Engineering Dispute

[National Review, Jan. 1898]

THIS dispute between the engineers' employers on the one side and the amalgamated engineers and some other Unions on the other side, has excited an exceptional amount of interest in the country, not only on account of the magnitude of the dispute, but also on account of the length of time, now over six months, which it has lasted. At the same time, as there is a great deal that is not understood by the public at large, it may be interesting to have it described more fully by one who has been concerned in it from the earliest stages.

As regards the history preceding the stoppage. The Amalgamated Society of Engineers, or, as we will call them, the A.S.E., which is one of the oldest and most powerful Trades Unions in the kingdom, has for the last seven or eight years been adopting a policy different from that of the other well-established Unions. During this period, a socialistic movement was set on foot which was commonly known as the "New Union Policy." The New Unionists taught the workmen to disregard the interests of both customers and employers and get all they could for themselves; they also taught them that the employers were their enemies and must be distrusted accordingly. Of course none of the old Trades Union leaders would approve of this. This view made considerable way among labourers, dockers, and many other branches of labour that had not hitherto been organized; but as a rule the old Unions stood aloof from it, with the exception of the A.S.E., which for some reason adopted a great deal of its policy, and from that time it began to interfere in the management of engineering works, and to encroach on the arrangements of employers in a way not done previously. On such matters as the trial trips of steamers, the allowance to working men away from home, and other matters, new and very formidable claims were put forward. They also tried to enforce very stringent regulations of their own as to who should work various machines, claiming the right of skilled workmen to work simple tools that had hitherto been worked generally by men who had never served any apprenticeship. Each individual claim was not a great matter in itself, yet the sum total of what was demanded amounted to a very serious increase on the cost of labour, and the constant interference made it excessively difficult for an employer to carry on his works either with comfort and profit to himself or with satisfaction to his customers, and early in 1897 the Employers Federation made a strong stand against these encroachments.

We should pause here to give a very brief history of the Employers Federation.

Prior to 1894, engineering employers, as a rule, were only associated in each locality, numbers of firms were not associated at all, and the localities had but a slight communication with each other, and rarely, if ever, made serious steps to support each other in disputes. For example, at that time the Tyne and Wear acted together, but it was not until 1894 that the works on the Tees joined them; and in 1896 these three rivers federated with the associations on the Clyde, Barrow and Belfast. Then in 1897 the demands of the A.S.E. became very pressing in the Lancashire districts, and Manchester joined the federated employers in April, and Bolton in June.

The position in April was this. Owing to the encroachments that had been made, and strikes having been threatened or actually begun, the federated employers decided in their own defence to lock out all their amalgamated engineers, but at the request of the workmen of the other trades engaged in engineering and ship-building, they suspended these notices, and agreed to meet the A.S.E. at a conference, which was held at the Westminster Palace

Hotel last April. This conference settled some points about allowances and other matters; but, on the question of interference with management, nothing was agreed, and the conference came to an end leaving these vital points unsettled, and these constitute what is commonly known as the machine question. What would have happened cannot now be known, but the A.S.E., who had been agitating in London in connection with most of the other engineering trades for an eight-hours day, made the definite demand that it should be granted by all those works in London that had not hitherto seen their way to give it; and then, seeing the serious nature of the demand, the Federation offered to help London, and a union between the London employers and those in the provinces was quickly effected.

The London engineers had hitherto worked fifty-four hours per week; the A.S.E. demanded that the hours should be reduced to forty-eight per week, without any reduction of wages.

A few words are necessary to explain the position of the engineering trade in London. Of course in a large town with a very large port attached to it, there is an immense amount of engineering work, especially repairs, that must be done on the spot, and for the employers who are so engaged, to give the eight hours meant that in the first instance they would have to raise their prices and throw the loss on to their customers; but in so far as the trade had to be done in London, they would not necessarily lose their business, because the customer would have to pay the extra price; and though this would ultimately tend to drive work away from the district, and in the meantime was putting a considerable extra tax on the customer, the employers possibly felt that the immediate loss to themselves was not sufficient to induce them to face the very serious risk and loss caused by a strike. But there were other firms on a wholly different footing, such as Messrs. Maudslay, Sons and Field; Messrs. Humphreys, Tennant and Co.; Messrs. Yarrow; Messrs. Thorneycroft; Messrs. Penn and others, who were engaged in contract work and had to compete with other districts; to these the concession would probably have been almost ruinous. It was difficult enough for them to compete at the high rate of London wages without this extra burden, and it must be borne in mind that shortening the hours of labour is a far greater loss to the employer than it is gain to the workman, because the whole of the machinery is for that time standing idle and unproductive. The Federation therefore signified at once to the amalgamated engineers and the other trades that were acting with them, that the demand was excessive, unwarranted by the state of the case, and could not be entertained; and that if they struck work in London, the federated employers would be compelled to lock out their men all over the country. The leaders of the workmen took no notice of this warning and struck in three of the London shops, and this was followed by the other works belonging to members of the Federation locking out all the men that belonged to those Unions.

It was soon seen that a trial of strength of the first magnitude was before the country. The organized Unions began to levy money, both in England and elsewhere, to the utmost of their ability, and collected very considerable sums during the whole of the dispute. The employers' support was of a different character. Numbers of other employers throughout the United Kingdom, who had suffered severely, felt that if the eight hours was conceded in London it would soon be enforced, as other encroachments had been, all over the kingdom, and become a general rule of the country, to the great injury of the trade; and therefore they cast in their lot with the federated employers, and the numbers of employers rose rapidly, till they probably reached something like 700.

Even this did not throw out of work half the members of the A.S.E., but it was quite sufficient to cause a very severe strain on their funds, and of course the loss to the employers was also great. But the employers on the one hand felt that in face of ever-increasing foreign competition, anything which caused a substantial increase to the cost of engineering manufacture would be a fatal blow to one of England's most important industries; and the workmen on the other hand, probably sincerely believing that a reduction of working hours would be a great boon to their class, and not believing, or not realizing, the dangers seen by the employers, strained every nerve to obtain what they wanted.

Now I hope I have said enough to show that it was no part of the employers' policy to smash the Union. Their action was entirely defensive, and if the A.S.E. Union has been injured, it has been by its own efforts against the federated employers. It is quite clear that other Trades Unions have no apprehensions on this score. A strike has rarely been seen where the other Trades Unions have been so lukewarm in their support, and hardly a single trades union leader of eminence, unconnected with the A.S.E., has identified himself with the movement.

Many employers hold that the members of a well-governed Union are more easily controlled than a body who are all non-Unionists. This depends of course on the prudence and experience of their leaders and the loyalty with which the men will follow them.

The first reason then that influenced the employers was the fear of foreign competition. The friends of the men often stigmatize this as a bogey or a bugbear, but how anyone who looks facts in the face can think this, is very surprising. No one has seriously tried to refute the view of the employers, who after all have most exceptional opportunities for studying this question, and most of whom spend constant time and attention in doing so.

One question which causes considerable discussion is whether the employers were justified in meeting the strike in London by a lock-out of the same society in the provinces. Now, as regards this, a common policy of Trades Unions has been to attack the employers of one neighbourhood with the whole of their national strength, beat them, and then make the demand elsewhere. The strength of the men on strike in London consisted of the fact that they had the whole funds and support of the A.S.E. throughout the kingdom and colonies to support them, and the only way the employers could see to avoid this was to consider the whole body as responsible and treat them accordingly. Had the A.S.E. throughout the country repudiated the action of their London members, and ordered them to return to work, there is no doubt they could have made them do so.

Now, first of all, as to the various disputes which led up to the present difficulty. One was the effort to limit the class of men that were to be employed on certain kinds of work, so as largely to increase the cost of doing that work. For example, they tried to stipulate that only skilled mechanics should be employed to do what an intelligent labourer could learn to do in a very short time. This is adding enormously to the cost of the work, and is very unfair towards the labourer. This demand gradually took the alternative shape that if what are called machine men, that is, more or less fully-trained labourers, were employed on our machines, they must be paid the same wages as mechanics. Now, the effect of this would be that an enormous number of men would have had to receive increase of wages of 10s. or 12s. a week at once; but, besides that, it is obvious that if you pay a slightly trained machine man as much as a highly skilled artisan, no one will employ the machine man as long as there are any artisans out of work, and the effect, in average time, would be to drive numbers of machine men out of work, for obviously you can deprive any man of his employment if you fix the scale of remuneration so high that it is worth no one's while to employ him.

In the case of the trial trips of steamers and other matters, demands for increases were made, which in some cases would seem almost incredible. It is right to say that when these matters were brought before headquarters in London many of the worst demands were abandoned and others very much modified, and at the conference that was held just before Easter, all questions, as far as the federated employers were concerned, were settled except the machine question, which was, speaking broadly, how far the men were to dictate to their employers as to what men were to be put to work the machines. The employers hold that if they buy a machine they have a right to put whom they please to work it; if the man spoils the work, so much the worse for the employer; and, practically speaking, experience has brought into existence certain fairly well-understood customs as to which machines might be reasonably expected to be worked by mechanics, and which might be worked by less highly-paid classes of men. The majority of employers had no wish to deviate very materially from what had been the practice in the past, but strongly objected to incessant new demands and encroachments; while for mechanics to monopolize all such work would take away from labourers all chance and hope of bettering their condition. There would not be mechanics enough in the country to fulfil, in busy times, all claims that would be made upon them if this principle were carried out so far as was demanded in many localities. As has been already said, we do not know how far these local demands were supported by the central authority of the A.S.E. in London; but the demands were made, strikes frequently took place, and the employers were harassed to a degree which was unexampled in the memory of any of them. It must also be observed that some of the men's authorized spokesmen avowedly say that the demand for eight hours is only the stepping-stone to further demands, and teach the men to look on their employers as their "organized enemies."

There was also a general feeling, which was constantly brought under our notice, that the A.S.E. unfortunately wish to restrict the amount of work that they turn out. Much resistance was shown to every effort to run machines at higher speeds and to make them do more work. In England, as a general rule, they refused to allow one man to work more than one machine, whereas on the continent or in America he will work sometimes as many as five or six, and that without any serious amount of labour to himself, for many machines once set will go on for a long time without being touched. In the Elswick works a body of officials were organized who are commonly called "feed and speed men." Their business was to see that all the machines in the place were turning out the greatest amount of work possible, and that the experience gained in one part of the factory should be at once applied to every other part. This, though it entailed no additional labour on the men, was very much resented, so much so that one of the chief officials of the A.S.E., in giving evidence before the Parliamentary Committee on fair wages, protested against it, and demanded that if it was continued the Elswick works should be struck off the list of government contractors. It has also been said by responsible trades union leaders that the more men they can cause to be employed to complete a given piece of work the better for them; and other instances of this doctrine, that the less work they can do for their wages the better, can be readily brought forward. Now it is hard to believe that these doctrines find favour with the more thoughtful and intelligent men, but they are certainly held by officials in high authority, and are acted on sufficiently to have caused very seriously increased difficulties in the management of works. The view of the employer is that the more valuable a man's services are the better remuneration he will get, and that if he can reduce the price at which he can sell his engines and machinery he could then very largely increase his trade, and thereby make a much greater demand for workmen. He also believes that skilled workmen will always command their price, and that the skilled man has nothing to fear from an intelligent labourer, who only began to learn the business after he had arrived at maturity. In every trade reduction of prices means increase of business; and in engineering it is especially so, for the majority of the products such as ships, railway materials, machinery, etc., are simply investments of somebody's capital for the purpose of earning dividends, and the cheaper these articles can be supplied the more they stimulate investments. If every workman tried his utmost to turn out the greatest possible amount of work at the cheapest possible cost, far more men would be required than at present, good trade would be much more lasting and bad trade far less common, and the amount of money that each man would take home at the end of the week would be very much larger than it is at present, with no more labour to himself.

As regards the danger of foreign competition, few people realize the magnitude of this. The most modern development of engineering is in electrical work, and in this the amount of work done in America, Germany and Switzerland, is far in excess of what is done in England; the quality equally good, and the price far lower; and this applies to many other branches of the trade. Generally speaking, in the largest and heaviest kind of work, England can still hold her own, but every year our trade is encroached on more and more, and, unless we can substantially decrease the cost of production, the consequences will be most serious, above all to the working engineer. In ships, even in Atlantic Lines, our superiority is seriously threatened, and in the manufacture of smaller and lighter articles we are losing ground every year.

Now as regards the eight hours. While it is obvious that no man ought to work, either in his own interest or in that of his employers, for such a length of time and to such an extent as to hurt himself, there is no evidence to show that the present hours are too long. We always find an abundance of men willing to work overtime, and we are not aware that they feel any ill effects as long as the overtime is not too frequent or too protracted. When the nine hours' day was obtained in 1871, the men certainly did not do as much work in nine hours as they had done in ten, and the deficiency was not made up till after long years of effort in improving our organizations and introducing new and better machinery. On the Clyde they reduced the hours to fifty-one, but they found they could not get on and were compelled to revert to fifty-four. In other districts not long ago, the hours were reduced from fifty-four to fifty-three by taking off an hour on Saturday. The effect of this, as far as can be judged, has been that on the first five days of the week there is no difference, and on Saturday the quantity is just diminished by the amount of time that they leave work earlier; and furthermore such has been found the frequent experience of almost every employer of labour who has from various reasons to work his men shorter hours. And those who have recently given the eight-hours day say that the men certainly do no more work per hour than they did before. It is curious to observe that the men specially claimed the eight hours in London on account of the distances they had to travel daily to their work, and yet at the three works where the men struck— Humphrey's, Thorneycroft's, and Middleton's—there is no difficulty in getting abundance of workmen's houses close to the works, and if the men live further off they do it by preference. Sometimes men work at places where, owing to trains or steamers, they can only work a shorter day; occasionally the factories are put on short time; there are frequent cases of men who, instead of starting at six, only come at half-past eight, and the invariable experience has been that when once the hours are short enough not to injure the man's health you will not increase the output by shortening them any more. Shorter hours are luxuries, and while we might be glad to see hours shortened if it could be done without injury to the men themselves, and if the state of the trade could warrant it, it is very mischievous to pretend that luxuries cost nothing, and to say that we can indulge ourselves without having to pay for it. Rightly or wrongly, the writer was one of those who was really glad to give the fifty-three hours instead of fifty-four, because it was a real enjoyment to the men to get one whole afternoon a week, which they could use either for their pleasure or profit as they pleased; but it is one thing to say that one was glad for them to have the pleasure and quite another to pretend that it did not cost anything to give it. As a general rule the firms who have given the forty-eight hours are those that are engaged on repairing and jobbing work, and numbers of these have very little machinery, so the question affects them much less; and also, in the first instance, they throw the burden on to their customers, and so do not feel the immediate effect, though, as I have before said, they may do so in the long run by the shrinkage of their trade. We are often told that we employers could afford to make this concession, but this could only be done either by increasing the cost of the goods that are sold or by paying it out of the profits. As regards the first, it has been pointed out that foreign competition is a most serious danger. At the time of the shortening of the hours from ten to nine, in 1871, foreign competition was for a very remarkable reason non-existent, because America had not become a serious competitor, and the whole energies of Europe were employed in making up for the great destruction of property caused by the Franco-German War.

In other words, the employers in this struggle hold that they are fighting not only for their own interests, but quite as much for the true interests of their workpeople, who are misled by erroneous ideas as to what the trade of the country can bear. Even in England there have been many cases of trades being injured and sometimes destroyed altogether because the workpeople would not look facts in the face. And the principal reason why shortening hours is specially injurious to the engineering trade is because, if the men are away, a large amount of costly machinery has to be idle. Probably an employer has about £150 of capital invested in his works for every man he employs, and not only does the absence of the man leave all this unproductive, but it in no way postpones the date when the machine will become obsolete and have to be replaced. Even as regards blacksmiths and other men who do hard manual labour, if, as the advocates of the eight-hours movement claim, the men would do as much work in eight hours as in nine, it can only mean that they must work harder while they are at it, rest less, and be more hurried, and this might do them far more harm than the additional leisure would do them good, and leave them more tired at the end of the day.

The fact is, that the shortening of the hours has been advocated on two opposite grounds: one is that the men will do as much in eight hours as in nine, which is improbable with men and impossible with machines, the other is that by reducing the amount of work done, employment would be found for more men; but the obvious effect would be to increase the cost of work very seriously, so that we could obtain fewer orders, and instead of employing more men we should employ fewer. There is no evidence that the present hours, fifty-three or fifty-four per week, are injurious to any man. Most of our men are eager to work longer hours (or overtime) for the sake of extra pay. To keep our trade going we must reduce the selling price of our manufactures, not by overworking our men or reducing their wages, but by their co-operating with us to get more and better work done by our machines.

And now it may be well to state what would be the probable effect if the eight-hours day were given generally throughout the engineering trade of England. The first effect, especially following a long strike, would be to make things extremely busy, because there would be large arrears to work off; and if, as most employers anticipate, the men do very much less work in eight hours than they do in nine, it is evident that the immediate requirements of the world would be worked off more slowly than heretofore; and as no one wants to wait for what is absolutely necessary to their existence, there would be considerable bidding among customers to get their work done, which would cause a large momentary increase both in prices and wages. But this state of things would not last. Every rise in prices would tend to make our customers go elsewhere, and probably, in two or three years at the outside, we should have depression of trade worse than even those very serious years 1877 and onwards; a large number of small and weak employers would be ruined; the old and the less efficient workmen would probably be thrown out of work, never to be re-employed, and a vast amount of suffering caused. Those employers that were left would no doubt strain every nerve, by the adoption of new appliances and by increasing their capital, to recover the ground that was lost; but numbers of men being thrown out of work, the men would have to submit to a severity of discipline to which they are wholly unaccustomed, and probably to what might fairly be called an amount of "nigger-driving," which would be hateful both to the employer and to the employed, and which would only be endurable in preference to the ruin of the one and the starvation of the other. This is what largely did happen after the nine-hours movement. To say that the country has got over it is only to say that the world sooner or later gets over all its great calamities; but to ignore these and to forget the effects of them can only be caused either by levity or heartlessness. There are no two opinions as to the superiority of the British workman, when he exerts himself, to any other man living; but if he ceases to exert himself, or if he handicaps himself too heavily by trade restrictions or shorter hours, he is like a horse over-weighted in a race where the best animal may be beaten by another altogether inferior if the conditions are too unfavourable, and the employers believe that they are fighting this question in the interests of the workmen quite as much as if not more than in their own.

VII

Presidential Address to North-East Coast Institution of Engineers and Shipbuilders

[Delivered in Newcastle-upon-Tyne on October 14th, 1898]

FORMER Presidents have addressed you on various topics: sometimes on the general state of our trade, and sometimes on some subject of which they happen to have made a special study; you also regularly hear and discuss papers by various members, on all that is best and newest in the construction of ships and engines, and from these papers we learn not only what to make and how to make it, but we are also instructed in laying out and managing works, in all that is new in machinery or buildings, and in everything which contributes directly or indirectly to the carrying on of our business. But as it is necessary that every President should speak of that to which he has given very close attention and study, I feel that I must speak to you on the subject to which I have been compelled to devote so much of my time of late years, namely, the human element in our works, or, in other words, the relationship between the employer and the workmen. I shall therefore speak of our workmen, of their legitimate hopes and aspirations, of those matters which are liable to cause friction between them and their employers, and the hopes of improvement. Nor do I apologize for this. One of the greatest, if not the greatest of the problems in the life of an engineer or shipbuilder of to-day is the labour question, and looking at this Society as a body mainly composed of young men, and of men of whom we may expect that the larger proportion will presently either have their own works or be responsible managers of works, I know of nothing more important than for you to form clear views on these questions, not only in the interest of the workmen themselves, but also in the interest of the employers, of the trade, and of the country generally.

Now, to put the matter on a broad footing, you may of course see that a man might be condemned as an unsatisfactory manager if he failed in any one of a great number of particulars; but whereas, with regard to all the mechanical part of his business, and even with regard to the commercial element, he can see a distinct line of training whereby he may know whether he is or is not qualified to undertake a certain position, and may compare his experience and powers with those of other men, yet with regard to the tact, judgement, and experience required for the management of his fellow-creatures, there is no such training and no such test.

We often hear of a manager who has had to give up his position because, we are told, he could not manage his workmen—could not get on with those about him—or because he was always offending the customers; and surely it is worth while to give some thought and study in order that we may qualify ourselves for these duties, without which a manufacturer and his staff will never be able to achieve any practical success.

The whole question of the relationship between employers and workmen is complicated by a great deal of feeling, which is unfortunate and unnecessary. When we consider the enormous number of workmen that are employed, each man with his own interests, his own difficulties, and the possibilities of misunderstanding, we see how very easy it is for friction to arise, and I sometimes question whether any transactions between man and man are, on the whole, carried on more smoothly than those between employers and workmen; even our great strikes, enormous as they are, bear a very small proportion to the large numbers of men in the country who are working peaceably and quietly; and when you think how often people quarrel with their neighbours, and sometimes with their customers, I am sure you will admit that the position I indicate is, to say the least of it, not untenable.

And furthermore, I am disposed to believe that the hostile feeling is not brought in so much by the workmen themselves as by well-intentioned but generally ill-informed outsiders; and while I fully recognize the excellence of their motives, I think it a pity that our disputes are sometimes intensified by the words of irresponsible people, who imagine that they are capable of deciding on questions about which an old employer of labour or a trades union leader of life-long standing would pause to think over very carefully before he gave an opinion.

On one of the commonest class of questions discussed, namely, wages questions, you will all find that before you can eventually give an opinion of any value on the merits of any case you must be sure that you very thoroughly understand the whole condition of the industry, the state of the order book, and many other subjects which are rarely known except to those engaged in the trade.

Those who are not engaged in the trade may study these questions or leave them alone as they please, or may keep what is called an open mind; but *we* have to face disputes and difficulties the moment they arise—they will not wait for our convenience, and we must be prepared to try and settle without delay or hesitation all points of friction that arise in our works. Probably much the larger proportion of questions are so settled. Some of the cases may be referred to an employers' association, a few of them may develop into strikes, and one here and there becomes a matter of national magnitude. But as you can only settle difficult technical questions quickly and without delay by having a mind trained in sound scientific principles, so you can only settle disputes between an employer and workmen by having carefully studied the broad principles that ought to underlie the employment of labour in such industries as ours.

I observe that many of those who broadly sympathize with the employers rather than with the workmen, talk as if all our disputes and labour troubles were owing to the existence of trades unions. But this idea has lost ground very much of late years. At the time of the late eight-hours strike, when a great cry was raised that the object of the employers was to smash the unions, our president, the late Colonel Dyer, kept to the front, both by statement and evidence, the fact that the employers had no such intention, and the working classes as a whole, and those unions that were not actually interested in the dispute, never showed much anxiety on that point, which they certainly would have done if they thought that the intention of the employers was to make an attack on the existence of trades unions.

Discussion and free expression of views on these questions used to be deprecated on the ground that it would never do to let the world know that employers held views different one from another. Very probably many workmen also felt that they had better not let their divergences of opinion be seen. But this principle is unsound, both for them and us; it is inimical to all effort to take enlightened and intelligent views of these questions, and only conduces to enforcing an unreasoning and narrow-minded tyranny on the minds alike of employers and workmen. No one can seriously believe that all the employers in 700 works (still less that 100,000 workmen) can all think exactly the same on every point, and it was silly to pretend that the impossible was a fact. And where there is a great amount of unanimity, as among the employers in the late engineers' strike, the more each individual is encouraged to express his personal views frankly, the more clear the strength of the whole body of opinion will appear to any thoughtful person. In politics most men act with their parties, and yet no one supposes that there are only two classes of thought on political questions; and so it is in labour disputes. Let us express our opinions freely and frankly, and then let the united body act on the resultant of those opinions, both as to direction and force. We must all give and take, and sink our own views in the average view of the body to which we belong.

Now to revert to the idea that there would be no labour difficulties if there were no trade unions. I think this view is wrong.
We are apt to fix our eyes on some earnest, self-reliant workman,
who thinks out every question for himself, and rises in the world
by his own exertions, and to say, "Oh, if there were no unions,
and all men were like this, how much better it would be!" But
what ground have we for thinking that if there were no unions all
men would be like this? I think all our knowledge and all our
experience go to show that at all times and in all countries,
among men and women of all classes, the natural tendency of most
people is to take conventional views (or in other words to adopt
each other's thoughts), to lean on each other, and above all to select
some one, or some few stronger natures, to guide them, preferring
to be led and to obey rather than to think things out for themselves and act on their own responsibility. Conventional customs,
conventional wages and hours exist where there are no unions,
and in case of dissatisfaction a number of men, hitherto disunited,
are liable at any time to hold a mass meeting, and, guided by
impulse, to elect the most plausible or violent men as their leaders,
and make demands of an extreme character, such as the leaders
of an experienced union would never adopt; and, worst of all, if an
employer comes to a compromise with these ephemeral authorities,
there is no safeguard that the men will not throw their leaders over
and adhere to their old terms, or demand something worse. Personally, I think we are safer in dealing with wise and experienced
union leaders.

But you may ask, am I not begging the question by assuming
that the unions and their leaders will be wise and experienced?
Quite true, we have unions and union leaders of both sorts. There
are those who, while making the best bargains they can for their
clients, still recognize that the employer has his rights, and that
trade is a delicate plant that may be injured if care is not taken.
All of you can at once recall the names of many leaders of the men
who try to meet the employers in a fair and friendly spirit, and

who often succeed in checking unreasonable demands on the part of their men. I don't mean to say that all their demands or positions are right, in fact they differ one from another; for example, you all know that some trades object to piece-work and others object to anything else. But as long as they try to act fairly, and recognize the interests of others as well as of themselves, it is possible to discuss amicably and compromise honourably. There is however another view of the question.

Some seven or ten years ago a new force came to the front which called itself new unionism. Despising the good work and experience of men who, as union leaders, had earned the respect of people of all shades of opinion and of all classes, its supporters advocated extreme demands, and some of them actually taught in many cases that employer and workman were natural enemies, and that there could be, and ought to be, nothing but distrust and hatred between the two.

Happily I believe this wicked nonsense has never taken a deep hold of the bulk of the working classes; but if so, it is not the fault of the advocates of such views. All I wish to point out to you is that unless we, as employers, really wish well to our workmen, and they to us, and both of us recognize our duty to each other and to the trade of the country, it is of very little use trying to establish amicable relations or to arrive at any settlement likely to be mutually beneficial; and I think we may say that all the sensible and experienced leaders of the workmen fully recognize this.

I would now say something as to the classes of demands that we receive from our workmen and the causes of friction; and, for simplicity's sake, I will try and classify them under four heads:

1st. Demands which benefit the workmen and are also beneficial or not injurious to the employer.

2nd. Demands which are beneficial to the workmen, and which, at a greater or less sacrifice, the employers can afford to give.

3rd. Demands which are beneficial to the workmen, but which

the employers cannot afford to give, either on account of their own interests or on account of the trade.

4th. Demands which are not really beneficial even to the workmen.

As examples of a benefit to the workmen and also to the employers come changes which are troublesome to make, but which afterwards repay the trouble. Personally, I think the weekly wages movement was a case of this. Speaking generally, I think that a workman's income goes further if he is paid every week, and, if so, weekly pay will make our service more valuable and attractive, while the extra trouble and cost are not very serious.

Under this head I myself am disposed to class a reasonable restriction of overtime. It is a point on which the opinions of employers are divided, but, personally, I favour a restriction of systematic overtime. I believe that to keep men on every evening till they are tired out, and perhaps all night on Friday, is bad for their health, demoralizing, and most wasteful. The men cannot give such valuable work, and the chances of accidents are much increased. Of course emergencies will happen when tremendous and special efforts are required, and everyone ought to be ready and willing in such cases to do their utmost. An occasional hard spurt will not hurt anyone; it is the systematic strain that is bad. Also, whenever a man is hard up or wants money, the temptation to increase his income by working overtime is very great, and it seems such an easy way out of his trouble; but it may be bad for him all the same. When the leaders of the men on the North-East Coast, in 1891, first tried to restrict overtime, they got the employers to agree to rules which were too tight and too inelastic; consequently the men themselves soon tired of them, and the employers found them injurious and sometimes intolerable, and in 1896 they were abolished. In legislating down an old and ingrained custom it is wise to fix the restriction so that it will only stop the very worst cases. Then, the majority of the men not being affected, you have the public opinion of the shops on your side, and you really do something to limit and reduce the evil. I hope it may prove that the present agreed rule of forty hours overtime in four weeks will prove a benefit to both the workmen and the employers. Personally, I think it will, though of course I may be wrong.

As regards the second head—a demand which is beneficial to the workmen and which, at a sacrifice, the employer can afford to give—an obvious example is a reasonable increase of wages, while an excessive demand for wages would come under the third head, of what the employer cannot afford to give. It is no benefit to anyone if the employer is too severely fleeced. Our ever-increasing population requires for its support ever-increasing industries, and if the return on capital is not enough to tempt employers to increase their works, or start new ones, it is a bad look-out for the future. Still worse is it, if prices have to be raised so as to diminish trade.

As regards the fourth head, or demands which are good for neither employer nor workman, a number of the recent points in dispute come, in my opinion, under this category. To some of these I must briefly refer, and you can judge of them for yourselves.

First and foremost came the recent demand which, stated roughly, was that all the engineering shops in London should only work eight hours per day. Now it was one thing for repair-shops, and shops that worked for London and had no competition with anyone outside, to give the eight hours, and quite another thing for those works, such as large Admiralty contractors, who had to compete with the Tyne, the Clyde, and other places, to give what would hopelessly handicap them. Personally I do not think the case for eight hours was made out for any of the works; but certainly it would have been ruin to such trades as I have mentioned. But I will not now discuss this, the more so as many of us published our views at great length during the struggle. Hours of labour however are just one of those things that probably could be better dealt with if we had no unions either of employers or workmen, for one firm might be able to do what another could not, and at any rate experiments could be tried.

5—2

But what really, in the eyes of the employers, had paved the way for, and led up to the great struggle, was the claim to interference in the management of the works. We held it as essential to success that the management of any works must be in one hand, and be guided by one who knows all the conditions, needs, and capabilities both of the business of our customers and of our rivals. This is no assertion of superiority. The workmen may be good and wise, but they have not seen the correspondence; they have no touch with the customers; and, above all, they are not, what employers essentially ought to be, men who devote their lives to the study of the general interests and conditions of the trade. Anything that would injure the trade would injure the men equally with us. On board a steamer we forbid the passengers, even in their own interest, to interfere with the man at the wheel, and in managing a business the wheel is and must be in the hand of the employer, or, to speak precisely, in the hand of the man who takes and is responsible for the execution of the orders.

Then, to pass on to other points. If in America one man looks after half-a-dozen little machines, we in England cannot compete if we put one man on each machine; nor should we be bound to put a skilled mechanic to a job that can be perfectly well done by a labourer. Some employers are said to press both these and some other points too far; but, if so, they will soon find it out by the work becoming inferior in quality, or too costly.

Again, we say that in the interests of the next generation, as well as of the trade, there should be no limit to apprentices, but that every lad ought to be allowed to learn some honourable trade for his support.

Another class of dispute is limits of demarcation. Is it right that if a pipe is three inches in diameter a plumber must screw it, while if it be a quarter of an inch larger he must not, but an engineer must be called in? Clearly there is a margin where both men are equally competent. No one wants to put on an engineer to solder a lead pipe, or a plumber to fit up a valve motion; but where both men are equally competent the employer ought to be entitled to employ either. In ship work these limits are an intolerable nuisance, and I have no hesitation in saying that they are without sense or justification, and are to the interest of nobody. The proper guide would be that a workman should be willing to do whatever can be done with the regular tools of his trade. Thus, either an engineer or a boilermaker may cut a hole in a plate, but an engineer should not, as a rule, be asked to work on hot iron, because he has not been trained to it.

I must however pass on to speak of the state of things that arises when, unhappily, workmen and employers cannot agree, and war is declared; for example in a factory the men of one trade strike, and their union, if it approves the action, supports them. The loss to the men is spread over a wide area, and is easily borne. The employer feels that he alone cannot compete with the whole resources of the trades union, so he appeals to his co-employers. They may help him in three ways: either by negotiation, in which their greater weight and influence may tell; or they may add to the burden and diminish the resources of the trades union by locking out all the members; or they may subsidize and give him such money compensation as may make him content to stand out. In the case of a lock-out, if large enough, the pressure on the men becomes very great; in the case of subsidy the union may be expected to get tired of letting its funds bleed away, if the only employer affected is quite happy. I must say I hope that as time goes on we shall more often see our way to adopt subsidizing instead of locking out, for however highly we may estimate the loss caused by a strike in a single works, the cost to other employers of reimbursing that amount by subsidy is very small indeed.

This leads me to say something as to the cost of strikes and lock-outs. Some extraordinary figures have been given as to what the late eight-hours strike cost the employers, but I will rather try and lead you into the way of making estimates for yourselves of these things. First, what does a strike or lock-out cost the men and their friends? After much thought you will probably come to the conclusion that it really costs just the amount of wages not earned by the men who are on strike or who are laid idle on account of the strike. If the trades unions allow the men so much, that means that the union shares the loss; but it neither increases nor diminishes the loss by a penny. So if other friends subscribe it makes it easier for the men on strike to hold out, but the loss (as I put it) to the men and their friends remains unaltered. So if 40,000 men are laid idle for 30 weeks, and their average earnings are 30s. per week, the cost for the 40,000 men is £60,000 per week, and the cost for 30 weeks is £1,800,000.

Then come two losses which I cannot estimate; one is the permanent loss to the trade of the country by directing that trade elsewhere. I think this is serious, and it is equally a loss to workmen and employers; a curse to both, a blessing to neither.

Next comes the loss to customers. A manufacturer who cannot get his steam engine, a shipowner who cannot get his ship to sea, anyone who cannot get his repairs executed, loses heavily. I am sure that these losses in the aggregate are greater than those of either of the contending parties. There again both sides are responsible, and the loss in the long run falls as much on one side as on the other.

Finally comes the direct loss to the employer. While a strike lasts this is difficult to estimate, but if any of us look back on strikes that happened, say two or more years ago, when all matters are things of the past, and all difficulties connected with them are at an end, it is not very difficult to make a rough estimate; and, as I have estimated the loss to the workmen as equal to the wages that would have been paid and are not, so (always in both cases including, for financial calculating, with the men on strike, those who are laid off on account of the strike) I reckon that the cost to the employer of his works standing idle, of interest on dormant capital, salaries of officials who must be retained, rent, rates, and all the other things we include under the head of working charges, is about one-half of the cost to the men. The permanent loss of connection to an employer is not often very great, unless in the case of an already decaying trade; but, to include that also, I think a liberal overhead estimate of the cost to the employer would be £1 per week per man for all the men on strike or laid off on account of the strike. Isolated cases may show special results, and here and there, owing to some peculiar circumstance, a special loss may be incurred, but broadly speaking I have no doubt that any strike or lock-out costs the workmen and their friends at least 50 per cent. more than it costs the employers and their friends, if not double. In the last strike, and as a general rule in engineering and shipbuilding disputes, the amounts paid in subsidies have been very small indeed, but in some trades, and in some cases, the system has been carried out very completely. Until recently there was a widespread dislike to combined action amongst employers. Thirty years ago there was very little of it, and it has increased gradually; and quite recently, stimulated, as I think, by the irritating attacks of socialism, it has grown rapidly. If employers wish for it, there would now be no serious difficulty in uniting all classes of employers for mutual support. Whether it would be an ideal state of things for the industrial world to be dominated by a union of capitalists is another matter, but, to my mind, it is simply a question of outside pressure. Trades union aggression and socialistic legislation have forced capital to combine, and if these forces became less powerful or less active, so far from capital becoming stronger, I believe our natural love of liberty would assert itself, and the bonds that bind us together would rapidly slacken and become weaker.

When I said I thought we got on better when our men were in well-governed unions, I was speaking of things as they are. I can well imagine a state of things where unions would be superfluous. Why is there this constant hostility between an employer and his workmen? We are indispensable to each other; we have our greatest interests in common; and, if we take a broad view of things, it is absolutely certain that it is a great advantage to work-men for their employer to be rich and powerful; while I should say it was quite as much to the interest of the employer for his men to be comfortable, prosperous, and, above all, secure in their employment and free from anxiety about the future; and if a manager can be, as he almost always is, identified heart and soul with the interests of his employer, why cannot a workman be the same, and whose fault is it that he is not?

If time allowed, I could enlarge on the causes that have put us on a wrong footing, but I will merely indicate one direction in which I have always thought we might rise towards better things.

There is no doubt the great evil of our large industrial organiza-tions is the loss of personal touch between employer and workman. It is both true and creditable that the more people know of each other the more they respect and like each other; but I will merely now, in conclusion, refer to one (perhaps one of many) means of narrowing the gulf between employers and employed, and that is by workmen becoming shareholders in the works that employ them.

In the South Metropolitan Gas Company, Mr. Livesey has not only, within a few years, induced his workmen to invest savings to the amount of some £50,000 in the shares of the company, but also holds out hopes of very soon electing a working man as a director on the Board.

To apply this to our own cases. We may say that for every workman employed in our trades there is about £150 of capital invested, and as the average wages paid (taking men, boys and labourers) is about 30s. per week for 50 weeks, it means that the capital required per man is about two years' wages—much the same as it costs a man to buy his house. Now it is not very difficult to see that if any man saved up 10 per cent. of his wages for 14 years, and could invest the money at 5 per cent. compound interest, he would then have a sum equal to two years' wages, or, as I have said, to the capital that employs him. If only a few of our men would do this it would be a step towards identifying our interests, and, besides that, the educational value of an investment is very great. You put money into something, and it is wonderful how quickly you will learn about it, and get rid of any unsound views you may have previously held. The workman-shareholder would be a connecting link between the capitalist and the workman, and if the men held a large enough interest, a share in the management must follow.

What England has gained by having made her railways out of the savings of the middle classes is simply incredible. That gave the class such a training as enabled us to take the lead in railway construction and all sorts of other public works all over the world; and what the middle classes did for the carrying trade of the world, I should like to see the working classes undertake for the manufacturing trade. I know that many, if not most employers would heartily welcome workmen as shareholders.

Meantime, we want if possible to establish a greater measure of confidence and sympathy between our workmen and ourselves. Our duty clearly is to give the sympathy and deserve the confidence.

VIII

Cost of Working the Workmen's Compensation Act

[JUNE 8TH, 1904]

IT seems to be desirable to arrive at some idea of the burden which is thrown on the employer by this Act, both as regards the increased cost of manufacture and the diminution of profit.

There are few, if any, figures in existence which will help us to arrive at a general view of the position, but the examination (for a wholly different purpose) of a large number of manufacturing businesses leads one to believe that, speaking generally, the actual capital of manufacturers is on an average about double the amount annually paid in wages. In this capital debentures and mortgages are not included, but the interest on them is included in the cost of manufacture, the same as rent, rates, and taxes.

If then the employer's capital is double his annual wages, we may consider wages as an annual average charge of 50 per cent. on capital, and any charge of, say, 1 per cent. on wages would be an annual charge of $\frac{1}{2}$ per cent. on capital, and any dividend would be reduced by that amount. We shall not be far wrong if (see rates of insurance) we take the cost of the Act as equal to ten shillings per cent. on wages, or—in other words—as a reduction of $\frac{1}{4}$ per cent. from profits or dividend.

Thus, if an employer would have made an annual profit of 5 per cent. on his capital, he will now make only $4\frac{3}{4}$, unless he can throw the burden on to the purchaser or someone else.

As regards the profits made by employers, it is very difficult to form any estimate that will be generally accepted as correct. But to take one instance, in a highly speculative industry like the Coal

Trade, figures (taken over more than 100 years) go to show that the average profits on capital invested are about 4 per cent. Of course, many enormous fortunes have been made, but on the other hand many investors have lost their entire capital; and there are many cases where an enterprise has been very unprofitable, and the colliery has been sold at a great loss, whereby the purchaser starting with a much reduced capital has made a fairly good investment. The successful men are easily seen; the losers, probably a larger number, are overlooked altogether. And even some of the most successful collieries have sometimes gone on for a number of years without paying any dividend at all. The same principles apply, more or less, to all manufacturing trades, and in confirmation of this it may be observed that only a small section of the public invests in this class of enterprise, and also, if a concern pays regularly much over 5 per cent., the shares generally stand above par.

Of course, beyond this, any employer who gives his time to the business should receive such a salary as his time and ability would earn in the open market; this is *his* wages.

We shall therefore probably not be far wrong if we accept the view, that on an average the shareholder or sleeping partner gets about 4½ or 5 per cent. per annum on his capital, reduced by this Act to 4¼ or 4¾ per cent.

But it must be noted that if two capitalists employ the same number of men, although one of them may make 50 or 100 per cent. profit, and the other is losing enormously, they will both contribute exactly the same to the cost of the Act.

But the idea of the Workmen's Compensation was that the employer would only compensate the workman in the first instance, and that he would reimburse himself by charging more for his goods, and this view must be investigated.

This is on the face of it improbable; a manufacturer will commonly sell his products at the highest price he can get, and this is limited by two things.

First, by the price at which someone will undersell him.

Second, by the price at which the consumption of the article will be lessened. (A reduced cost will enable a manufacturer to sell at a lower price, but an increased cost will not enable him to secure a higher one.)

English manufacturers work so much for foreigners, and in competition with foreign manufacturers, who are not under English Acts of Parliament, that if they raise their prices to cover increased costs, they simply lose orders to a greater or less extent, by being undersold in competition; and all commercial experience of all ages and countries shows that every increase in the selling price of an article reduces its consumption.

Of course, though these principles are true, the cost of working the Act is very small compared to the variations that frequently take place in the rate of wages and cost of material.

But though of small application, we must follow the principle further. If the price is raised, there will be less manufacturing and fewer men employed. If the price remains where it is, those manufacturers whose costs are highest, and who can bear no increases, must cease to manufacture; and, again, fewer men will be employed.

Thus in this, as probably in all commercial vicissitudes, the rule is that immediate and temporary gains and losses fall on the employer (and may be sufficient to ruin him); but, in the long run, permanent improvements and permanent burdens in any trade are borne, to a great extent, by the working classes.

IX

Three Articles on the Workmen's Compensation Act

[Written for 'The Times Engineering Supplement']

I.

[Nov. 29th, 1905]

THERE are at all times matters, besides buying, selling, and labour questions, which very materially influence the profitable character of every trade.

One of these, which is of great importance, is the Workmen's Compensation Act of 1897 and 1900. This Act has been productive of much good, but also of some, possibly serious, harm. A committee was appointed by the Home Office to inquire into the Act in 1904, and an amending Bill was brought before Parliament last Session, which was, however, with other measures crowded out for want of time.

The recommendations of the committee on the Bill only went into the question of amending details, and did not touch the main principles.

It will be remembered that this Act introduced a new principle in making an employer liable for accidents to his workmen, over which he had no control, and for which he might not be in the slightest degree to blame. The logic of this is, of course, that if a workman has an accident for which he is not to blame, he should not bear all the suffering and loss. Rather let it be borne by the community, or at any rate by the trade as a whole. The employer therefore compensates his workman, and seeks his remedy either by insurance or by taking his own risk, and must recoup himself, if he can, from someone else, and as he is only in direct touch with his workmen and his customers, the burden must fall either on one of these or on himself. We will investigate this hereafter.

Now in the case of a large employer the matter is tolerably simple. Taking one industry with another, we may consider that he can insure against all the risks under the Act for about 10s., or ½ per cent. on the amount he pays in wages, while to the workmen the benefit of the Act involves, in case of accident, the whole difference between tolerable comfort and utter ruin; and, as long as the Act is worked fairly and compensation is given justly, it is a distinct step in the right direction. But it has many difficulties. Sometimes it is used as a means of blackmailing or of extortion; if the employer is a poor man, he may be unable to pay the compensation, and the difficulty of making small employers pay has restricted the Act to a very moderate section of the working classes. And the most serious effect of the Act is that small manufacturers and farmers are becoming increasingly unwilling to employ men more than they can possibly help, and it is becoming more and more difficult for middle-aged, infirm, and one-eyed men to get work at all.

This probably tells seriously on the question of the unemployed. Although trade is on the whole improving, we find from this cause that in some country districts the increase of able-bodied vagrants is most serious. Now, no evil can be so bad for working men as to be shut out of employment altogether. A farmer, or small contractor, with £300 to £500 of capital, might be absolutely ruined by an accident to a workman, over which he had no control; and, on the other hand, some small employers so carry on their business that practically no workman could get compensation out of them, even though he had a perfect case, as there would be no available assets.

A very sad effect of the Act is, as is well known, to make it very risky to give a day or two of charitable employment to some casual poor man, for fear of his having some slight accident and making a very exaggerated claim.

But in large industries there is a much brighter side. The employer can take better care of himself, and if the injured workman puts himself in the hands of a strong trades union, he usually gets a fair settlement without litigation; and employers have very seldom had to complain of unions supporting unreasonable or excessive demands. Where employers are wealthy, and trades unions are powerful, these questions, like many others, work smoothly, except in rare cases.

The chief problems of the Act are:

1. The case of small employers who cannot or will not pay.

2. Obscure accidents, possibly complicated by previous bad health or injury.

3. Blackmailing.

4. Excessive awards.

5. The position of insurance companies.

These last are complained of as being harsh in settlement, and unfavourable to small employers, while, on the other hand, the insurance companies complain that they are looked on as fair game for everybody.

Employers who cannot or will not pay are necessarily small men, and the insurance companies do not lay themselves out for the smaller class of business. Unless compelled by law, probably many of these small employers never would insure, even if the process were easier than it is, while in this as in any other class, compulsion is very unpopular. A small employer may insure his one or two regular men, but will often muddle on anyhow rather than employ an extra hand. His own interests may suffer, but he does not see it, and the man who might have got a job goes to swell the ranks of the unemployed.

As regards both large and small employers, much harm has been done by excessive awards. If an employer believes that in case of permanent injury the most he will have to pay will be £400, he will arrange his estimates accordingly, but if a soft-hearted judge awards some man £800 instead, all employers will put up their estimates, and thus will now and then lose orders, whereby their men lose employment.

Insurance companies necessarily fight their claims much more than an employer would do, and this makes them unpopular with the average workman, who dislikes fighting and litigation.

A remedy recommended by some of the labour leaders is Government insurance. How the Government would like this it is hard to say, but they could work it far more cheaply than insurance companies, and might fairly make a small profit, while a strong, uniform, impartial hand would be an enormous boon to both employers and workmen. The logical sequence would be compulsory insurance, but, in adopting this course, consideration would have to be given to the question of how far it discouraged casual employment.

II.

[DEC. 20TH, 1905]

We now have to consider the actual cost of this Act to our industries, and to study where the burden falls. The first cost is, by law, thrown on the manufacturer (coalowner or other employer), and the first point is to estimate the direct cost to him, and we must then consider the possibility of his passing on the loss to either his customers or his workpeople.

Taking only our large industries, such as engineering, ship-building, and coal mining, we shall not be far wrong if we assume the following figures as roughly correct: average weekly wages earned by mechanics, labourers, and boys, £1. 10s. 0d., or (say) per annum, £75 per head; amount of capital per man employed, double this, i.e. £150. Therefore an increase of 1 per cent. on wages is equal to an annual charge of ½ per cent. on the capital employed.

It has already been stated that the average cost or rate of insurance is about 10s. per £100 paid in wages; it will accordingly lessen any annual dividend on capital by ¼ per cent. per annum. Thus if without the Act a company would pay 5 per cent. per annum, it will now pay only 4¾ unless, as shown above, it can pass on the loss to customers or workmen.

The next question is, what are the probable average profits of employers? This is a very difficult question to answer accurately, but we must try to make a rough estimate. Take one instance, the North of England coal trade. Sir James Joicey wrote a letter to *The Times* (May 21, 1901), in which he showed that the profits of the coal trade as a whole, for fifteen years, had been 6·11 per cent., but this allowed nothing for amortization (or annihilation of capital by working out the coal), nor for those unsuccessful efforts to sink collieries which come to nothing. These would reduce the 6·11 per cent. considerably. Figures kept for over 100 years, for the Newcastle district, go to show the average profits at about 4 per cent., which is probably much the same as 6·11 with the above deductions.

Political economists teach us that wherever possible profits are highest, average profits are lowest; and, though it is difficult to prove the fact absolutely, there is the strongest probability that in no trade, as a whole, will the average profits in the long run exceed the interest on good securities. It is generally believed that the more speculative kinds of mining are carried on at an absolute loss. A few capitalists make enormous fortunes (as in gambling), but poor investors, and those without good information, have no chance at all. In every line the few successful men are conspicuous, while the large number of losers remain unseen. Probably we may say that the real average return on capital, in labour-employing investments, after allowing for depreciation, is not much above 4 per cent. If a company can be relied on to pay 5 per cent., its shares will stand above par—*e.g.* railways.

Of course, beyond this, an employer has a right to a salary equal to what his time and ability would command in the open market. This is "wages," not return on capital. So we will assume the average profits to be $4\frac{1}{2}$ to 5 per cent., reduced by this Act to $4\frac{1}{4}$ to $4\frac{3}{4}$ per cent., unless the burden can be transferred elsewhere. This is equal to an extra income-tax over the whole trade of 1s. in the £. But it must be observed that if two manufacturers employ the same number of men, the Act costs them each just the same, although one may be making large profits and the other may be losing money.

Can the manufacturer throw this extra charge on his customer? Let us consider one or two cases for and against. In work for the British Government, as a general rule, no foreigners are employed, and no foreign material is used. Therefore, if the Government asks for tenders for, say, a ship, all competitors are equally subject to the Act, and the work must go to one of them. They each quote slightly higher than they would if there were no Act, and the cost of the Act therefore may fall, in this case, on the customer. But this applies to very little of all the work that is done. In most cases foreign competition comes in; even when foreigners are not directly asked to tender, their prices are always in the background as possibilities, as in the case of steel plates, forgings, and castings, and even electrical machinery and locomotives. But of course England could not get on at all, and masses of our workpeople would starve, if it were not for the manufactured articles that we supply to foreign countries; and here we compete with others who may not have to incur this expense, or may have wholly different ones (as a matter of fact, most countries have a Workmen's Compensation Act); but, obviously, whatever adds to the costs of manufacturing increases the irreducible *minimum* below which work cannot be taken, and therefore is liable to cause orders to be executed abroad, or, which is far more perilous, not to be executed at all.

The last contingency is much more serious and common than the general public appreciate. For example, people will often argue thus—"If a man wants a ship, he must pay at least the lowest price at which he can get it, and if all the builders who tender put up their prices he must pay more accordingly." But this is quite an unsound view as far as commercial work is concerned. What the shipowner wants is an investment, not a ship. He sees what the net earnings of a possible ship will be, and if the capital required is so large that the dividend will not be satisfactory, he will not order the ship at all, but will invest his money in some other way. So both employers and workmen must observe the need of keeping down the cost of production as low as possible.

III.

[Jan. 3rd, 1906]

In order, moreover, to consider the possibility of an employer increasing his prices so as to throw the cost of the Act on his customers, it must be constantly borne in mind that a manufacturer will always sell his produce at the highest practicable price; and although a reduced cost will enable him to sell at a lower price, an increased cost will not (or will only rarely) enable him to get a higher one. So generally the increase of cost ends by throwing men out of work, unless they will either take lower wages, or, by working better, restore the low cost.

We must again however repeat that the Act, where it works tolerably well, is an immense boon to the workmen; and, as far as large works are concerned, it ought to be possible to remove, or greatly alleviate, the evils; but in the case of small employers it is to be feared that the whole position should be carefully reconsidered.

Nothing will help the small employer except such a system of insurance as will make him absolutely certain that, once having paid his insurance, any injured workman will get his compensation direct from the insurer without causing the employer to be troubled in any way, or rendering him liable to get lawyers' letters.

Now, to assume the possibility of Government universal compulsory insurance. It might work out to something like this:—

Every employer might have to get a licence to employ one, ten, one hundred, or one thousand workmen for a week, month, or year. The cost might be *nil*, but the condition would be that the employer either had insured or could give security that he was good for any possible claim. (There are many cases where employers have to give security for large sums, and this would be no trouble.) A small employer would probably have to pay as insurance, either ten shillings per year, or say 2½*d.* per week, and then his policy ought to secure him against any claim or trouble of any sort whatever. It might include giving a ticket to the workman, who would be instructed to make any claim direct to the Government (say to the nearest post-office). As far as can be seen, the trouble of taking out a licence to keep a dog does not count for much. This licence would be taken out just as easily, and it may be hoped that this system would tend to remove much of the present unwillingness of poor men to be employers.

As regards large works, if manufacturers and others could insure old, one-eyed, and infirm men at the same rates as others, all the objections to employing these men would vanish at once, and a terrible injustice to a most deserving class of men would be removed. As it is, if such men are disqualified from employment, they must at last come on to the poor rates—*i.e.* be supported by the nation—but in the meantime they have to undergo the protracted misery and bitterness of slowly sinking from a position of honour and comfort into dependence and poverty and to the workhouse, while their children's whole prospects are blighted and their future ruined. This could be saved by universal compulsory insurance, and a considerable deduction would be made from the ranks of the unemployed.

How would it affect the Government? The rates of insurance above quoted are what are actually paid, and include a profit to the insurance companies, which the Government might get. They could probably work the insurance more cheaply, and would have less litigation. Very soon a number of fixed rates would be established, such as death, blindness, loss of limb, and so on, each bearing a fixed proportion to the sufferer's weekly wages.

Failing Government insurance, it would seem to be worth consideration for every responsible trades union to insure its own members. This would only apply to the most prosperous and united of the working classes. But a trades union is responsible for the future of its own members, and if they are rendered ineligible for employment, either they or their union have to bear the loss. As in the case of the Government, the union could insure at a profit, and the union would have one great advantage over the Government, which is that, as insurers, they could take exception to anything, either in structure or management, which made employment more dangerous than it should be. They could, better than the Government, fix scales of compensation with their own members, so that they would have absolutely no legal expenses on either side to allow for.

Either of the above methods would, as far as it goes, ensure the two things that are needed to make the Act satisfactory, viz.:

Every injured workman would be absolutely certain of his compensation.

Every employer would know exactly what he had to pay, and, having paid it, would be free from all further claim and anxiety.

X
Alms-giving

[MARCH 24TH, 1906]

I FEEL that this is one branch of a much larger and more important subject that can only be dealt with as a whole. The question is sometimes raised whether a Christian man ought to give away a certain proportion of his income, say one-tenth, but while each man may find a special rule useful in his own case, we must not let any such statement obscure the broad guiding principle.

In our Baptism, we devoted ourselves entirely to the service of God—soul, body and possessions—nothing to be kept back—absolute surrender. We are placed in all sorts of positions, and have all sorts of duties, but we all agree that our duty is to perform even the smallest and most worldly business as part of the work that God has given us, and to do it in the full spirit and wish to serve and please Him; in short, to try and let each thought, word and deed be done as we believe our Lord would have done it had He been in our place.

It may be asked, why do I presume to put forward these ideas, which we all know to be the ground-work and basis of the Christian life? Merely because I have spent my life in business, and I know how very hard it is to incorporate these principles into our financial arrangements. I was made very sad in my youth by hearing, from two leading business men, that they thought it was not possible for a man to live up to as high a standard of honour in business as in private life. To my mind this is simply to say either that the world is stronger than the grace of God, or, if that section of the world were such that the grace of God would not go with us to guide us, that it is no place for a Christian. Some of us are very apt to mark down certain careers and positions as unfit for a Christian; many think the Stage, the Liquor Traffic or the Army unfit for a Christian to touch. We must each judge for ourselves, and we are promised guidance for ourselves, but I do not see that we are promised guidance for other people; and I am satisfied that not only is it impossible to judge what is, or is not, someone else's duty, but, to revert to our special subject, it is equally impossible to form any idea as to how my neighbour ought to spend his money, how much he ought to give, and to what objects.

But that which is of sin cannot surely be consecrated to God, and before we talk of giving, we must make the income itself pure. This is indeed a great difficulty, and especially for those who carry on the trade and commerce of the world, although, in a less degree, for all of us it is the steep and difficult path on which we have to learn to deny ourselves and bear our Cross; and if, out of the mistakes and experiences of a lifetime, I can bring any ideas which may help and encourage others, I ought to be deeply thankful.

Some may say, why not leave it? Why mix up with this money-grubbing? Why meddle with the muck rake (as Bunyan calls it) when the golden crown is held out overhead? The only answer I can give is, "to one he delivered five talents, to another two, to another one"; and the talent, small as it is, is not to be laid up in a napkin.

A business life does not attract young men, however eagerly it may be clung to by old ones. The excitement of the army or navy, the fascination of far travel and discovery, the brilliant career of the lawyer or the statesman, the refined charm of the student or artist, or, on the other hand, the glorious self-sacrifice of the priest or the missionary, all appeal to the higher or lower enthusiasms of youth more than the confinement and monotony of the high stool and the ledger. Often and often the man who ends his days in wealth only entered this path after the other half-dozen doors had been closed against him. Few curates become Bishops, few subalterns become Generals, and quite as few of the humble denizens of the counting-house or the factory emerge as Capitalists or large Employers.

Now, to understand the philosophy of either getting, or disposing of, money, I must pause to impress upon you one economic fact which is often forgotten, but without which all consideration of money questions is unintelligible, and that is the position of Capital. Mr. McCarthy says that, for want of understanding this, the Roman Catholic priests, with the best intentions, are ruining Ireland. Whether capitalists happen to be good or bad, whether the world could dispense with them or not, Capital, the *thing*, is of vital necessity to the human race, and the more there is the better off the people are. Capital may belong to the wickedest and most selfish man in the world, but he cannot make a profit on it without employing labour, and when we think of 1000 unemployed, we must remember that if someone started another large factory worth say £150,000, he would at once want just about 1000 men for whom there was no demand before. It is all very well to talk about finding work for the unemployed, but the man who wants to employ his capital will and must employ labour. Even if he is a usurer it comes to the same thing—he lends money to others that they may employ labour. And if Capital is destroyed, the poor very often suffer even more than the owner. Suppose a factory is burnt, it takes a year to rebuild it; very likely it is insured, and the loss to the owner is small, but the poor people who are thrown out of work may starve for a year. To take another case, the railway from here to London has an enormous money value to all of us, not only to the shareholders. I will not dwell on this, but it is of vital importance to bear in mind when we come to talk of giving, spending, and investing, that the first duty may perhaps be *to create Capital.*

I shall have more to say later on as to making the income, and making it honourably, and I will here venture to impart some practical experience. For convenience, I will divide a man's income

under two heads: first, what is necessary to keep him in that state
of life in which he is placed, and, second, all beyond this. To
many the second has no practical existence: to most it is small:
to a few it is large. Of course it is trite to say how much it relieves
anxiety to live on a smaller instead of a larger scale, to which
I would only add that a man is much less tempted to what is
doubtful in money matters if he lives within his resources; the first
step to which is to try how small, and not how large, a house he
can manage to live in. I was always brought up on the principle
that every increase of income brought increased duty and responsibility; that no matter how much was given one, it was not given
for one's own pleasure, but to be used for the good of others, and
that therefore wealth was not at all a thing to be desired, so long
as one had enough, and "enough" depended very much on one's
own industry and self-denial. In fact, I was taught that, given
food and raiment, wealth was a duty and a responsibility rather
than a blessing; and if, among those who listen to me, there are
any who are actively engaged in the pursuit of wealth, I would
suggest to them what a great help they will find it, if, more than
other men, they try and discourage themselves from associating
the idea of wealth with the idea of enjoyment. I would suggest
no Puritanical ideal, but I am sure that, if a man is mixed up with
money-making, it is a great thing to take as detached a view of
money as possible, and not to look on it as the principal source
of one's pleasures, since many of the greatest pleasures, such
as social intercourse, reading, some forms of travelling and even
of sport, are inexpensive. As a rule I would advise the man
whose duties compel him, night and day, with sleepless vigilance, to be watching in either the exchange or the workshop,
to train himself to lean on and love money as little as possible.
I remember once talking to a cellar man who was stacking bottles
of wine, and he told me he was a total abstainer; on my expressing
some surprise, he said he did not in the least wish to judge for other
people, but as he was all day and every day among wine and

spirits, he felt it a good safe rule never to touch them himself. I commend this view to the money-maker. I would not, in the faintest degree, hint at the condemnation of innocent pleasures, nor would I pretend to judge for others, but I think it a sound principle that the man who is in special temptation should strengthen himself by special self-denial. A very present and subtle temptation is to think "if I had money how much good I could do." It seems to me that this idea has no support from the Bible or the Church, and is against all Christian experience. I would pray that if it pleases God to give me wealth He will give me wisdom and self-denial to deal with it, but I am a steward and not an owner. He can give the money where He sees best, without my intervention, or He can carry through the work without any financial assistance from anybody.

Once allow yourself to wish for wealth for any purpose, however noble or plausible, and you take the first step towards driving hard bargains, crushing weak competitors and grinding down wages. By this wish we have seen not only individuals but whole churches demoralized. The purification of one's income is far more important than the dispensing of it. I should like to quote the four beautiful maxims of Thomas a Kempis:

1. Be desirous, my son, to do the will of another rather than thine own.
2. Choose always to have the less rather than the more.
3. Seek always the lowest place and to be inferior to everyone.
4. Wish always and pray that the Will of God may be wholly fulfilled in thee.

One more word of secular economics. It ought to be clearly understood that the essence of true commerce is that everyone is enriched and no one is impoverished by it. A man orders a ship, an engine or machine; the greater part of the price is paid in wages which would not otherwise be paid, thus making work for the unemployed, and tending to raise the rate of wages. The employer makes a profit, and yet the purchaser considers that he is better off for having the article than he was with the money he has paid for it. This is of course often a very difficult ideal to live up to, but only business that carries this out is legitimate, and it applies probably to an enormous proportion of all the business in the world, even though the people who buy, make, and sell, never trouble their heads about it.

But I must now pass on to the disposal of the income and the giving of money in charity.

I quite agree that for a man's own guidance, it is well to have a hard and fast line somewhere of money set apart to be given, and I daresay a tenth may be a suitable minimum. But really very much must depend on a man's immediate circumstances.

Having first purified the income, and having saved what ought to be saved, then, and not till then, do we come to expenditure in giving. And here it must be borne in mind not only that widow and children should be provided for, but that of all the millions of poor men in this country practically none can be employed unless somebody has first of all saved up a substantial sum of money called Capital; and I may add that to employ a man in England, in the twentieth century, generally needs an amount of Capital equal to from once to double his yearly wages.

Now every man must decide on his own scale of living, assuming that in no case must it exceed nine-tenths of his spending income, and probably if he is wise it will fall far short of it. For though salaries and safe investments may be reasonably secure, wages, professional incomes and business profits are very uncertain, and a man must be prepared for years in which he may have a reduced income, or very possibly none at all. But you will see that I am still reserving the one-tenth as a minimum.

If my experience is correct, I think, in a place like Newcastle, most men, even careless and irreligious men, give away more than one-tenth, but the human and secular claims are very large and urgent, and show for nothing, which is one reason why I say it is absolutely impossible for any man to judge as to what another man gives or ought to give.

Then, assuming a man to have a more or less varying income, he will give his regular tenth *plus* a much larger proportion of his surplus income in good years. Suppose a man has an average income of £1000 a year, varying from £500 to £1500, he will set aside £100 as his regular offering, will save something, and spend the rest. In a bad year he will draw out of his savings enough to live upon, *plus* the hundred, but if he has a good year he will very likely give away a great deal more than one-tenth of his extra £500. The large, and often unsolicited, donations that rich men occasionally give are frequently connected with some rare windfall, and of course cannot be repeated unless the windfall is repeated.

And now, how and to what shall the money be given? It seems to me that here again it is impossible to make rules, and utterly presumptuous to imagine one can judge for anyone else. I knew a man, anxious to relieve distress and make work for the unemployed, who came to the conclusion that if he moved into a larger house and entertained more, he could meet more of the class from which his customers were drawn, increase his connection, get more orders, and employ far more people. But, as a matter of fact, he decided that his habits were formed, that his gifts did not lie in the social line, and he took the, to him, easier course of spending less and giving more. I knew another man, of great wealth, who had the reputation of giving away nothing. But at length I heard his apology, and it was this—"I spend very little on myself" (which was true): "I want to benefit, both temporarily and permanently, as many people as possible: I lay out all my money in works of general usefulness, factories, railways, mines, ships, etc.—they all employ labour to make, they all employ labour to carry on, and they are all permanent benefits: they make coals, corn and travelling cheaper, wages are higher, and more and more people are comfortable, both because they have more money and because each shilling goes further." The natural retort was—"All this goes to make *you* richer." "Yes, but I spend no more on myself: the richer I get the more men I employ, and the more I improve the world."

Whether you take his view or not, it must never be forgotten that no man can be employed unless somebody has had enough self-denial to save up Capital to employ him.

But passing on to consider claims—feeding the hungry, rescuing the sinful, guarding the young and the weak, helping those in difficulties, supporting education in its endless forms, and furthering Church work at home and abroad—all these demand help. On the evils of indiscriminate almsgiving a very great amount has been written and reiterated during a generation or more, but whatever we may think about giving money to strangers, most of us have before us many cases of distress as to the reality of which we can have no doubt, or if this is not so, our clergymen can show us where the needy are to be found.

As to how to apportion our gifts between these objects, it is very difficult to make any rule. Personally, I think I would say that hunger or acute distress must always have the first claim on everybody. As regards Church work, of course every congregation ought to try and provide for its spiritual needs being met, and its own services being carried on decently and in order; but beautiful buildings, music and what may be considered luxuries I would put on a different footing, which I would try to explain thus:

A Christian ought not to wish to see his own house better cared for than the church where he and his brother Christians meet and worship together, and we make our churches stately, beautiful and restful, so that they may be a home and a rest to the weary in spirit, and that these may feel that here is an atmosphere altogether different from that of the world. But we beautify as a pleasure and a thank offering.

I feel most intensely that all dispensing of money given ought to be guarded by the most rigid economy. Numbers of Christian people give only through great self-denial. The few pounds which are accepted as a matter of course by a committee may mean that an overworked man has relinquished his much needed holiday, or that a mother has not got that equally needed new dress. I have heard collectors sneer at what they call "the stereo-typed guinea," when they little realize what a number of these the average middle-class man gives away, and what a gap they make in the family income. It is easy for men and women of energy and influence to start new objects, and perhaps raise large sums, but the necessary effect of this claim on willing givers often is to leave them unable to support perhaps more deserving, but less brilliantly exploited, objects. Are not such new objects the obvious cause of the diminished income of our older charities, such as the S.P.C.K. and others?

Personally, I doubt the wisdom or propriety of ever *begging* hard for money. Mention the object, but don't press it: the responsi-bility lies with the steward of the money to dispose of it. And I greatly admire those Christians who will not ask a man who is leading a godless and careless life, to give money to a religious object, and will not even accept money from a man who is living in open sin.

First draw the heart, and then I suppose the gifts will follow, but that is a very small matter in comparison. Kindle in our hearts the love of God: teach us that all we have is His: make us realize that all these things are as nothing if only we may serve our Lord. I cannot believe that the money is worth having without the willing heart. Surely the Bible teaches this, and some of its most plain teaching is to tell us not to trust in riches, and that the gift of God cannot be purchased with money.

XI

Four Articles on Labour Problems

[WRITTEN FOR 'THE TIMES ENGINEERING SUPPLEMENT']

I.

[DEC. 12TH, 1906]

IT is obvious that no engineering works or appliances are of any value excepting subject to the skill and energy of the human beings who are occupied upon them, and therefore it is impossible to consider any engineering questions, especially with reference to cost, satisfactorily, unless we take account of labour problems. In recent times these have become very conspicuous, and there are few manufacturers who have not studied the question carefully. As a rule, the general public also take a considerable amount of interest in them. I therefore offer no apology for occupying a small amount of space with the consideration of these problems. The most conspicuous recent development in the interests of the working classes is the powerful and energetic party in the House of Commons known as the Labour party, in which we may include those trades unionists who are identified with the Government, but who, on broad issues, practically agree with the others. Although Radicalism and Socialism are two very different creeds, yet, as far as practical Parliamentary work is concerned, the two are substantially acting together, and it is well to consider the effect that their action is likely to have on the trade of the country. My point of view is represented by the engineering trades, to which, therefore, I shall as far as possible confine myself.

A few months ago some articles of mine on the Workmen's Compensation Act were published in *The Times Engineering Supplement*, and nothing has happened since to alter materially the position or the views as laid down in those articles. I would merely repeat that the great weakness of that measure is that an enormous number of small employers will probably be unable to pay compensation if their workmen are injured, so that their workmen, at any rate, have been given rights which they will, in numbers of cases, be quite unable to enforce. If the very small employers are allowed to insure in the Post Office this will be a distinct step in the right direction. To take up another very important bill, the Trade Disputes Bill; the main points of this bill are twofold; one, the protection of union funds; the other, the freedom of picketing. Of course, this bill only comes into effect when labour disputes have reached an acute form—that is, when there is either a strike or a lock-out. Furthermore, as we see that in the case of large stoppages the employers usually make no effort to fill the places of the men who are out on strike, the bill will have no effect in these cases. But where strikes are very small, and where it would be easy to replace the men on strike by the importation of others, where the employers are weak, and the unions, or workmen combined in any other manner, put strong pressure on them, the effect of the bill may be very considerable. Even where workmen are replaced from a distance, by what is commonly called free labour, if the employers are wealthy and powerful, and supported by others of their class, it is very likely that their position may not be very seriously prejudiced, because it must be borne in mind that an employers' association is a trades union within the meaning of the Act, and therefore they are free to do many things from which hitherto they have been legally debarred. What these are it is perhaps not my business to specify; they will probably find them out quite soon enough themselves; but if free labour is brought in under precautions, and in considerable numbers, it is probable that no extra picketing, short of downright rioting, will have any great effect.

It has been pointed out already that where this bill will act most prejudicially will be in the case of such works as railways, gas companies, electric light companies, and others whose stoppage is not so much an injury to the employer as a calamity to the whole community. It certainly seems to me that some provision ought to have been made to save an innocent public from suffering the appalling evils that might be brought on by a cessation of the supply of food and of other necessaries to an inland town, or even a city from being plunged into darkness at the caprice of either a trades union or an obstinate employer. As the Act is sure to be passed, probably the best way out of the difficulty would be if, in the case of those companies who exist under special Acts of Parliament (which would practically cover all those indicated above), no stoppage of work should be allowed, and every dispute should be compulsorily referred to the Board of Trade for settlement. This would be a serious evil, but nothing like so great an evil as would be involved in the stoppage of such industries.

I consider that the point to be arrived at should be that those industries which have a monopoly in serving the public should not be allowed to stop work on any pretext whatever. The employers have enormous advantages from their monopolies, and the workmen have the very great advantage that they have no slack times and are not subject to the vicissitudes of industrial competition; therefore, as their work is regular and continuous, they ought to be bound to accept the position and make it such.

I fancy the time is far removed when anything like compulsory arbitration could be applied to ordinary industries, but there are a great many points in connection with strikes and trade disputes which are very often overlooked, and on which I may have something to say on a future occasion.

II.

The real question involved in the Trade Disputes Bill is whether it is wise of Parliament to establish rules for the conduct of disputes which are, admittedly, to the advantage of nobody. It is questionable whether the working classes have not, in the long run, lost far more than they may have gained by strikes and lock-outs, because even their victories always have to be paid for in dislocation of trade, which really means diminished employment.

As far as can be judged, fewer and fewer strikes now terminate in favour of the workpeople. This is probably owing to the fact that employers as a class are far wealthier in proportion to the number of men they employ than they were thirty years ago. To build a factory at the present time would probably require at least half again as much capital per man employed as it would have done a generation ago. Besides that, whereas in those industries in which we are chiefly interested (engineering and shipbuilding), it was very common in those days for the customer to make liberal payments in advance in order to help the manufacturer, it is far more common in these days for the manufacturer to give long terms of credit in order to help the customer. Therefore, of course, should it be worth his while, the employer, being richer, can hold out much longer against a stoppage of work than he would have been able to do in old times.

In speaking of strikes, it must be borne in mind that a strike is not merely a cessation of work, but an organized cessation of work in which the workmen not only decline to work themselves but refuse to allow others to take their places. If workmen simply considered the wages too low, or the work distasteful, and quietly left without taking active measures to hinder others from succeeding them, that would not be a strike. It is the interference by workmen with their would-be successors that constitutes a strike, in favour of which the whole of this legislation exists.

Of course an organized strike carries with it the disability that it is exceedingly difficult for the men on strike to obtain employment, whereas, if they simply left their work, every other place would be open to them if their services were required. Nearly all the most experienced trades union leaders of the country look on strikes with the strongest aversion; and those of them who have been most successful in raising the wages of their members and of improving the conditions of work are very generally those who have the greatest objection to coercion and stoppage of any kind. In fact, if we trace the history of strikes, a large majority of them are probably caused, not by the deliberate policy of experienced leaders, but by the general irritation of a body of men which betrays them into ill-considered action.

It is remarkable how very little thought has been given to what may be called the strategy of strikes on either side; yet, in a war of this description, thoughtful and well-considered tactics are probably quite as important as they are in a military campaign. Hence we see anomalies like the following: should there be a strike in a given district, employers very often try to induce other employers to close their works so as to make the area of the strike as wide as possible, thinking that it is to their advantage. On the other hand, it is equally common for workmen, when on strike, to try and induce other workmen to leave work also, seeming to think it is also to their interest that the area of the strike should be as wide as possible. Now, it is quite obvious that both cannot be right, but if we look to irritation, and not to calculation, as the guiding principle, we see clearly how these results are brought about. Other instances of this can be given, but it is to be hoped that before long this form of private warfare will cease, as another form of private warfare, called duelling, ceased, not only because they are both wrong and evil, but because, generally, they utterly fail to carry out the object which they are supposed to serve.

It must further be remembered that there is a very distinct limit to the pressure that any body of working men, however strong, can bring to bear upon their employers, because when employers find the business is not worth carrying on, the rich ones gradually reduce their operations, and the poor ones probably succumb altogether. The consequence of this is that men are thrown out of work, and, in the long run, where there is insufficient employment, it is almost impossible to keep up the rate of wages, and quite impossible to raise it.

Probably the commonest cause of a rise of wages is that the general body of men in any trade really adopt experimentally a certain standard of wages, and employers must either pay this or dispense with their men's services. Of course, the science of the union leaders is to adopt the highest rate which employers will pay, so long as it is not so high as to diminish the number employed.

Again, in considering the question of an advance of wages, a trades union leader may be safely guided by the following rule. He naturally desires the total amount of wages paid to his class of workmen to be as large as possible. If by getting a 5 per cent. rise of wages he throws only $2\frac{1}{2}$ per cent. of his clients out of work, he has on the whole gained; but if by getting the 5 per cent. advance he throws 10 per cent. of the men out of work, his men obviously lose more than they gain.

As employers are always anxious, for other and obvious reasons, to do as much work as possible, and as the men want as many of their number to be employed as possible, the interests of the two are up to a certain point identical. And, even beyond this, most experienced employers know that in labour, as in material, the higher prices are generally the cheapest in the long run, so that the interests of employers and workmen are by no means so divergent as is commonly supposed. This is borne out by the fact that, considering that perhaps 70 per cent. of our population belong to the working classes, labour disputes, though large in themselves, are really very small indeed compared either with the interests involved or with the amount of fuss and trouble that there is over other much smaller matters.

III.

[February 6th, 1907]

In case any of my readers should think that I have minimised the importance of strikes and have taken too optimistic a view of the relations between employers and their workmen, I should like to point out the unique position that England, as a manufacturing country, holds in the trade of the world, and show what great results have been achieved by the co-operation of employers and workmen, whether compared either with present countries or with past times. Now, these results could not have been obtained by two enemies who were always ready to attack one another, nor does the stability of our position remind us of "a house divided against itself."

If anyone reflects on the state of large bodies such as the Northumberland or the Durham miners, and how they have gone on now for a number of years without any serious difficulties, the owners making fair profits and the men having steady work, it seems to me that the popular view of the difficulties between capital and labour is extremely exaggerated, and that Parliament has given an undue amount of attention to perpetuating and stereotyping a class of dispute which really ought to cease to exist altogether, and which certainly bears only about the same proportion to the general mass of good work done in the country as lawsuits bear to the general body of our trade.

It is often considered that trades unions are organizations existing mainly for the purpose of quarrelling with the employers, but this is a very unfair view to take of them. Where one thousand or one hundred thousand workmen have common interests, it is far better that they should act together, under trained and experienced leaders, than that each man should act separately, or that the whole should be swayed by mere passion or prejudice, which is always liable to be fermented by ignorant and unscrupulous agitators, or which is apt to attach undue importance to some misunderstanding or some ill-judged action on the part of an in-considerate employer. The difference between unions and no unions is very much the same as the difference between an army and a mob. If an army sets to work to do wrong, or to use force to do what is right, it is far more powerful than a mob; but, nevertheless, as a rule, we look on an army as a protection and on a mob as a danger; and since the working classes were better organized, their demands have been, as a rule, far more moderate and their action far more thoughtful than in olden times, when they were unorganized. And although people may point out certain wicked and foolish things which have been done in the name, and with the influence, of trades unions, this is only the same as pointing out what crimes have been committed in the name of liberty, and yet nobody would say that liberty was an undesirable thing. It may be added that boards of directors and other organized bodies sometimes do unwise and absurd things, but we do not therefore seek to abolish them.

To revert to the illustration already made use of, I have no hesitation in saying that the North Country coal trade has worked far better and more smoothly, under the firmness and tact of half-a-dozen leaders—most of whom happen to be also members of Parliament—than it would have done had the two counties been entirely unorganized and acting upon impulse led by inexperience.

Nearly all large unions in these days are guided by men of great ability and knowledge, and although, of course, both as regards unions of workmen and unions of employers, the machinery some-times makes it difficult to effect experimental changes, and some-times fetters originality in thought and action, yet on the whole I think there can be no doubt that we are a great deal better with them than without them.

Unionism has some obvious faults, which conceivably might be mitigated. Like all large organizations, unions are too fond of cast-iron rules, and do not appreciate that their very strength would enable them to make exceptions, when desirable, without fear of their going too far. There is also, of course, the question of jealousy between one trade and another, which comes out in the limits of demarcation as to which of two trades has a right to a certain class of work. These probably ought to be dropped entirely. The work ought to go to that trade which is best qualified to do it, and things would very quickly adjust themselves; and it is far better for those who work, so to speak, on the fringes of the trades to be on friendly terms with each other, so that every workman gets a certain amount of knowledge of the work of those with whom he necessarily has to co-operate. Besides this, disputes tell very seriously against that universal friendliness which ought to exist among all sections of the working classes.

I often regret, moreover, that unions have been so firm in discouraging, and generally in abolishing, sub-contractors, or cases of one workman taking a piece of work and employing others. No doubt this practice was open to grave evils, but it may be accepted as a universal maxim, both in industries and in politics, that where people are strong enough to abolish a custom they are also strong enough to reform it. I believe that sub-contracting not only enabled a great many of the workmen to make money and to rise in the world, but it also gave the working classes generally an insight into certain problems which their employers have to face, and had it been fostered instead of abolished, I think it is very probable that by this time large sections of industry might have been carried out by workmen in groups, in a way which would have been extremely profitable to them.

This brings me to the consideration of an individual who, though not usually very popular, is really exceedingly important, and that is the small employer. We shall probably hear a great deal more of him under the new Workmen's Compensation Act, because there must be millions of such small employers in the country who will be quite unable to pay compensation to their workpeople, and this, while disclosing their numbers, will very likely add to their unpopularity. Large employers very often dislike small ones, because they give way to the pressure of labour instead of standing firm, and where there are considerable numbers of them this makes it impossible for the large employers to resist the pressure without them. The workmen say that they are much more exacting and unreasonable to deal with on account of their impecuniosity, and I have more than once heard a union leader say to me, as an employer, "You don't like them, and we don't like them, and we very much doubt if they like themselves, because they have very struggling lives and great difficulties; and would it not be as well if they were abolished?" But the real fact is that they fill an exceedingly important place in our national economy, not only because, among them, they probably employ far more workmen than the large employers do, but also because in consequence of having been small employers, enormous numbers of working men rise in the world, and it is more and more obvious that the capitalist class wants to be incessantly recruited from below.

No doubt some young workmen and a great many working apprentices get into the drawing office, or in some other way get out of the workshop and rise to be managers, and very often become employers of labour, and this is excellent; but a still greater number probably save a little money, or join with some friend or friends having money, and thus become small employers, and then gradually grow into larger ones, and in the second generation they not infrequently hold important positions.

IV.

[MARCH 6TH, 1907]

We now come to the final point of passing judgement on the Labour party, and the value of the work they have done in the past session. In this case it is fair, first of all, to consider what was their ideal, and, secondly, how far they have acted up to it.

For their ideal one cannot do better than place on record the businesslike and manly words, extracted from a recent address of

Mr. Alexander Wilkie, M.P., to his constituents, which are as follows:

As we stated during the contest, we went to Parliament to do business, not merely to talk, and in this respect the Labour party have led the way, by the method they adopted of appointing committees for all matters before the House, in which Labour was specially interested, and likewise by having one or two spokesmen thoroughly conversant with the questions at issue as their speakers in the House; and the general adoption by all parties in the House of such a method would save time, facilitate business, and avoid useless repetition in debate.

And again, towards the end of the same address:

Labour questions have been pressed forward by the sympathetic attitude of the Government, but the Labour party have not narrowed their patriotism to a class, but have endeavoured to maintain and improve the national welfare, and foster comradeship amongst all classes; they have assisted wherever possible the cause of international peace, whilst at the same time maintaining the rights of our countrymen, whether at home or abroad.

These statements represent a high ideal, and there is no doubt that, as far as good intention and good faith are concerned, the Labour party have tried to act up to this ideal. This is no question of the desirability of having working men in Parliament. I think that there is only one opinion—that there is not one working man too many in Parliament. Probably everybody would be glad to see a larger number of them there; and this is borne out by what many of us can remember—namely, the cordial reception that was given by all men, of all shades of opinion and social position, to Mr. Burt and others when they were the first working men to enter the House of Commons. But this also ought to show what is likewise clearly proved by the action of Parliament during the present session—that the working class, as such, have no enemies, that everybody receives them cordially, and wishes to do them the fullest justice in the most friendly manner.

Now, what have the Labour party achieved? They have merely passed two bills, both of which were practically unopposed. I have pointed out in previous articles what seems to me the great weakness of both these bills. The new Workmen's Compensation Act is almost valueless without further legislation in the direction of compulsory Government insurance, or of some efficient substitute. To this statement I would only add that, as the employers of the country as a whole could probably insure against all the liabilities of the Act by a payment of something less than $\frac{1}{2}$ per cent. on the wages paid, so the benefits to the working classes cannot be more than that amount, and, therefore, if one working man or woman in two hundred is thrown out of work by the bill, the working classes positively lose more than they gain, on the whole, by the Act, especially as the sufferers would probably be the weakest and most defenceless.

The Trade Disputes Bill, as I have pointed out, enormously increases the fighting efficiency of both employers and workmen, and is, therefore, calculated to make our miserable trade disputes more common and more serious than heretofore.

The thoughtful part of the country has long felt that the House of Commons was getting increasingly careless in practical legislation. We never know now what an Act of Parliament will do, or will not do, till it has been through the hands of the Judges—hence the ever-increasing amount of what is called Judge-made law—and certainly the two bills mentioned above, in their final form as passed, give one the idea that very little thought has ever been expended in considering how they would work out and by what difficulties and pitfalls they were encompassed.

We want, in fact, to get our working men in Parliament back to Mr. Wilkie's ideal:—

not to narrow their patriotism to a class, but to endeavour to maintain and improve national welfare, foster comradeship amongst all classes, assist the cause of international peace, and maintain the rights of our countrymen at home and abroad.

The only amendment I would make would be in the last line, for "our countrymen" to read "all men of every nation."

Probably seven-tenths of the nation are of the working classes, and practically they are, therefore, more interested in national and Imperial questions than anyone else. It has sometimes been suggested that the Labour party might support whichever political party would do most for labour, but this is fallacious. No mere labour questions are so important to the working classes as their own general well-being, and they are pre-eminently the nation; they are, under another name, the General Public.

Can they not see from the cordial and courteous welcome they have had in what has been called the pleasantest club in London what reception they may expect whenever and wherever, either singly or in a body, they rise upwards? Can they not see that every workman who can either accumulate capital or raise himself is making more employment for others, and making it still easier for the next man to rise?

There is absolutely no limit to the possible expansion of our engineering trade, provided we can produce cheaply enough. Every reduction in selling price, however small, makes an increase in the demand, and this reduction will be brought about not by lower wages, but by better methods and by more efficient organization.

Every question in politics, be it military expenditure, fiscal policy, religious education, or coloured labour, ought to be looked upon from the point of view not of what will pay best, not of what is to the interest of ourselves and our fellow-subjects only, but of what is to the true interest, both temporal and eternal, of the whole human race.

The working class are not only the great majority of the nation, but they are the recruiting ground from which the other classes must be constantly renewed. Upon their breadth of view and their unselfishness depend the future of the Empire, the happiness of humanity, and, if they will only believe it, the most certain road to their own prosperity.

XII

Commencing Business

[READ TO THE NORTH-EAST COAST ASSOCIATION OF SECRETARIES,
APRIL 6TH, 1907]

IN taking as my subject the idea of a man going into business for the first time, it is necessary to take some one particular business as an illustration, and I have preferred to take engineering as being a typical business of Newcastle. Shipbuilding is equally bound up with the trade and industry of the district and is very similar in its conditions, but simple manufacturing engineering will best serve my purpose in illustrating what I have to say. First of all, then, when a man is going into business for the first time, he must remember that there are three essential qualifications for success. I don't say one man will have all three of them, but they must be there, if not in himself, then in somebody else. These three qualifications are the power of designing, the power of manufacturing economically, and the power of selling. I might almost add the knowledge of finance, but of this I will speak later. One of the most important elements in success is that the man commencing business should form a really honest opinion of his own qualifications. There are some men who very foolishly think and say that they can do as well as anybody else many things in which they have never attained eminence. To act on such an assumption is a most ruinous policy, for once you begin to deceive other people you deceive yourself also. I will try to illustrate this. I daresay I see before me several gentlemen who, besides being secretaries, are also athletes. These will know that athletes have their limitations, and that they must know their own form exactly. No runner who had made a speciality of 100 yards could expect to do so well over a mile as he does over his own distance; no light weight boxer could expect to be on equal terms with a heavy weight. And so a man commencing business should ask himself in all honesty and fairness whether he can design, whether he can manufacture cheaply, whether he is well qualified to get orders. If on all or any of these points the answer is not satisfactory, then the question arises—Who is going to do these things for him? Practically very few young men have more than, at the outside, two out of these three qualifications. Meanwhile we must consider the condition of the business which any of you gentlemen may be asked to enter. You may have to create an entirely new business, or you may be asked to carry on an old business, either an old business which may be doing well or one which is doing badly. You will see at once that taking over an old business involves a widely different set of conditions from beginning a new one. You may be asked to continue a successful business or one which is unsuccessful. The first task sounds easy, but you must remember that a successful business chiefly depends upon the arrangements and vitality of those who have gone before, and that you have the rather difficult task of finding out the secret of the living organization which has achieved the success, of understanding the vital elements which keep it in a healthy state, of considering how they might be lost, and, if lost, how they might be replaced. It may be that in this successful concern there is manufactured one special article, say, a locomotive or steam crane, for which there is a steady and well recognized demand. It is well then to remember that this demand may not last for ever, that there may come a time when the once popular article is regarded as just a little bit antiquated. It is well, at the outset, to be ever on the watch to see if this or that article is being superseded, and to have in your mind's eye some other article which will replace the decreasing trade. See, then, what the mainspring of the success is, and how far due to design, to workshop economy, or to business connection, and take care that all is kept working smoothly.

And now I will come to the case of a man who goes into a business which is not successful. Here you must be careful to see what the weaknesses are, and consider how to remedy them. As you go along, minor defects will present themselves, but you must try from the very first to find out what the fundamental defects are. A friend of mine, who went to manage a large business, set himself to work at once to discover what was wrong. He said, "There are three things wrong with this business. First of all, the articles we make are absolutely antiquated in design; secondly, the workshops and the machinery are inferior; and, thirdly, the men are altogether in a disorganized state and without proper discipline." He determined to sweep away all this at once. His friends counselled him to be cautious, to be quiet for a while, to take care not to bring a hornet's nest about his head. "Take," they said, "one point at a time. Deal first of all with the article you manufacture, re-design it, put it on the market in the best possible form, and be content with that for the present; and, meanwhile, take the opportunity of thoroughly weighing the wheat and the chaff, the good and the bad, alike as regards men and methods and material, and gradually introduce your new ideas and better system as opportunity offers. To do it at one fell swoop will disorganize the place, will pull it to pieces, and will raise up a lot of hostility from both high and low." Unfortunately, my friend took his own line; he tried to deal with all the three points at once, and before he knew where he was his services were dispensed with. It is very often by the mistakes of others that we learn where to find our own power of success. A much more interesting and a much clearer field for business ability is provided in the case of starting new works altogether, but in these typical instances of old businesses you will see that the first care is to look towards the rejuvenation of the concern, department by department, and, where money is being lost, carefully and gradually to reorganize and place everything on a fresh footing.

One great secret of success in business is to give your customers what they want. If a man says he wants a machine to do something in particular, and you have got something on hand which is rather better than he wants, it is quite right to show him what you have got and explain to him exactly how it will meet his requirements. You have here a proper opportunity of pushing a standard article. On the other hand, if he persists in asking for an article of quite a different type, then remember that the customer knows best what will suit him. It may be that you really think you have something that will suit him better, and it may be, in many cases, that you are particularly wise and he particularly foolish, but still it must not be forgotten that, in the long run, it is the customer who has to decide, and that it is an unwise policy to press him to take something which he has no intention of buying. If you can alter his decision without any pressure, that is another thing, for often the preference of a man for a particular article rests on very slight grounds. It may be because his men are familiar with it, and he does not care to incur the trouble of a change. And it may really not be worth his while to make a change. I have often heard a customer say, "My men can understand the machine I ask for, and I don't want to buy a different one and so disturb the whole of my working arrangements for the sake of saving a few pounds a year in one particular department."

Supposing you are going to start a business, make up your mind first what you are going to make, and, secondly, on what scale you are going to make it. You may decide, for example, to make a lathe or some other tool that has a market; you may decide to make your particular article a size larger or a size smaller than that in general use; but, whatever you choose to make, you must see to it that that article has the best design possible, that it is made as cheaply as possible, and that you find out exactly how much it is going to cost you to produce in the first instance. Then it is always wise to look to expansion. If ever a works is put in the market, or is going to take in a new partner, one of the first questions asked is whether there is room for expansion; this, I think, shows that it is well to have more land than you want and to have room for expansion. Remember that one of the most important essentials for expansion is capital, and that if you spend all your capital at once you may have difficulty in carrying out extensions. An important thing to consider also is what may be the smallest unit on which you can manufacture economically. Having found that out, you should first of all adopt that unit, and then, when you are sure everything is right, expand upon it according as you see your power of selling increase. As you go on you will learn how to be more economical, until, by degrees, your business will expand and you will be able to manufacture many articles where you used to make one. It is a great thing to begin in a small way and expand by degrees, taking the utmost care that every article you manufacture is the most efficient article possible for its purpose, and that it is made in the most economical manner. Unless you do that, unless you work cheaper and better than other people, you cannot expect to make money. Now, in saying that your article must be the most efficient article on the market, I do not say that it must necessarily be the best article. In some cases, as you perhaps know, the best article is not wanted. For example, your customer may be a contractor who has a large contract that may take him two years to complete. The contract may be in Africa or some other distant place whence it is difficult to remove or sell his plant at the end of the contract; so he prefers his articles to be of a less permanent character. A locomotive or a set of waggons that will last him a couple of years is all that he requires; something which will suit his purpose at a lower price is quite good enough for him; and to bestow extra finish and perfection of detail in such cases would be a waste of money. About eight or nine years ago, when the great controversy concerning English and American locomotives was exciting attention, much was made on this side of the greater durability of the English-made engine. The Americans admitted it, but they said, in effect, "We don't want that extra quality of engine, we think it better to use our loco-

motives up quickly, to sell or scrap them and buy more, and save
the money on repairs. We are a large country, pushing and ex-
panding in new directions, working under different conditions, and
we think that the best engine for our purpose is the cheaper engine
which will run for a certain time, and which we can replace when
it shows signs of weakness." That, of course, does not affect the
general rule that you must manufacture your article as efficiently
and as economically as possible. It only means that every now
and again we are confronted by a mere commercial question decided by the customer according to his judgement.

Very often the young beginner is unnecessarily jealous if orders
go past him. But he should remember that one does not want all
the orders in the world, that what one wants is sufficient orders,
and that other people must live as well as oneself. He must remember that there is always some little corner in production which
he must try to hold for himself, some little speciality which he may
make better than anyone else. It may be on that very account that
he may lose customers, people who want something rather different
from the article in which he has specialized. In such cases there
can be no harm in saying, "That is not the article I make." My
advice is, that the manufacturer commencing business should make
up his mind as to the amount of his proposed output, and the exact
article or articles he intends to make. Let him fix the limits beyond
which he will not go; let him tell the customer who is ordering
below or beyond his regular size that it is entirely out of his line.
Let me give you the instance of a shipyard. Perhaps the berths
only take in ships of from 300 to 400 feet in length, and enquiries
come for vessels very much longer than that. The shipbuilder
would naturally say at once that he could not do it. Such an
illustration may not be so strikingly brought out in the case of an
engineering order, but the same principle very largely applies.
There is a limit within which the manufacturer can manufacture
economically, and it is at this limit that he must firmly draw the
line. You please your customers far more when you tell them

frankly that the article they want is different from that which you have standardized, and that it will not pay you to make any change. The question, of course, arises as to how far it is worth while to modify standard types for the sake of customers. Generally speaking, if you find a certain standard of article fulfils its purpose better than any other, it may not be worth while, for the sake of a chance order, to alter it, because it is very possible that a man who gives a special order is only a theorist who will hereafter find out his mistake, and then in the long run he may be annoyed at your giving him something which turns out unsuitable. There is always room for a good deal of tact in these cases, but it is an unassailable principle if you choose to take the line of saying, "That is the article I manufacture; it is a typical article, and I am not prepared to make anything different." At the same time you must remember that in every case the article should be something which is perfectly suitable for the purpose it has in view. And if, after all, the customer prefers something else and takes his order past you, you must not blame him, but help him cordially to find what he wants elsewhere, and then, though you do not get a customer, you probably gain a friend.

But the question is—how are you going to begin? You have got to make a system and to choose a site, and both these matters are subjects for separate lectures. As to the site it is almost impossible to lay down general rules. Of course, it should be accessible by rail or water and should be within reach of a good supply of labour. With these two conditions, it is perfectly astonishing to notice how good businesses have been built up in a comparatively short time. On the other hand, during the last few years, we have seen a great number of people remove their places of business to what they considered better sites, only to find that they have never done well afterwards. For the sake of an ideal site they have sacrificed a good old business; they have lost something in the act of moving which no enterprise has been able to replace. How can one account for it? Who can say, unless it be that they have upset their old organization and removed out of the way of their customers, and very likely lost some of their best workmen. Accessibility to customers and a set of good workmen may have outweighed all the disadvantages of the old site. Still, I have seen in practice that while some firms which have removed from London have done badly, others have done well. The opportunity of going to a place where labour is cheap and land is cheap is one inducement, I know, which is very apt to appeal to anyone starting in business. At the same time, he must remember that, while there may be plenty of cheap labour, it may be also inferior labour, and that while the land may be cheap, it may be so far out of the world as not to be likely to be reached by customers. A customer will not readily go far out of his way to visit works which are near no recognized centre. It used to be a saying that if you wanted to start as a carriage builder you must establish yourself in Long Acre, in London; and so, if you start a shipyard on the Tyne or the Clyde, you would have a better chance of getting customers than if you started in some out-of-the-way place which nobody visits.

The next point is the question of capital. That, of course, must depend upon the size of the works. I shall give you some exceedingly rough figures, and ask you to bear in mind that as an approximate estimate it must not be confused with an actual estimate. The approximate estimate is the sort of thing which the director or secretary should carry in his head; the actual estimate is that which has been carefully drawn up to show the exact cost in a particular case. We get approximate ideas of cost in many rough-and-ready fashions, such as by taking the cost of a tramp steamer at so much a ton, or of an engine at so much per horse-power. All such methods are sufficient to inform us whether it is really worth while going on with an undertaking, and whether it will pay to take up a matter seriously. So, generally speaking, you may take it that as regards the ratio between size of works and the capital required, the approximate estimate is something like £150 per man employed. The exact cost, of course, must be given

by an actual estimate. Another rough estimate which may be
carried in the head is that your pay bill, including that of boys,
mechanics and labourers, will average out at something like 30s.
a week per man, which is an amount equal to half your capital
account. Practically you pay half your capital account in wages
every year. And so we come on to what sometimes is a more distasteful figure—I mean the profit-earning figure of the business.
I think you will find it to be the case that this principle holds good:
that no business, no class of business, pays on an average more
interest than that earned on first-class securities. I know that
some people will hardly agree with this rough estimate; but taking
all the businesses together, good, bad and indifferent, I think you
will find that this is not far from the mark. You must always remember that enormous amounts of capital are sunk which never
pay anything at all, that numbers of men have invested their little
savings and got nothing in return, and that many concerns have
been obliged to write down their original capital considerably.
We have a very high authority for saying that over the last hundred years the capital put into the Northumberland and Durham
Coal Trade has not paid, on an average, more than 4 per cent. per
annum, in spite of the enormous dividends which are known to be
paid in individual instances. This comparatively low average
dividend has been paid notwithstanding the large dividends;
I am rather inclined to say it is low because of the large dividends.
Where large dividends come out in a particular industry you will
always get more people to put their money into it than if it had
paid a steady 4 per cent. all along. An extreme case is an Austrian
Government Lottery. Here, for a small venture, you may happen
to get a castle on the Rhine, though you are well aware that the
Government are making a substantial profit on the whole, and
that the prize list is very much less than the whole money subscribed. In the same way the gambling element unfortunately
comes into many of our industries. We see it in the high prices of
shares in copper mines, always a more or less risky business. The

fact that someone makes a large fortune in a business does not
mean that everybody will have the same success. Personally, I am
certain that in those businesses where the largest profits are
possible you will get the smallest average profits. Therefore,
I would advise the beginner to regard a dividend of 5 per cent.,
after allowing for depreciation and other charges, as a fairly liberal
estimate. To proceed with my approximate estimates, I would
ask him to bear in mind that the paying away of half his capital
in wages, means this: that for every £1 that goes to the employer,
£10 goes in wages. This I know from experience to be a fair
estimate of the way in which the money is divided. Here then is
another rough figure which you should bear in mind: that in
engineering businesses the yearly sales may probably be somewhere about equal to one-and-a-half times the amount of your
capital. As to borrowing I need say little. I have already pointed
out that it is preferable to start your business on a small scale. It
is certainly better to do so than to attempt to borrow too soon. If
possible you should keep your borrowing powers in reserve for the
time when you feel sure you are going to succeed and know exactly
what you intend to do with the money. A man may ordinarily
count on borrowing half the amount of his capital expenditure,
but he would be wise to wait until he feels perfectly safe in going
forward.

I assume that you have got your works started. The first thing
you must then do is to see that you have an able man to design.
Whether you are going to build ships or engines you want a man
who can design your particular article efficiently and economically.
Remember that in designing, sound theory is, if anything, more
important than practical experience. You cannot do without a
really scientific man when it comes to designing work, and though
science alone will not make a place successful, the designer must
have sound scientific views. The next man you want is the man
who manufactures, and here probably science counts less than
experience and wide and varied shop knowledge. I was speaking

the other day to the general manager of a very well-known shipyard. He said, "I have nothing to do with the booking of an
order. I never think of the design of a ship that I may be called
upon to build. That is all done without my having any knowledge
of it at all, but from the moment the drawings come into my possession I take complete charge and responsibility." His business was
simply to see that every man turned out the maximum of work at
the minimum cost and of the highest quality, that he had the
best labour-saving appliances, and that the material was always
on the spot; and to arrange carefully that there was the best
possible organization. And my own impression is that this is the
department where English manufacturers fail more than in anything else. It should never be forgotten that designing is really
the work of the draughtsman, and that in the drawing office a man
learns nothing about manufacturing. I remember in my younger
days that there was a great idea that it would pay public companies
and boards, such as the Tyne Commission, to carry out large undertakings without a contractor and so save contractors' profits. The
idea was born of the implicit faith which these bodies had in the
gentlemen at Westminster, the scientific men who designed the
work. But it seemed to be forgotten that though these scientific
men knew what the finished article ought to be like, they had no
experience whatever in carrying out the work. They did not know
just exactly how the work, as it progressed, could be got through
most economically and efficiently. When the work applied to
higher mechanics they were even worse off. But they knew perfectly what the work should be when it was finished, though they
did not know what and how many men ought to be employed.
The difference between the designer and the contractor was that
one knew *what* had to be done, and the other knew *how* it was to be
done. Many of the first judges of painting in the kingdom are not
themselves actual artists, but they are judges of painting. Many
a man may be a first-class judge of wine, and yet have no idea
how to manage a vineyard. And so these London engineers were

good designers; they were good inspectors; they were perfect
judges of what the finished article ought to be; but they could
hardly be called the best men to superintend the doing of the
actual work. As regards England, I believe no foreign nation
has beaten us in designing machinery, but as regards economy of
manufacture Americans are certainly ahead of us. Personally,
I do not think we give the actual manufacturing part the attention
it deserves, for I am convinced it is the key to success in every
business.

The great thing is to use other people's brains as well as your
own. Do not be conceited. Do not be above consulting anyone
who may know more of a particular matter than yourself. Suppose
you are buying your castings and it occurs to you that it might pay
you better if you had your own foundry. Suppose your manager
says he can design a foundry, and you allow him to do the work.
The chances are that if he has never designed a foundry before, he
may do the work apparently all right; but it is certain, if he should
ever have to design a second, that it will be better than the first,
and therefore it probably would have been wiser in the first
instance to call in a man to lay out your foundry who had laid
out other foundries before. There is always a danger in a man
saying about a particular piece of work that "there is nothing in
it." Whenever you catch yourself in that frame of mind, whenever
you find yourself saying that such and such an engineering job is
easy, you must say at once, "That proves my ignorance." In
giving this warning I am not going to say that you may not have
some special knowledge on a particular subject which makes you
rightly conscious of knowing more about it than your neighbour,
but this hardly implies that you know about everything else with
the same thoroughness. There must be certain subjects about
which it would be better to consult other people. A man called
upon to design any new type (for example) of locomotive would
surely do well to call in a man who understood locomotives, and
consult with him. The principle that two heads are better than

one should never be forgotten. The most scientific locomotive manufacturer of my lifetime, Mr. Beyer, of Manchester—(I cannot remember Robert Stephenson)—once said that "it was all very well for people to be able to design, but that the man he preferred was the one who could find out what other people were doing." Other people's brains are always at work, and if you can find out what they are doing you will save yourself some serious mistakes and much humiliation.

In economy there is no finality. No one should be content with the results he is gaining. When he has reduced the expenditure down to half, let that give him courage to see how he can still further economize. Here comes in the advantage of specialization and careful organization. In Adam Smith's *Wealth of Nations* there occurs the following passage: "A common smith, who, though accustomed to handle the hammer, has never been used to make nails, if, upon some particular occasion, he is obliged to attempt it, will scarce, I am assured, be able to make above two or three hundred nails in a day, and those, too, very bad ones. A smith, who has been accustomed to make nails, but whose sole or principal business has not been that of a nailer, can seldom, with his utmost diligence, make more than eight hundred or a thousand nails in a day. I have seen several boys, under twenty years of age, who had never exercised any other trade but that of making nails, and who, when they exerted themselves, could make, each of them, upwards of two thousand three hundred nails in a day." This is a most striking passage on the necessity for specialization. When you find that your balance sheets are bad you begin to see that there is no wisdom in an output of two hundred nails per day per man when that output might as well be two thousand. You may not be able to make the change all at once, but you may do something towards it. It is within the experience of every manufacturer that now and again he finds things that once cost a shilling are being done for a penny. Many things which once cost an enormous amount of money are now done for next to nothing, solely through good organization, good machinery and good design. I remember the manager of the works where I served my time,—I owe him a debt of gratitude for it,—once saying to me, "Look here, my lad, I want you to remember that every time you take up a thing and put it down again, you are putting half-a-crown a ton on to its cost." It is essential to avoid unnecessary work and manipulation. The care shown by my old manager, running through a whole shop, must mean in the end large dividends. Above all, I want the man commencing business to remember this: that one of the great secrets of economy is extreme accuracy. I do not think that because a job is supposed to be a rough one it is cheaper to make it roughly. As regards essential features, keep to the great art of standardization, make everything accurately interchangeable, make every part fit exactly. What matter if a standard article intended, say, for the Colonies is rough, still the holes ought to be true and the various parts should fit accurately. In the long run, I am certain that good work comes out cheaper than bad work.

And remember this—and it is a most essential point to bear in mind—that economy in the cost of production does not mean either less men employed or lower wages. People suppose that the more economical the conditions in a workshop the more men are thrown out of work. That is absolutely untrue. If we could manufacture at 10 per cent. less than we do now there would be a labour famine in this country. We should not be able to get sufficient men to execute all the orders we should receive. Let us take, for example, the shipbuilding and engineering industries. You will agree they do not make luxuries, nor do they chiefly make things that are absolutely necessary. I dare say you think they do, but they do not. Is a railway in Africa, is a ship trading between Sumatra and the Cannibal Isles a necessity to the English investor? Not in the slightest. But in the sense that a new railway in Africa or a new ship for the East may bring me orders, they are of great importance to me. You must remember that ships and railways are all ordered and purchased for money-making purposes. Almost everything that we engineers make is made for the purpose of investments. You might divide engineering manufactures into three classes. First of all comes the material of war. This, however, is only a small element in the great production of the kingdom. Secondly come repairs, which are really necessities, for they would doubtless have to be done when required, no matter how high the cost. A railway company keeps its engines in repair whether the cost is high or low. It may be that they spend no more than they can help, but the traffic must be kept going. But what we really depend upon for the main employment of ourselves and our workpeople is new work, such as new ships or machinery; we are, in fact, dependent upon the expansion of our trade and the appliances connected therewith. Fortunately there is no fear that this expansion will come to an end, if only we can produce cheaply enough. Everything depends upon the cost of production. The capitalist carefully bases his chance of a dividend on the prime cost of an undertaking. It may be a railway in Africa. We will assume that the capitalist can reckon on bringing so many tons of goods from the interior to the coast for which he will be paid so much a ton. Half this will, perhaps, pay the actual cost of carriage, and the other half is the fixed amount on which he can rely to pay a dividend on the capital cost of the railway. Now, if the capital cost is so low that the above amount will make a dividend of 5 per cent., very probably the capitalist will succeed in raising the money; but if the cost is so high that it will only pay 4 per cent., probably he will not succeed in raising the capital, and the railway will not be made, and all the locomotives, rolling stock, rails and other things that go to make a railway will not be ordered, and all the men who would have been employed thereon are left as unemployed. In fact, nearly all the things that we, as engineers, make are "investments." Ships, locomotives, engines, machines for spinning cotton and textile goods, rails and steel, these are all ordered by people who want to make money out of them; and

whether we think of it or not, the ordering of them all depends upon
the price. It is the price which shows the investor whether he is
going to get a return for his money, and which determines him to
buy or to hold off. If, then, we can manufacture more cheaply,
and, by making capital go further, convert a 4 per cent. dividend
into a 5 per cent. dividend, so much the more numerous will be
the orders. Sir David Dale once said that only 10 per cent. of the
human race really used iron and steel. If the other 90 per cent.
ordered it, just think what an enormous amount of work it would
make for the world. In this connection let us look at the United
States. Was there ever such an increase in production? Yet they
are consumers, and as they increase in production so they increase
in consumption. Apply this increase to other parts of the world,
and we may go on for hundreds of years without showing the
slightest signs of diminution of orders. When you think that every
person in this kingdom requires, to keep him or her going, about
three hundredweight of steel or iron every year for an average
lifetime, you may imagine the strain which would be put upon the
powers of production, if the inhabitants of all the rest of the world
had the same proportion of the railways, tramways, etc., in comparison with population. I doubt whether you could imagine it.
I doubt whether our manufacturing powers would be capable of
dealing with even double the present demand for steel and iron.
So we may see that there is no fear of overdoing the market if we
can only work sufficiently cheaply. There is plenty of occupation
before us if we can but secure it by low prices. Only remember
that economy is most emphatically not carried out by reducing
wages, but by increasing the quantity of work turned out by each
man, and by turning out the best possible work in the cheapest
possible manner.

XIII

On the State of Trade

[SPEECH FROM THE CHAIR AT THE COMMERCIAL TRAVELLERS
DINNER, DEC. 20TH, 1907]

I HAVE been asked to give my views as to the state of trade. Of course I may be right or wrong, but my own view is that the state is peculiar; there is a good deal that is encouraging, but there are serious difficulties which, it seems to me, ought to be capable, if not of removal, at any rate of alleviation.

To look at our own district, the coal and iron trades are good: shipbuilding is in a state of extreme depression everywhere: engineering is very much depressed here, but it is fairly good in Lancashire, in the Midlands, and wherever they are engaged on textile machinery and general trade.

The two chief causes of the evil seem to me to be a general want of capital and want of confidence, intensified by the high price of our raw material, which is almost universally steel and iron.

But, to take a wide outlook first. I think it was Sir David Dale who pointed out that not more than 10 per cent. of the whole human race really use iron and steel in the full sense, and that if the trade could be extended to a second tenth it would create a demand more than all our present appliances could possibly meet. There is every sign that both foreign countries and the Colonies are increasing their demands more and more, and this might go on for centuries, because, as their wants seem to be supplied, they go on increasing and widening in other directions. As an illustration, I may point to the United States. We have always been told how much they were increasing their output, to meet the requirements of the world; so that very soon their powers of production would be so great that they would supply all the world. But what we were not told, and what has happened, is that though their powers of production have increased, as was expected, their powers of consumption have increased quite as fast; so that, in reality they are to an enormous extent their own customers, and this would be so all through the world—they would all consume, but by no means all of them could ever become producers.

Now, if this were the only factor, it would simply mean that you, gentlemen, the commercial travellers, would be the only men we should want, and prosperity would solely depend upon your exertions. It would be for you to travel over the face of the world, point out to people the advantages of our manufactures, book the orders, and we should all be happy together. In fact, the commercial traveller is the pioneer and the missionary of industrial civilization. He is the life, the soul, and the parent of all sound trade and commerce.

But now to the difficulties. I think you will all agree with me that the taking of orders depends almost entirely upon the price at which you can supply the article. Many an article for which you might book orders, almost without limit, at a certain price, would be refused altogether if the price were 20 per cent. higher; in fact, it does not seem to be sufficiently observed either by statesmen or by manufacturers, that our individual prosperity does not consist in taking orders away from other people and in bringing trade here which could be done elsewhere; but in calling trade into existence which never has existed before, opening out the resources of the world, giving people facilities to which they are not accustomed, and comforts and luxuries which they have never before enjoyed. Ships are only the packing cases in which other goods are sent about the world, and, given the passengers and the cargoes, the orders for ships will follow, provided the passengers and cargoes will pay sufficient freights to make a reasonable return upon the capital.

I should like to point out that the profits on a manufacturing or carrying trade are much more far-reaching than appear at first sight. If you take the case of a railway—say the North Eastern—the amount which goes to shareholders in the form of dividend, which is all they get in return for their capital, is absolutely paltry compared to the enormous benefit in the shape of convenience which the community gets. Were the North Eastern Railway to stop work it would be, of course, a considerable loss to the shareholders, but that would be as nothing compared to the general ruin and paralysis which would come upon all of us in the three North East counties.

Now, there are two things which keep us back:

1. Too little capital.
2. Want of confidence.

What is capital? Capital is not money—it was money once but is so no longer. See how the capital in one of our large industries is represented. Probably a great deal more than half is represented by land, buildings and machinery: in fact, by the tools which the workman uses. The other and smaller part is represented by the unfinished work for which the material and labour have to be paid as the work progresses, and for which the capitalist is not paid till the work is finished. If, on the other hand, you turn to the customer, he may feel the want of ships or a country may feel the want of railways; but they cannot get these things unless they either have the money or are able to borrow it. We are told now, by people in the City, that many foreign countries are very anxious to raise loans which would be spent on industrial enterprises, but they cannot get the money. Now, why is this? Why are we short of capital?

To explain this I must go into the second reason, which is want of confidence. I am aware that I cannot speak my mind on this subject without trenching on political questions, which are very thorny and very tender, but if I speak I must say what I think, and I believe myself that we are suffering very seriously from the

political action of this country. I may say I don't blame one side
of the House of Commons much more than the other. The faults
which exist on one side, exist on the other side, but I think the
consequences are very serious indeed. If you look over the history
of the last century, and see the giants that ruled the two
political sides in those days, you will see they all gave a strong
and consistent lead to their own side, but discouraged the extreme, violent and unreasoning section of their followers. Now
that is quite changed—not only is there a bitter hostility between
the two parties, but also each of them seems to foster and be
guided by their most extreme and violent members. These people
generally, I think, are those who, not being by any means the
wisest men or the deepest thinkers, take very extreme views of one
side because they are absolutely ignorant of all that there is to be
said on the other side. The effect of this is that careful people feel
a sense of insecurity: they may not think the country is going to
be ruined—probably very few think that—but they do think, what
is perfectly true, that reckless legislation and mischievous agitation
may make it extremely difficult to carry on trade prosperously; so
instead of investing their money in English industry, they take it
elsewhere.

To take an illustration: without giving any opinion as to the
merits or otherwise of the war, there is no doubt that the South
African war, like every other one, destroyed a large amount of
property (that is of capital) and money was spent on the war which
otherwise would have been saved up and employed labour. After
it was over, the party in power set about, in their own way, to
repair the damage, and did what presumably they thought best
to bring back a return of prosperity. But the other side came into
power, upset those methods, and took up a wholly different line.
Now, whether the new way was better than the old way or not,
there is no doubt that a great deal that was done by the former
party was reversed and entirely wasted by the new one. That
was all destroying capital. Gentlemen, do remember that capital

simply is another name for the workman's tools. It means his workshop, and the machinery and the tools that he uses, and if it cannot be produced or created, these cannot be found. Furthermore, capital is absolutely useless without labour. No man, however wicked and selfish, can get a proper return on his capital unless he employs labour, and in the same way labour cannot be employed unless there are suitable places and suitable tools provided for it.

But, now, there is worse to follow. We have people advocating a panacea like Fair Trade on the one hand, or like Socialism on the other—vague, extreme measures which they say would regenerate humanity, but which in the meantime upset our trade. I will not now enlarge fully on the mischief that is caused by Socialism, except to say that the very talk of it certainly tends to check trade and to throw more men out of work. The idea of a very large income tax, the idea of legislation which cripples the efforts of the industrious; such things make people unwilling to invest their money in the employment of British labour.

I will only point out two things in connection with Socialism which are not perhaps sufficiently observed. Great stress is often laid on the fact that all men ought to have equal opportunities. So be it: that is exactly what, for more than a generation past, we have been trying to get for them. We have not succeeded in all cases, but, as regards the large majority of the human race, we probably have succeeded very fairly, and in consequence now, more than ever, the capable, the energetic, the industrious, the talented boy shoots ahead at once and goes ahead more and more every year that he lives. Therefore we see, of two boys who started equally, one of them becomes a large capitalist, the other remains an ordinary workman, and that is really exactly what irritates the majority of people more than anything. But it is what we have been trying to produce, and it is not easy to see the injustice of it.

I know the capitalist is often spoken of as if he was a dishonest man who has taken his money away from the working classes, but now let us look at it from that point of view. An orator stánds up in Hyde Park, points to the West End of London, and complains of the people who live in those large mansions, and he thinks they do not at all deserve what they have got. But when that man says that their money ought to go to the working classes of England, that is quite a different matter. One man has made his money entirely in foreign countries or the colonies; if his property were re-distributed, not a penny of it would go to the English workman—it would go to the people of those countries. Another man has made his money by speculating on the Stock Exchange, and such like; his money cannot be claimed for the working classes. A third man has bought things at fair prices wholesale, and has sold them retail, and thereby made very large profits; that has not been taken from labour. The fourth man is a manufacturer, and it is to the wealth of this man alone that the socialist workman's claim can apply.

Now, could the working classes have got the use of their tools and machinery—without which they could not produce anything—any cheaper? I have spent all my life among manufacturers and large industries, and I think you will find the following figures are fairly correct:—that in our ordinary industries the annual amount paid in wages is equal to about one-half the capital value. The profits of these concerns do not, on the whole, average more than 5 per cent. if you put the losses and gains together; and the number of people who are willing to invest their money in manufactures is very small compared to the enormously larger number who will invest in railways, foreign loans, and numerous other things. That means that the profits are one-tenth of the wages. If all the profits went to the workmen, it would only give them a 10 per cent. rise of wages, and it is obvious that not one person would find a single penny piece to provide their tools or machinery, or in fact to employ them at all.

Another remedy which may have something in it, but which

I think, is doing incalculable harm from the way in which it is put forward, is Tariff Reform. We hear a vague talk about putting taxes on all sorts of foreign products; we are not told how much; all that we can see is that there is a general desire to put our trade into the melting-pot and see something entirely different come out. Is it possible that this talk can go on, and be believed, without making people timid in pushing their business? Would any of you gentlemen care to nurse up a trade which consists of importing something from other countries, to find out that as soon as the present Opposition get into power the trade you have laboured at will be at once taxed out of existence? Rather, as I have before said, what we want is not to tear away the trade from other people, but to create new trade, so as to enhance the general prosperity of the world and to employ a larger number of people altogether.

Of course, taxation is a complicated question, and probably it is more important to put on taxes in a way that will irritate the public as little as may be, than to aim too much at any specially scientific method, or at any ulterior object. Probably very small taxes may be treated as comparatively unimportant, even if they are unsound in principle. For example, the 1s. a quarter which a short time ago we paid upon wheat, was really felt by nobody, but if we put on an amount which would enable the British farmer to compete with foreign wheat markets again, we should have to put on at least 10s. a quarter, and that would utterly dislocate an enormous number of our industries.

It seems to me obvious that in a country like England—an old and complicated civilization, perhaps the only really large community which is entirely unable to feed itself—all changes must be made with the greatest care and the greatest caution, and above all it is most undesirable that people should try to make violent changes without very careful thought as to how they would affect, not merely the majority of the nation, but even the various minorities. Each of us, as far as our particular trade is concerned, is a very small minority of the whole British nation, and yet it is in the sum total of the prosperity of minorities that the prosperity of the country as a whole consists.

I have no objection to your preaching to me, or to any other capitalist, about our responsibilities. I will yield to no one in my feeling of the obligation that lies upon every man to make the best use of his money and talents, not for his own pleasure but in the interests of his fellow-men. I will admit that all property is a trust; but, while you may say so to the capitalist, it is no use to go about telling other people that the capitalist has no right to his money, because I have never been able to see any system whereby the workman could get his tools and appliances any cheaper, or which would make him any better off. In fact, as regards Socialism, Fair Trade, and all other extreme methods, to my mind the tendency of them all is to injure the working classes, for whom, as all experience shows, the greatest prosperity consists in the most steady and uniform progress.

I will say one more word as to the capitalist. How did he get there? Take the case of three workmen, all earning good wages. One spends his surplus income on his amusement; the second one spends it on increasing the comfort of himself and his family; the third one saves it up in order to purchase the means of production, to find employment for himself and his fellow-workmen; and this third one is the one who is abused and called a thief. A capitalist is simply a man who has worked while his fellow-men played, who has saved while his fellows spent, who learned to do what he did not like, and, if he has a fourth qualification, it generally is that he has backed his own opinion by buying something, or doing something, which other people thought was not worth buying or doing. Many a man, in doing this, is ruined, and gets no pity, so if he succeeds he ought not to be grudged his success.

I believe nobody more than the capitalists would welcome any and every scheme for enabling workmen to put money into their own works, and to share profits. To share profits means sharing losses; becoming a partner means saving money; and I see little or no evidence that the majority of the working classes wish to do either one or the other. I believe, as a rule, they prefer the safety of being outside the risks and anxieties of business, and, as regards their happiness, I don't say that they are wrong.

My own feeling is that if people would only remember that every question has two sides to it, that all changes ought to be made gradually, and that fortunes are not composed of other people's misfortunes, we should get on a great deal better; there would be far more wealth, far more employment, ever increasing as years went by, and then you, gentlemen, the Commercial Travellers, would have a fair field for all your energies.

XIV

The New Army from an Employer's Point of View

[Feb. 1908]

WHATEVER form the Army of the future is to take in this country, it is quite clear that it will be based upon some principle of retaining in civil occupations a large number of men who can be called upon to become soldiers at the shortest possible notice. For this to work satisfactorily depends upon how far the converse is kept in view, that is to say, upon how readily it will be possible for men, when they are dismissed from the Army, to return to their old positions in civil life with the least possible loss and inconvenience to themselves. People often say that for this they must rely on the patriotism of employers; but that probably means that they themselves are not prepared to make any sacrifice, and won't even take the trouble of thinking about the matter, or they would see two things. First of all, that a large majority of the wage-earning men in this country are employed by small and poor employers, who cannot make any very great sacrifices; and, secondly, that to keep a job open for a long and uncertain period, for one man, and to be able to re-absorb him at a moment's notice, is, in most industries, practically impossible.

To save trouble, I propose to talk of militia, volunteers, reserves, in the old army phraseology. Of course all these have been thrust into the melting-pot, but as we do not really know what the names and conditions of the new kinds of soldiers are to be, it is safer to confine ourselves to words that we understand, and we may assume that if the varied conditions of the men in the old classification could be adapted to civil life, there would be no serious difficulty in adapting any modified conditions that may be created under the new organization.

Before we go further, it may be well to look at the question of compulsory service, which of course would affect this matter very considerably. It would probably be no hardship in nineteen cases out of twenty for schoolboys to be taught a certain amount of shooting and drilling, and, judging from the analogy of other countries, it would be quite possible, in almost every case at any rate, for a young man to devote a short time to barrack or camp life, without serious loss either to himself or the community, and in many cases it would be very beneficial.

But the objection to compulsion is that, as a rule, Englishmen are particularly averse to being coerced, and though the majority may take to it very kindly, a really bitter minority would be a serious trouble in carrying out the scheme; and there are three motives which, though they would only act on a small number, would be a tremendous force within those limits.

There are, first of all, those boys, and often their fathers, who bitterly hate any kind of discipline or authority.

Secondly—and this is a class much to be pitied—there are a certain number of men who really are so timid that the idea of being soldiers would terrify them and make them perfectly miserable. People may call these men cowards, and may not be disposed to have much compassion on them, but, after all, we are only what God has made us, and while you may justly blame a man for taking up duties which, owing to his constitution, he is incapable of carrying out, you cannot blame him for being unfit for the position which somebody else has coerced him into occupying.

Thirdly, there is a small, and very real, class who honestly think all war wrong, and that it is wicked to be a soldier, and these people's opinions are entitled to due respect. Possibly some scheme might be devised whereby any lad objecting to military training could be made to perform some other and more onerous service to the State, to which he could not in any way object, but such a scheme ought not to be relegated to a postscript but should be kept well in view from the beginning. We might then estimate that nineteen out of twenty, or, possibly, ninety-nine out of a hundred, would accept their military training as a matter of course, and we will then assume that it is with this majority only that we are dealing.

Probably, on the Continent, the authorities would ignore those who so strongly disliked military service, and would coerce them into the ranks, but this is undesirable on two grounds:

First, it is exactly the sort of thing that gives the House of Commons the handle, which they are only too ready to use, to delay the estimates and injure the army.

Secondly, such men in the army are probably a very great evil. We have always been informed that cowardice is contagious, and as regards the man who disapproves of, or dislikes the service, he is simply a centre of disaffection. It is notorious that the Austrian army in 1859 was terribly weakened by the number of unwilling soldiers in the ranks, and, even in our own army, there is at least one case of a regiment having to be disbanded on account of the insubordinate men, who practically acted as missionaries, and infused their own dangerous spirit into their fellow-soldiers.

After the late war, there was a great deal of disappointment at the difficulty which many officers and men found in returning to civil life, and I fear that many of them never recovered the positions that they then gave up in order to serve their country. This ought not to be, and I think it has caused a feeling that whatever the Government may talk about or promise, when a war is over it does not really much care whether the men get comfortably settled again or not. I believe that in the conviction that the Government really cares, lies the secret of the whole thing. If men thought that the nation would see them back again into their civil life, they would volunteer, or go away, with far more confidence. Of course some employers undertook to take back every man on his return, to his old, or to an equally good place, and probably, where the works were well organized, this was managed by large employers without serious difficulty, but certainly many employers who had only, say, one man, found it perfectly impossible.

Now, a military career will interfere with a man's civil life in various ways. We may divide them under three headings, which we will call:

(a) Training the youth.

(b) Keeping him available for service; and this may be divided into regular calls for training and special call for war.

(c) Finally, restoring him to civil life.

At this stage we must ask ourselves how many men the country really wants, because it always seems to the civilian employer and taxpayer that it is no use training more men than you can possibly need. Make up your mind that the army you want to put into the field is half a million, or any other figure you like to call it, and then work for that figure. If you have more men coming on than you require, it is easy, by giving some advantage to the young soldier, to select the best and keenest men and pass by the others.

The training would seem, from a civilian point of view, to come under four heads—First, rifle shooting. Lord Roberts seems to consider that if a man or boy is a fairly good shot with a rifle, he is more than half-way to becoming a really useful soldier, and possibly, mixed up with better men, or behind a wall, or in a house, he would be of real use from that moment onwards. But of course it is far better if, secondly, he has also learnt a fair amount of simple drill, such as boys at school could learn very easily, and which could be kept up by an occasional evening afterwards without being an appreciable tax upon anybody. But these two really give us only what ought to be the normal recruit, and no doubt it would be better still, and necessary in most cases, for a man, even if he did not become a regular soldier, to go into either camp or barracks for a longer or shorter period, as a third step, and be trained so that he could really take his part in the field; and though probably he would not be equal to a skilled soldier, he would be a very useful man for the defence of his country. Fourthly, this training would have to be repeated at regular intervals.

If a man and his employer knew beforehand how much training was wanted, this could probably be arranged without serious difficulty, and here comes the key to the whole position. Whether a man is a militiaman, a volunteer, a reservist, or anything else, the important thing is that he should be, as it were, ear-marked, so that his employer should know what he is, and if he is liable to be called out at short notice, in order that he may provide for this contingency. It would be most unreasonable to drop down suddenly on a household and say that the coachman or the cook had to be called away instantly, but if you told the householder that these officials were liable to be called away, he could then think out the question and know how to provide for their absence. A theatrical manager of necessity provides an understudy for every single part in his play, and an employer could, in almost every case, provide an understudy for every reservist, or volunteer, if he knew beforehand and could work it out quietly. But nobody knows the incalculable loss that may be caused by an important man being called away quite unexpectedly; it is as bad as if he died; his place has to be filled, and then it is not there for him to return to.

As regards the classes from which our soldiers ought to be taken, looking at the matter from a civilian point of view, it always seems to me as if the position were this. We will roughly divide the community into four classes, which we will call, to save trouble, the upper class, the middle class, the mechanics and the labourers. As a rule, in a regular army, nearly all the officers come from the upper class and nearly all the private soldiers from the labouring class. Now these two classes are both getting smaller, while the two intermediate classes—the middle class and mechanics—are getting larger and larger, and comprise the greater part of the energy and power of the community. The volunteers have a good deal bridged over this difficulty, because the officers and men, respectively, come very much more from these two classes, but, certainly, any national army must be necessarily based on the strongest forces in the country.

We do not know how the army of the future will be organized, but we will assume that whatever branches there are must be, roughly, in the nature of:

1st.   Regular soldiers.

2nd.   Reservists, who are called to the colours for uncertain periods.

3rd.   Militia and yeomanry, who are called out for longer and regular periods.

4th.   Volunteers, who are called out as little as possible, but who have to keep up their training and efficiency.

Of course no civilian can see things from a really military point of view, but may it not nearly always be taken as a corollary that no military man can really see things from a civilian point of view, and that therefore, in restoring men to civil life, the opinion of the civilian must be taken as an important factor, just as the officer is the person to decide who and what is required to make a soldier?

To go into details of the future of old soldiers, whether liable to be recalled to service or not. Surely common sense and patriotism would equally say that the State ought to give the preference to soldiers for all the employment at its disposal, and that every civilian employer ought also to be distinctly disposed to favour the men on whom he relies to defend him in case of war. But, alas, the question is not to describe an ideal state of things, but to discuss the defence of England, its vices, follies and prejudices being what they are. To the ordinary unmilitary student of history, it always seems that the unwillingness to prepare for war while it is yet afar off, and the indecent haste to get rid of the soldiers at the end of a war, without any regard to gratitude and very little to justice, are inherent faults in the country that repeat themselves century after century. No doubt we ought to strive to infuse a better spirit into our people, but, though we may try to reach a very much higher standard, we have to start at this moment from things as they are.

Now, to return to the old soldier. Of course, a large proportion of them do find profitable and honourable employment, and we hope lead useful and happy lives. It is not easy to find out what proportion these bear to the whole, but I think we may assume that they are a substantial majority. However this article is not written to discuss them, but rather to discuss the large minority who are not so fortunate, and whose troubles and difficulties after the South African War were certainly a scandal to the country.

It is no use for the country to dismiss the question by what they call an appeal to the patriotism of the employer. It is rarely realized, but it is a most unquestionable fact, that a very much larger number of men work for small employers than for large ones —probably far more than twice as many—and the small employer, who is often not much more than a working man, cannot have heavy burdens thrown upon him with impunity; and furthermore it is among the large majority who are engaged in small employments that the soldier is far more likely to find work than he is among the minority who are in large factories, collieries, and such like. For one thing, almost all large industries are governed by trades unions, and among small employments very often you will find enormous districts where the words "Trades union" are never heard, and that is, in most cases, a great advantage to the old soldier.

To compare our position, for one moment, with that of Germany. The writer, on a recent occasion, had an opportunity of rendering some small service to a large body of Prussian trades union officials, and he took the opportunity of asking them to sit down quietly and give him a deliberate opinion as to what was their experience of military service. With one exception they had all served, and

when I asked as a final question whether they considered it a
hardship, they gave as their well-considered opinion—"No, not
a hardship. Probably a young man is glad when it is over, but on
the whole it does him good, and as he serves young he very soon
regains anything that he has lost at his trade. In some cases, as
when men have been working underground in collieries, it is a real
advantage to them, just when they stop growing, to be drilled and
set up and disciplined; and," they added, "we believe the English
Government would be wise if they introduced the same system
into England." I give no opinion as to their views, but they are
interesting, and worth recording.

What the Government ought to aim at is to bring about such
a state of things that certain employers would absolutely prefer
old soldiers to mere civilians. If this was the case with the employer of one man in twenty, it would probably be sufficient to
absorb all the old soldiers about whom we are writing, and it must
always be borne in mind that all the workman wants is for some
one employer to be really anxious to obtain his services. One very
simple way to effect this would be to do as is done with horses, and
allow the employer what might be called a registration fee of say
1s. a week to be able to produce the man whenever he was wanted
and to keep him employed in the meantime. A small employer
in many cases probably does not make more than 1s. a week clear
profit upon every man he employs, and to double this would be a
very strong inducement, and having once got hold of a soldier he
would do the best he could, in his own interest, to teach him and
make him as useful as possible.

In the same way, when a man leaves the army his employer
might be allowed so much a month for a few months if he keeps
him in continuous employment. After the soldier had been in
regular work for that time he would probably have no difficulty
in finding permanent work along with other people.

Another point which has often been discussed is how far it is
possible to train soldiers, while they are in service, to be valuable

after leaving the army. In considering this it is interesting to compare the case of sailors. The experience of employers in general, is that sailors hardly ever have any trouble in getting work on shore; and that is because they possess certain qualifications, such as being able to climb, to work at a great height from the ground, to sling, to tie, and to do many things which give them a special value over other labourers. Very possibly if an enormous number of sailors were thrown out of work, the special demand for this class of labour might not be equal to the supply, but so far that has not happened.

In training soldiers there are two principles which ought to be borne in mind: one is, not to train too many men in any one line; rather, if possible, to try to encourage every man to be useful according to any knowledge he may have possessed before he went into the army, or according to his present tastes and aptitude. A far more serious consideration is this. People often think that, with soldiers, or schoolboys, or anybody else, by giving them a few hours in a week when they may play with, say, joiners' or some other tools, they will make mechanics of them. This of course is impracticable. A modern mechanic is one who, as boy and man, has given his undivided attention and his most strenuous efforts, for a great number of years, to learning his trade, without doing anything else; and who, in a large and ever-increasing number of cases, has also had a certain amount of theoretical training to fit him for his work. It would be quite impossible to give this to a soldier who has his own work to do besides.

It must also be borne in mind that, as things stand, a large majority of our soldiers come from the labouring class rather than from the class of skilled mechanics, and would be quite satisfied if, when they left the army, they could get regular work at reasonable wages, at some special branch of what is commonly called unskilled labour. Instead of trying to make a soldier a joiner, a painter, or a mason, try and make him a joiner's labourer, a painter's labourer, or a mason's labourer. This is comparatively easy, and, as an example, many an intelligent and obedient joiner's labourer, if he gets a job in the country, will very soon rise up, under the instruction of his employer, till he becomes a semi-skilled man and quite equal to doing a great deal of the simpler forms of joiner's or carpenter's work.

A certain number of soldiers get into large factories, and from the lowest kind of labouring gradually rise till they learn to work some of the simpler machines, such as drilling, planing and slotting machines, after which their position is an assured and comfortable one, but this is probably more difficult to do in a factory than it would be in the very much larger field of small employments. Of course, many soldiers take such posts as domestic servants, warehousemen, clerks, shopmen, chemists' assistants, and others too numerous to indicate. The great thing, however, is that the Government ought to let it be understood that they will not cast off the soldier without taking any interest in his future, but, when they have done with him, will honestly and sincerely try both to improve him and to give him the best opportunity for finding some sort of honourable employment, whether they require his services or not. I believe what we want is to teach the soldier that he may trust the Government to do their very best to look after his interests. The cost of this would be very little indeed. Even if, as is suggested above, the Government made a payment of £2. 12s. 0d. a year for each soldier, it would be a small matter compared to the disgrace and humiliation of having these unhappy men wandering round the country, in the ranks of the unemployed, or breaking their hearts in our workhouses, as is so often the case at present.

We believe something of the same sort might be said for those young men who did good work as officers either in the militia, yeomanry or volunteers, during the South African War, many of whom have never been able to get back into their old employment. That is a separate question, but it is one well deserving the thought of all those who have at heart either the well-being of our Army or the honour of our Government.

XV

On the State of Political Parties

[LETTER TO THE EDITOR OF 'THE SPECTATOR,' APRIL 18TH, 1908]

I BELIEVE there is no doubt that a large proportion of the
people of England are very tired of the extreme hostility
which has existed for some time between the two parties in the
House of Commons, and of the violent counsels which have more
or less prevailed in the leadership of both sides; and would very
gladly welcome a government which, while carrying out its own
policy, would aim to do so on the principle of carefully listening
to the view of the other side, and trying to compromise and modify
so as to cause the smallest possible amount of injury according
to the view of the Opposition, instead of ignoring and defying
their ideas altogether. Such a position could only be held by a
Moderate Liberal Government, which, while sympathising with
the views of all sections of the community, would work on the
principle of trying to carry out the resultant of a number of unequal forces acting round one point.

If, as is feared, Sir Henry Campbell-Bannerman is unable
again to lead the party, it must be remembered that his personality was extremely popular with the labour members, and this
feeling would most distinctly not be extended in anything like the
same degree to any other probable successor. Recent events have
also shown the difficulty of the Liberal party marching any longer
abreast of Socialism without a serious rupture; but on the other
hand, I believe that many of the Conservative party would gladly
compromise on a number of burning questions, and that although,
when once a strong cleavage is made between the two sides of the

House, the leadership necessarily falls into the hands of the extreme men of each party, it would be more natural and more proper if, instead of such wide cleavage, there was an effort to bridge over the difficulty more or less, and to establish a *modus vivendi* between the moderate men of all parties. As illustrations the following four points might be taken:

1st. The first extreme party that has to be reckoned with is Socialism. As the formation of a policy it is difficult to make anything of it, but there is no doubt that it is the expression of a real complaint against many things that are wrong and getting worse in our ordinary organization. It is, in fact, a genuine cry of pain, though it is useless as a prescription; but in some of its forms it might be dealt with sympathetically. For example, municipalization may not be altogether wise in principle, but in many cases it works very fairly in practice; and there is plenty of room for progress without at present considering at what point that progress should stop. The more reasonable men of any party will be tolerably patient if they see their views are being considered and tried, however slowly.

2nd. Fair Trade. The great difficulty of this movement is that while in general terms the leaders clamour for all sorts of duties on foreign articles, they have never definitely formulated exactly how much duty they would put upon any given article, or exactly what change would be produced if they did. Now, while all the older traditions of England are in favour of free trade, a very large portion of the population of the world are Fair Traders or Protectionists, and their views may therefore claim courteous consideration if nothing else. Might it not be well to ask the Fair Trade party to specify exactly what they think would be a very strong case for the protection of some one industry, and if a suitable case could be found, let that one case be tried to see what it is worth.

3rd. Education. There can be little doubt that a large majority of churchmen would gladly co-operate with a large majority of nonconformists to bring about a measure tolerable to both parties, if only the extreme men of both sides could be silenced.

4th. Licensing is a most burning question and one well calculated to upset a Ministry. Much blame has been thrown on the late Conservative measure[1] which, no doubt, had serious defects that have been shown in practice, but which nevertheless did a certain amount of real work in the right direction. Might it not be possible to get over the evils of that measure by a time-limit longer than fourteen years, and also by fixing some point beyond which the value of a licence could not rise?

These are only rough indications of the sort of way in which the various questions before the country might be bridged, but I believe there is a large and rapidly increasing party which would be only too thankful to see statesmen of opposite opinions trying to work together to make uniform and patriotic progress, instead of continuing the present wasteful and weakening strife.

[1] The 1904 Licensing Act.

XVI

Two Letters on
Tariff Reform & Free Trade

I.

[NEWCASTLE DAILY CHRONICLE, OCT. 1ST, 1908]

I AM one of a not very small class of people who, having been whole-hearted Conservatives under Lord Salisbury, did not see our way to follow the doctrines, now called Tariff Reform, that were brought forward by Mr. Chamberlain and are now adopted by so many of our old comrades. Perhaps you will allow me space for a few remarks as to our reasons for rejecting these views, with a slight sketch of how I think these proposed reforms would affect some of our local industries.

How would Tariff Reform affect engineering and shipbuilding and other industries connected therewith? It is rather difficult to criticize Tariff Reform closely on account of its vagueness. We want to know, at any rate approximately, what articles would be taxed, and how much? What would be prohibited, and what would be more or less heavily handicapped? Of course, much depends on this. It may be wrong in principle to tax, say, wheat, but if the advocates of Tariff Reform propose a tax of only 1s. a quarter it would really not be felt by the consumer; on the other hand, it would be no help to the farmer. If they put on a tax of 10s. a quarter, it might help the farmer very much, but it would be a most terrible burden on the working classes, and destroy a great many industries altogether; and, without tying down the advocates of Tariff Reform too closely, we have a right to demand that they should give us some idea of what their ideal budget would be.

I take it the central principles of Free Trade are:

1st. That all taxation is for the purpose of raising a certain fixed revenue which is required for the necessary expenditure of the Government.

2nd. That this revenue should be raised so as to cause the least possible inconvenience and loss to the community as a whole.

For a tax to be popular is almost as important as for it to be scientific. For example, the penny stamp on cheques and receipts is, theoretically, a tax on industry, but it brings indirect advantages which are a very great convenience, and a fair set-off against the amount that is paid.

I think it a pity that the question has been complicated by the cry of "Free Food," because, if you damage a man's income, it is exactly as bad as taxing his food. If Tariff Reform could really give work to a large number of unemployed, and substantially increase wages, even a tax on food might be very well endured. Indeed, we all accept taxes on tea, coffee, and the like.

So the simple question is, can we, by taxing certain articles that are made abroad, improve the condition of the working classes, either by making work for more of them or by paying them higher wages?

It is common to begin by saying that raw material would not be taxed. But what is raw material? To take our local industries:

The coal owner raises coal as a raw material, and manufactures coke, which is, to *him*, the finished article.

The blast-furnace owner buys coke (and ore) as raw material, and produces pig iron as the finished article.

The steel manufacturer buys pig iron and sells steel plates.

The shipbuilder buys steel plates and sells a finished ship.

Now, are coke, pig iron and steel plates to be considered raw material or finished articles? In other words, are they to be protected?

As the one farthest off the raw material, we will take the case of steel plates, and suppose that a tax of £1 per ton is put on these. Not much foreign steel plate for shipbuilding is imported, but if the English makers combine to put up their prices, then the foreign plates can come in and keep the price reasonable. As things stand, to keep out foreign plates would not really find work for very many steelworkers, while a rise of £1 a ton would hinder a vast number of ship orders for foreign countries coming here, and, as far as can be estimated, far more men would be thrown out of work in the shipyards than would be employed extra in the steel works. The people who would gain are the capitalists who own the steel works. They would gain £1 per ton extra price. On the other hand, the capitalists who build ships would lose very seriously—more than the others would gain. Therefore, directly you begin to put on tariffs to protect certain trades, every employer and workman strains every nerve to get his particular trade protected, no matter what may be the effect on other trades, and so you encourage a most selfish and unpatriotic attitude, and open the door to endless jobbery and corruption.

In most large British industries, all the chief manufacturers are more or less acquainted, and the facilities for making combinations and rings would be terrific, while, to a struggling manufacturer who is responsible for an enormous amount of capital, of other people's as well as his own, the temptation to combine to raise prices is very great indeed.

But, now, would the steel maker employ more men and pay higher wages? I believe the Tariff Reformers say that he would. If he made more steel, of course he would employ more men, but the question in this case is, would his increase exceed the decrease in the shipyards? It seems to me that it would not. And, as regards higher wages, no doubt he could afford to pay more, but would he do so? If labour is plentiful, employers do not pay higher wages just because they are rich, and they do not pay less because they are poor. Everyone who wants to employ labour has to pay the market price for it, and no more; and anyone who reads the papers can see for himself on Tyneside to-day that some works are making large profits, others are suffering serious losses, but both pay exactly the same rate of wages, just as they pay exactly the same for the materials they buy.

If it is said that we will even treat steel plates as raw material, then the only finished article to tax is the ship, and as practically no English shipowners get their ships built abroad, this ends the question; while certainly an extra £1 a ton on steel plates would have kept away a number of orders in recent times.

To turn to an entirely different case. We hear complaints of windows, doors, and other joiner work being imported ready-made from abroad, and the Tariff Reformer says these things ought to be taxed and work thereby made for more joiners. But it must be remembered that these things come in because they can be sold cheaper than those made in England. To keep them out would be to increase the cost of houses, and therefore raise rents, and, while a few joiners would doubtless gain, the working classes, as a whole, would lose much more. So with every article that was protected, each tax would enrich a small class and impoverish the whole, and the aggregate would be that the country, *i.e.* the working class, would lose nearly as much as the total increase in the selling price of all the protected articles.

Thus, as protecting steel plates would cause fewer ships to be built, protecting joiner work would cause fewer houses to be built. In each case, while one trade was protected, other trades would suffer, and I believe the total effect would be to increase, and not to diminish, the amount of unemployment.

II.

[NEWCASTLE DAILY CHRONICLE, OCT. 23RD, 1908]

I fear I must apologize for having been a long time in replying to the letters of those gentlemen who have written to comment on what I wrote to you on the 1st October, about Free Trade. Without attempting to answer each letter in detail, I think I may say that the dispute focusses on these points.

The Tariff Reformer by what he does would increase the selling price of certain articles. In so far as he does this, the purchasing power of the general public as a whole is less than it was before. I understand he claims that this is a small price to pay for the great advantage of making work for a number of men who are now among the unemployed, by manufacturing things at home that are now made in other countries. But it seems to me, and to most Free Traders, that he overlooks the fact that while work might be found for some men, a great many more men who are now fully employed would then be thrown out of work, and trade would, as a whole, be diminished; and that would do more harm to the working classes than the artificial fostering of certain industries would do them good.

The present extreme depression of trade, and the number of un-employed, are serious, but nobody can deny that during the sixty years of Free Trade the prosperity of this country has increased, probably beyond the hopes of even the most enthusiastic Free Trader, and, serious as is the condition of the unemployed, I doubt if it is as bad as it was even as recently as in 1885 and one or two years before and after that.

To touch for a moment on the supply of shipbuilding plates. As I have already said, far the greater part of the plates that are used in England are made in England, but the price of them is con-trolled by the price at which they can be bought from other countries, and if there is a duty put upon them, large or small, I think the English manufacturers would charge us exactly that much higher.

I cannot think what one correspondent means by being so shocked at my speaking of rings, either of employers or workmen. He must surely know that there always are a number of combina-tions of employers in one trade to keep up their prices, and these, as a rule, are limited either by the price at which the article can be got outside the ring, or by the danger of people opening new works. Within the last few days I happen to have heard of a certain article extremely important to the working of collieries, in which all the manufacturers have combined and have practically agreed to double the selling cost. Nor am I aware that the people who do these things think that they are doing anything unfair or wrong. Personally, I doubt if these combinations are in the long run to the advantage of anybody, but perhaps my opinion that way is exceptional. As regards labour, I think any trades union leader will say that he considers it his duty to raise the wages of his clients as high as he can, and he would be coming short of that duty if he did not take advantage of any legislation, or anything else, that enabled him to raise the rate of wages still higher.

I may further say that, in considering this question, we may pretty nearly confine ourselves to the way it affects the working classes. Experience shows that the manufacturer or capitalist can easily take care of himself whatever happens.

Now, as regards the joinery work for houses. A builder tells us that the saving by using foreign material is only 30s. on a house that costs £441. 10s. 0d., and another writer says that the joinery work from abroad is not so good. It certainly seems to me that this is a case where, if there was a little confidence and energy, the British manufacturer might manage to work as cheaply as the foreigner, and so get the trade on to a sound footing and do the work here.

It is impossible to touch on every trade, but I should like to give an instance from one of the very few cases where I myself have ever bought foreign goods as against English. The matter appeared in the newspapers many years ago. When steel castings first began to be very largely used in locomotive work, the English makers produced an article which was harder than the foreign, but was practically hardly ever free from honeycombs. The ordinary railway inspectors objected to these honeycombs, and we manufacturers were therefore obliged to buy our castings from abroad. But this lasted a very short time indeed; when the English makers found the orders were actually going abroad, they set to work to find out how to produce the steel that the customers required; and my impression is that within a very few months the greater part of the trade had come home again, and it has remained here ever since. I imagine that where a Fair Trader would have secured his object by putting on a tariff, a Free Trader secured it by bringing more intelligence and energy to bear on the business.

Whatever is said by Mr. Samuel Storey deserves most serious consideration. He is a gentleman of the greatest and most valuable experience in every kind of business, and also in Imperial and local politics. I should like to point out to him that I absolutely in no way deny, but quite agree with the fact, that one of the very first objects of a statesman ought to be to enable the people to provide a plentiful subsistence for themselves. I was writing at the moment about Adam Smith's second principle, but that did not imply that I denied, or ignored, the first one. I cannot admit that I am a heretic. Till Mr. Chamberlain brought forward the views associated with his name, just after the death of Lord Salisbury, our knowledge of what is now called Fair Trade was chiefly derived from the Colonies, and though I have never been, as one correspondent suggests, at the making of a protective tariff, I have had the good fortune to converse with colonial statesmen, and, especially, very fully with the Prime Minister of one of our Colonies which has been generally considered, under his guidance, to have taken the very front rank in the protection of local industries; and it was after mixing a good deal with influential colonials, that I came to the conclusion that their teaching would not be a blessing if applied to England.

As regards what Mr. Storey says about the tax on corn. Not long ago, of course, there was 1s. a quarter tax on corn: this had very little effect on the trade either way, and if Mr. Storey could guarantee that they would never charge more than 1s. on colonial corn and say 2s. on foreign corn, it might be no worse to bear than some other tax for which it was a substitute; but is he sure that Mr. Chaplin and the Agricultural Party would be content with this? If we could get that from them officially I shall not have written my letter in vain.

I see another writer says that Tariff Reform would only be 10 per cent. on our imports. This would not be a serious burden, but, on the other hand, it would do very little to bring trade from foreign countries into England.

The whole question comes to this. They want, in the case of each trade, to benefit a certain body of workmen by throwing an apparently slight burden on the whole community. They would then benefit the next body of workmen by throwing another slight burden on the whole community, and it seems to me self-evident that the sum total of these burdens, each slight in itself, would do every man more harm than the possible protection of his trade would do him good, even if it were not that a number of men would probably be thrown out of work.

Another correspondent has pointed out that the tendency in France and Germany is for these protective duties to keep rising, and certainly, if the effect of them is to make people depend on legislation instead of on their own energies, nobody can deny that the harm would be incalculable.

I deny altogether what yet another says, that Free Trade is a more cold, selfish and unsympathetic doctrine than Tariff Reform. I claim that we want to supply the poor people with what they want at the lowest possible rates; and, furthermore, that under Free Trade the rate of wages has increased enormously, as has the population of this island. On the whole, distress has diminished, and the working classes are far better off, and have far more chance of rising in the world than they had before. I do not see that countries like, say, Australia are doing as well as they did before they became such strong Protectionists, and I certainly believe that the working classes as a whole would be poorer, and not richer, if any serious scheme of Tariff Reform came into existence.

Of course we may go on disputing this matter for ever. We have set forth our respective views, and all we can hope is that as many individuals as possible will think for themselves and study the question on its merits.

XVII

The North-East Coast Strikes & Sir Christopher Furness's Scheme

[The Times Financial and Commercial Supplement, Nov. 18th, 1908]

THIS year there have been two serious strikes on the North-East Coast—the one in the engineering, and the other in the shipbuilding trade. Although quite distinct, the two strikes affected very much the same employers, as so many of the shipbuilders are also marine-engine builders, and the history of them was very similar indeed.

In both cases, owing to bad trade, the employers demanded a reduction of wages, which demand they reduced to what they considered the smallest possible amount. In both cases the majority of the men in the works agreed to the reduction, but in each case an important section refused. In the shipyards, the carpenters and joiners refused to accept any reduction, and in the engine works, the three engineers' unions did the same.

In both cases it is generally recognized that the leaders of the men would have agreed, but the great body of the men they represented overruled them. In the shipyards this happened before the strike began, and in the engine works it happened with the Board of Trade intervention, just as the strike was beginning.

In each case the local employers were confronted, as soon as the strike began, with the whole power of the national organization and resources of the workmen. In each case, after a protracted struggle, the local employers appealed to the Federation, *i.e.* the national body of shipbuilding employers in the one case, and the national body of engineering employers in the other. In the case of the shipbuilders, the national body of employers carried out a general lock-out: in the case of the engineers, the same body threatened a lock-out, and there the two matters ended, and in each case the men returned to work at the reduction.

Now, to add up the cost of these strikes is a very serious matter. In the case of the engineers, Mr. Frank Rose, who ought to be a good judge, estimates that the cost to the men was over £400,000; if so, we may probably take the direct cost to the employers at one-half that amount.

In the shipyard strike fewer men struck, but many more were laid idle on account of the strike, so we might probably take the cost of the two at about the same, and consider that these two strikes on the Tyne, Wear and Tees cost the employers about £400,000 and the men about £800,000. This of course takes no account of the indirect losses to both bodies caused by orders being driven away and trade generally injured.

But, besides this, there is a very great loss to the customers to be considered. This it is almost impossible to estimate, but it is easy to see that every succeeding year, owing to the greater magnitude of transactions and the greater complications of trade, the loss to customers is becoming more and more serious. A new railway may be paralyzed for want of its locomotives, or a colliery may be absolutely ruined for want of its pumping engines. A curious but instructive case is that of a ship built and engined on the Clyde but unable to be completed for want of its steering gear, which was ordered on the Tyne where the men were out on strike, and which therefore stopped the whole ship. It is probable that customers will get increasingly impatient of these losses, especially foreigners. These are more and more resenting the strike clauses in English contracts, and in this way the possibility of strikes is an ever-increasing burden on English trade.

Compared to all this, the apparent amount in dispute is very small indeed. To avoid a reduction of 1s. a week on his wages, each workman loses the whole amount of 35s. per week. This may, in part, be borne by his Union, but that is only another way of saying that it comes out of his savings and those of his class. We have already said that the employers' loss is estimated at half that amount, or, say, 17s. 6d. per man per week. If this was all, the fight would be absurd, but the real motive power is that the men feel that if an employer can insist on even a small reduction just because he chooses and without regard to what they may say, he might then enforce other reductions, shilling after shilling, at his own pleasure; and the employers equally feel that if the men absolutely refuse to accept reductions, however bad trade may be, it creates a difficulty of the most injurious character to the interests of both of them.

It would be one step in the right direction if the principle that ought to underlie all reductions of wages were more universally and formally recognized, for it is a fairly obvious one. Of course workmen want all the employment they can get, and it is always to an employer's interest to keep his works as fully employed as he can, therefore the following principle may be recognized:—

That it is to the interest of both sides for the total amount paid in wages to be as large as possible. If a 5 per cent. reduction will enable the employer to lower his prices so as to employ 10 per cent. more men, it is to the workmen's interest to accept the reduction; and not only so, but if they were as familiar with the state of trade as they might be, and ought to be, they would not, if they were sure of this point, oppose a reduction, and indeed they might ask the employers to put it in force, because employers themselves practically always reduce their own profits, and perhaps annihilate them altogether and take work at a loss, before they ask the men to accept a reduction of wages. In both cases it is simply a question of enlightened self-interest versus a short-sighted policy. Similarly, an advance is only good for the men if it does not seriously reduce the number of men employed. To reverse the above figures, it is no use for the men to get a 5 per cent. advance of wages if it is going to throw 10 per cent. of the men out of work, for thus the total amount to be paid in wages is less than it was before.

Of course, it really comes to the old story, that each side wants to be a little stronger than the other, and this is exactly what the wisest employers and trades union leaders have tried to avoid. The proper course is for the two sides to negotiate across a table, on a basis of perfect equality, and the leaders of the men ought to have the power to settle. Had this been done, both these strikes would have been avoided, and to appeal from the higher trained few to the untrained multitude who have not even had a chance of hearing the employers' reasons and arguments, is certainly a step in the wrong direction, and, if persevered in, not only is it death to what the men call collective bargaining, but it will sooner or later destroy trades unionism itself, and leave all these questions to the chaotic risk of mob law, momentary impulse and clamour. One form after another of private warfare has been annihilated, to the unmixed benefit of the world at large, and public opinion ought to render strikes and lock-outs impossible.

Without being able to give a panacea for all disputes, it is quite obvious that in wages questions, whatever may be the faults or uncertainties of arbitration, the benefits would enormously outweigh any possible evils. In the first instance, it does not raise any question as to which side is the stronger; and, secondly, whichever way the matter is decided, it saves those enormous losses borne by the customer, which no doubt indirectly have to be paid for by the employers and workmen afterwards, in diminished trade and other losses. This is only one illustration. The whole question of whether strikes can be got rid of altogether is a much larger one.

But there is one consequence, if it may be so called, of the strike, which is deserving of separate and very serious consideration, and that is the proposal of Sir Christopher Furness to his men, which we now propose to investigate.

Sir Christopher points out, very properly, that all wealth is the result of three things—capital, enterprise (which of course includes organization) and labour. Some people are fond of saying that no wealth can be produced without labour, and that labour is entitled to all the fruits of it; but this is just like saying that all the credit of a cup of tea is due to the hot water and nothing at all to the dried leaf. The co-operation of the three is essential, and among the three the profit must be divided, though not of course necessarily in equal shares.

Sir Christopher proposes two schemes by which the workmen are to be interested.

The first is that the trades unions should buy his shipyard. This probably he never seriously expected the men to accept, but thought it right to make it in order to prove to the men that he, as an employer, was quite willing to give place to them if they were prepared to accept the position that he held with all its responsibilities. There is no reason why workmen should not in time own works entirely, but probably, if that ever happens, it will grow up by degrees under something more like Sir Christopher's second scheme, viz.:—

The workmen will have 5 per cent. deducted from their earnings, to be spent in buying shares in the company for which they work. On this money they get, if we understand correctly, a minimum absolute rate of interest of 4 per cent. (like borrowed capital). Then capital (the old capital) gets 5 per cent. The board of directors, whose powers remain as at present, decide what amount to set aside for depreciation, reserve, development, etc., as in any ordinary balance sheet, and salaries will presumably be paid both to officials and directors.

After all this, whatever is left is the divisible profit, just as in an ordinary company, and this would be divided between the workmen's shares and the ordinary shares, on the basis of the individual holdings. We understand this to mean that if the ordinary share capital is nine times the workmen's capital, the latter would receive one-tenth to the ordinary shareholders' nine-tenths. As we understand, every employé must be a shareholder—mechanic, labourer, or boy.

Next comes a very special feature. Sir Christopher proposes to have a works council, elected or selected, of equal numbers of officials and workmen—a court of reference and committee of council rolled into one. Sir Christopher is not yet prepared to have working men directors, and this council has apparently no real power; but its members can have things explained to them, they can represent the men's views, they can advise, criticize, and ask questions. Besides the above, he proposes to have on this council some of the officials or representatives of the trades unions principally engaged in the works. This would appear to an outsider to be the most doubtful point of the whole scheme. Some trades union leaders no doubt are excellent business men, and can give very useful advice, but it does not necessarily follow that they are all so, and we think Sir Christopher might easily be landed sometimes with a man whose advice he could not follow, whose interference might be indiscriminate or dangerous, but whom having once admitted he could not remove without great awkwardness. Furthermore, if other works were to adopt Sir Christopher's scheme, one could not avoid these men passing from one works to another, and this might obviously open out positions of great difficulty.

But here, as in everything else, it is quite clear that the scheme has been very carefully thought out, and it may be that where we see the difficulties Sir Christopher may see the remedies, and no doubt everybody will watch the scheme with great interest, and everybody will be pleased if it succeeds.

It may be well to point out very hurriedly a few of the schemes of the same kind which have been tried before, though it is impossible to enumerate the whole of them. Thirty or forty years ago, some works began by giving the men a share of the profits—perhaps half of what was made over 10 per cent.—on condition that the men did not belong to any trades union, but in this case the benefit to the men was so infinitesimal that it was not worth their consideration when weighing the far more serious question of whether they should, or should not, belong to a trades union.

It is generally recognized in all investments that the higher the possible profits the lower the average profits, and an enormous number of shipbuilding and engineering works are carried on at a very small profit indeed; therefore, in any profit-sharing scheme, there is a great probability that very often the men for many years together would get no interest at all on their moeny.

Sir Christopher, very wisely, insists on his men depositing part of their wages in return for shares. This has been tried in Lancashire, we believe with fair success, and there is certainly one well-known works on the Tyne where a very similar, but not absolutely identical, scheme is exceedingly popular. When once a man has shares in a business he cannot easily throw the arrangement overboard, and even a small investment has a considerable educational value. This, coupled with the committee of council, ought to diffuse among the men a better knowledge of what is going forward, and should make them more tolerant of those endless difficulties, of which the whole burden is at present borne by the employer.

Whether it is wise to make it compulsory for every man to become a shareholder is a question which may have to be modified by future experience. Some men, from outside causes, cannot afford to save, and in every works there are some floating men who come and go very quickly and easily, whom it really does not seem worth connecting so seriously with the establishment.

But if England was not short of capital there would be no unemployed, and there is every sign that we are also numerically short of people who can organize labour and capital so as to make profitable industries; so a scheme which first of all makes working men save, and, secondly, makes them take more interest in the conditions of the industry upon which they live, is certainly a move in the right direction. We are glad to see that the men have adopted it, though a year is too short a time in which to try it.

It is impossible to close an article on this subject without referring to Sir George Livesey's success in the South Metropolitan Gas Works. There he made his men first of all shareholders, and then made a certain number of them directors, but it was often thought that the success of this movement was due very much to his own strong personality, energy and ability. Sir Christopher Furness probably has all these qualities, but we must remember that many a thing will succeed in the hands of a man of exceptional ability which would not succeed in ordinary circumstances. However, Sir Christopher may be quite sure that the whole industrial world will watch his scheme with great and friendly interest.

XVIII

Unemployment

[LETTER TO THE EDITOR OF 'THE TIMES,' NOV. 14TH, 1908]

THERE is one most serious and obvious cause of unemployment which appears to be altogether overlooked, and yet which is capable of a considerable amount of gradual alleviation.

To use Sir Christopher Furness's expression, all work is a combined effort of labour, capital, and enterprise. Now at present we have a terrible surplus of labour which cannot be employed for want of the other two. Labour requires workshops and machinery and raw material to work upon, which all need money, also someone to pay wages till the produce is completed, sold, and paid for. This is Capital. But these together can produce nothing without Enterprise, that is, the trained employer or manufacturer. To know how to get orders, what to make, and how to make it profitably, to arrange the workshops, recruit the labour, and manage it when collected, besides being able to raise the necessary capital, are qualities which require training and experience which are possessed by few men.

And I think it is evident that the country is short both of trained employers and of investors in the employment of British labour. The socialist view is that Government ought to do all this—but that brings us no further. Government has men at its disposal who can manage dockyards and arsenals. Corporations can manage, more or less, such things as gas and water works and tramways, and in most countries the Government manages railways. But Government has no one at its disposal who can travel for orders, please all sorts of customers, advise them as to their difficulties, give credit safely to shaky people, build up a trade by working at cutting prices, and discharge all the other functions which make the difference between employment and non-employment, starvation and comfort, to millions of our population.

If anyone says they might get men out of the present employer class, I reply that probably all the men who may be said to understand the science of employment, are as busy as they can be, but there are far too few of them.

This evil is very seriously felt in two directions. First, the small employers. I fear these are getting rapidly fewer. Now, though we have no actual statistics, I think there can be no doubt that, taking the whole kingdom, far more than half the workmen and labourers are employed by very small employers of perhaps twenty men or less.

Not only are small employers necessary to make work to employ labour, but they are often the material from which more large employers can be formed, and the position is one of the best from which a working man can rise.

But there is another kind of small employer—the people who take shares in industrial companies. Without these the professional capitalist cannot collect the necessary money for new enterprises. They are a very timid class, and rash or harsh legislation and the talk of the various kinds of Socialists have a most practical effect in causing these people to invest their money elsewhere and not in the employment of British labour. If we take the somewhat low estimate of £100 of capital for every man we want to employ, it is easy to see how an orator, by frightening a few timid investors, may and actually does increase the number of unemployed, and therefore increases the amount of starvation and misery in the country.

The ideal paradise for the working classes is where, as we see occasionally but rarely, two employers are competing for each man's services.

If Government likes to become an employer on a much larger scale than ever before there is ample opening for them.

The need for British products is enormous; the practical demand is limited by the world's power of paying for them. But I doubt Government having the men or the experience, and, as many local bodies have found to their sorrow, the capital at the disposal of Government is only what private individuals are able and willing to lend them.

For one man who can manage 1000 men, there are many who can manage 100, and almost any skilful workman can manage three or four.

What we want is more employers, beginning with small ones, who ought to be encouraged both by the Legislature and by trades unions.

Also, and above all, we need more capital, and this can only be got by saving. Every man who saves money, at a time like this, is a public benefactor. It is almost impossible to invest money without making more employment, and we want it invested in England.

XIX

Co-partnership and Unemployment

[PUBLISHED IN 'THE ENGINEER,' DEC. 4TH, 1908]

THE acceptance by his workmen of Sir Christopher Furness's profit-sharing scheme makes it interesting to go a little into the question of other efforts which have been made in this direction in times past, so as to form an idea how far Sir Christopher's plan is likely to be successful in the future.

It is impossible to give all the schemes, but the following may be taken as samples. In many cases it is perhaps undesirable to give the names of the works where these schemes were tried—successfully or otherwise.

In the early seventies one or two firms offered the men half of all the profits that were made above 10 per cent., on condition that they did not belong to any trades union. This failed, for the obvious reason that so very few firms pay more than 10 per cent. that the men got nothing at all in most cases, and where they did the amount was not sufficient to interest them either way in the question of whether they would, or would not, belong to unions. These attempts may all be brushed out of the way as unsuccessful.

Another class of proposal has had some measure of success; namely where works have allowed the men to leave money on loan, on which they get probably 4 per cent. interest whatever happens, and, as in one case in the west, if the ordinary shareholders get dividends of more than 4 per cent., the workmen's interest is made up to the same amount. In another works in the east, which have always paid extraordinarily well, the men get half the difference between 4 per cent. and the dividend. But whereas the ordinary public has to buy these shares at an enormous premium, the workman gets them at par. I believe, in both these cases, that when a workman leaves, he can by some process get out his money, which is in fact really a loan with a varying rate of interest.

This is good as far as it goes, but it does not give the workmen a real interest in the business. Probably only a minority would avail themselves of the opportunity, and there is neither sufficient hope nor sufficient fear to induce the men, as a body, to act differently from what they would do if there were no such arrangement. At the same time, it is probably an encouragement to a few of the leading and keener men to save money and rise in the world, and it will, to that extent, lead to a better feeling between employer and workmen.

There is, however, one episode in history which is worth describing much more fully, because, though the outcome was disastrous, it was full of interesting lessons, and this was the rise and fall of the Ouseburn engine works, which were started in Newcastle, on a co-operative basis, in 1871. At that time the great nine-hours' strike was in progress. Twelve firms in Newcastle and Gateshead were affected. The majority of the men were non-unionists, and so were about half their leaders. There was nothing like the organization for raising money for men in those days that there is now, but the prospects of trade, just after the Franco-German War, were exceedingly good, and it occurred to some of the friends of the workmen that they might start works independently of the masters, and so get their own way about the hours. Dr. Rutherford was the head of this movement and chairman of the company, and the capital was very largely found by the various co-operative societies, and to some extent by friends and sympathizers—political and otherwise—of the workmen on strike.

The Ouseburn works at that time were closed, and the new company rented them with all the machinery complete. Probably

Dr. Rutherford's chief problem was how to get orders; there was a feeling abroad that the capitalists, as a class, would all stick together, and that therefore shipowners and shipbuilders would not give orders for marine engines to the Ouseburn works, and this was apparently a great anxiety to the company. However, things turned out not at all as they expected. Two large shipowners each gave them orders for six sets of engines, and one shipbuilder did the same, so they had a magnificent order book of eighteen sets to start with.

It is very difficult at this length of time to arrive at exact figures, but there is strong reason to believe that these gentlemen really got their engines at what was, even at that time, a very low price, and as the prices after that rose very rapidly, these engines ultimately had to be built and delivered at prices which probably were simply ruinous. I may say that when the strike began, the price of engines was about £45 per nominal horse-power, and very soon after the strike was over—it lasted a little over four months—the price had risen to nearly £60 per horse-power.

The terms on which the men worked were these: they were to work nine hours a day, or fifty-four hours a week instead of fifty-nine, as had been the case up till then. They got the standard wages, but they had to leave 10 per cent. of their wages in the business, which became actual share capital, therefore every man had an ever-increasing financial stake in the company, and I suppose that if he left he would have to sell his shares in the ordinary market. The directors were nearly all working men. It seems to be agreed on all hands that the quality of work they turned out was just about equal to the average good work of the district; in fact, there were no complaints whatever.

Probably the employment of so many men contributed very much to the workmen winning the strike, which they looked upon as a great victory, but after no very long time the Ouseburn got into greater and greater difficulties, and ultimately failed, and the shareholders, at any rate, got nothing at all. Many old workmen who had invested all their savings were absolutely ruined, and of course the whole of the 10 per cent. of the wages which the men had put in was lost for ever.

The practical effect of this seemed to be thoroughly to disgust the working classes with the idea of being their own employers, and I think that for a long time it hindered the growth of any co-operative movement in engineering production throughout the country.

It should be observed that, as far as one can judge, where the men failed was not in doing the work, but in taking the orders; in fact, they were absolutely without commercial experience and knowledge of the trade. Whether the men at the Ouseburn worked as hard as, or harder than, in ordinary works is a point on which there is the greatest divergence of opinion. Some managers have said that they worked enthusiastically, and others that they were very idle. One can only suppose that different usages grew up in different parts of the works, but on one point there is no doubt— that the men were willing to leave this much money in the business if they had sufficient inducement; and, had the concern paid well, and the money accumulated at 5 per cent. compound interest, which ought to have been possible in that case, every man would at the end of fourteen years have had a sum equal to double his wages, which is, practically speaking, the amount of capital which is necessary in an engine works for every man employed.

The great misfortune was that so interesting an experiment was tried during the strike, as, at any other time, most employers would have been only too glad to have given them friendly and sympathetic advice, and to have co-operated with them just as they do with each other; but the starting of these works was an avowed act of war on the part of the men's leaders, and therefore, of course, employers could not be expected to take any friendly action towards them, when such action would probably have been altogether resented.

It seems to a great many employers who have thought about it carefully that it would be possible for an employer to induce his men to leave 10 per cent. in the business as above, and gradually to bring working men into the management, letting them benefit by his experience, and succeed him, just like his own sons or any other younger men who might, in ordinary cases, step into his place. People often say that no workmen are capable of managing a large business, which is probably perfectly true, but it is equally true that there is no possible reason why they might not learn to do so in the course of a few years, if they had the same opportunities as the sons of the capitalists, or other people who actually do rise to that position. The best of us were wholly ignorant once, and there is no reason why selected workmen might not learn as well as any-one else; in fact, as everybody can see for themselves, numbers of our best employers have either been workmen, or are the sons of workmen, and there are probably as good fish in the river as ever came out of it.

Following this, it is interesting to refer to Sir George Livesey's experience with the South Metropolitan Gas Company. His scheme, which began in 1889, has been so great a success that the terms must be carefully set forth.

Leaving out certain technicalities, which apply only to the sale of gas, the point is that whenever the shareholders get an increase of $\frac{1}{4}$ per cent. on their dividend, the workman gets a bonus of 1 per cent. on his year's wages. But the courageous act on Sir George—then Mr.—Livesey's part was, that he handed the men at once a bonus for three years back, which gave them for the first year 2 per cent., for the second year 3 per cent., and for the third 4 per cent., making in all 9 per cent. on one year's wages, so that a man earning 30s. a week received a bonus, or, as Sir George called it, a nest-egg, of £7, and other men in proportion. It need hardly be said that few boards of directors would have the courage to recommend, and few shareholders to adopt, a system which began by such a large out-of-pocket payment. This money was put to the credit of the men, and was to be left undisturbed, at compound interest, for three or five years as might be thereafter decided, and was not to be drawn out except in case of death, superannuation, or leaving the service in an honourable manner. At the end of five years this nest-egg became an absolute gift, and the men after that might either draw it out, with the interest, or leave it in at interest. Every man would then get 4 per cent. on the money that was lying to his credit, and, of course, would receive any bonus that was due, as stated above. The details were settled by a standing committee, composed of equal numbers of workmen selected by themselves, and officers chosen by the directors, presided over by the chairman of the company.

There are other clauses to deal with what might be called casual men, and various minor matters, but with these we need not concern ourselves.

Under this scheme the men accumulated large sums of money, which, we believe, were, to a very large extent, changed into share capital, and Sir George very soon began to wish to have the workmen represented on the board of directors. This was carried out, and it is generally believed that no directors ever worked together more harmoniously than Sir George, his old directors, and his working men directors.

This scheme might be looked upon as one suitable, with modifications, for general adoption; but of course we can never know how much of its success was due to the charm and personal influence of Sir George Livesey, to whom all his men and officials were devoted, and who certainly had the most extraordinary power of influencing other people to do what he thought right.

From this we pass on to Sir Christopher Furness's scheme. He has clearly grasped the point that the men must become true shareholders; he does not make them directors, but he has a carefully considered committee, which will form a connecting link between the Board and the works. This is of the greatest importance; probably all who have ever worked in a shop have often wondered at what seemed the inconsistency and inconsiderateness of the governing body; and this was only due to the fact that they did not know the difficulties and ever-changing conditions which the employers had to meet in dealing with their customers. To take an extremely common typical case: most men and boys know what it is to be hurried and made to strain every nerve to finish some work by a certain date, and then suddenly to be taken off it and the work allowed to dawdle on for a month. They say how inconsiderate masters are; but the obvious reason is that the employers were most anxious to get the work sent off by a certain steamer, which suddenly disappointed them by filling up with other things, and they were perforce obliged to wait a month for the next ship. So the reasons why men are paid off, and why changes are made, are all capable of explanation, but are very apt to be looked on as foolish or inconsiderate, if the explanation is not given. Among the many advantages of modern industry, no doubt one of the chief evils is the greater gulf which now exists between the owners of works and the actual workmen.

But, to return to Sir Christopher's scheme. There are probably very few men in business who have not often and often wished with their whole hearts that they could get themselves and their money out of it. Probably most men have many times during their middle age said that if they could only get out the money they put in, they would be thankful to cry quits; but the great blessing, both to themselves and everybody else, is, that they cannot get it out. The money is there; they have to watch it, and they have to work. They have incurred liabilities which they cannot shake off, and therefore, tired, weary and almost heart-broken though they may be, they have to go toiling on; and probably, in most cases, this ultimately leads to a life of reasonable comfort, sometimes of course to considerable wealth, while in an infinitesimally small number of cases the man may become a millionaire.

The obvious tendency of works to group together into a few enormous organizations is a very serious one. The small employers are crushed out, and a large number of men, who would have been moderate-sized employers a generation ago, are now represented by highly-paid managers—men who do most admirable technical work, but who have nothing like the same power in organizing and developing fresh branches of industry. One of the greatest reasons of there being so many unemployed in the country is that there are far too few employers, and it is very probable that one of the happiest means of getting over this difficulty is by interesting the working men themselves in the works.

Besides being short of employers, we are terribly short of capital, and this is made worse and worse by the appalling fact that such a large amount of the money of the investing classes is being invested abroad. We cannot shut our eyes to the fact that the blustering talk of the House of Commons, and the threats of the Socialists, have frightened capital to a very serious extent. When a member of Parliament deliberately threatens people with an 8s. income tax, many investors think that though it may never come to that, it may easily mean a very serious increase, and they will do wisely to invest their money in, say, Canada. Now, none of us would grudge Canada anything that is done, but in sending so much capital there you are sending it where the labour is not, instead of where the labour is. The bearing this has on a scheme like that of Sir Christopher Furness's is this, that every pound of capital that is saved—and every workman under this scheme has to save 5 per cent. of his wages—is doing something to employ somebody. Capital cannot be utilized except by employing labour, and labour, as we can see by the unemployed, is of no use whatever without an appropriate amount of capital.

Now it takes, roughly speaking, an amount of capital equal to two years' wages for every man employed in shipbuilding and engineering works, so if a man invests 5 per cent. of his wages, he invests an amount equal to $2\frac{1}{2}$ per cent. of the capital that is required to employ him; and this will continue to accumulate, and for every £150 or so left in the business by the workmen, there is permanent work for one more man.

This, as far as it goes, is a very sound manner of making work for the unemployed. Furthermore, in so much as the men give less trouble to the employer, and possibly come to take more interest in his business and help him in other ways, so far his energies are free to hunt further afield in search of work, to organize schemes which will keep his works busy, and, generally speaking, to add to the prosperity of the world.

It must never be forgotten that until every part of the world is as crowded and as well-furnished as England, there is an absolutely unlimited demand for our manufactures; but this demand is, to a great extent, of no avail, because, while many people are anxious to get what we can make, we can only supply them in so far as they are able to pay for the articles. Here again comes the need of more capital, and the only way to get capital is to save money. In the average manufacturing business of this country, probably the shareholders get about one-tenth of what is paid in wages. If wages, therefore, really began to be saved, and every working man began to exert himself, we should put a far greater force in motion towards furthering work and prosperity than anything that can be done by the present race of employers. Besides this, there would be the great advantage that, instead of wealth being accumulated in a few hands, it would be diffused over the largest number of men possible, the average comfort of those in work would be materially increased, and there would be fewer and fewer men out of work, which is what we all wish to see.

XX

Christian Politics

[Read to St Paul's Church Literary Society, Newcastle, Oct. 8th, 1909]

IN addressing a Church of England society, I make no apology for assuming that I am speaking to a body of men who will accept as an abstract principle the fact that in every relation of life what we do, say, and think must be guided by those eternal truths which have been taught us directly by God, which we have all accepted in our baptism and confirmation, and which we all admit, in theory at any rate, we ought to carry out in our daily lives.

I think sometimes thoughtless people fancy that because men do not talk much about religion, it therefore has far less effect upon their conduct than it really has, but this is false reasoning. To take a similar case, a very large proportion of the men we meet every day are married men with families; they rarely, if ever, speak about how much they love their wives and children, and yet we can see at every turn how much they are influenced in their business, daily conduct, and everything else, by the interests of their families. In the same way, a true Christian, though he may not be always talking about his religion, ought always to be thinking in every transaction of his life how to do his duty towards God and towards his neighbour.

To put the matter in a practical form, certainly no Churchman, and I do not think any Nonconformist or member of the Church of Rome, will quarrel with me if I take what the Catechism lays down as our duty towards our neighbour, as a simple and handy statement of the principles which ought to guide all the relations of our lives—including politics.

I remember some years ago a cry was started at one of our elections, that religion had nothing to do with politics. It seems to me that people might just as well say that religion has nothing to do with business, that religion has nothing to do with social and domestic life,—or any similar fiction. I think that in managing the affairs of a State we ought to be just as anxious to be scrupulously truthful and honest, and to do that which is for the good and happiness of the whole human race, as we should be in the conduct of our families. Some people say that is impossible, but this I do not believe. That it is difficult, of course I admit, but is it not the whole point of a Christian's life to be always doing things which are difficult, and which would probably be impossible if he did not know that he might seek for a higher strength than his own, both to guide and support him?

We should always remember that as politicians, from the Prime Minister down to the humblest voter, our business is not to stand up for our own rights but to do our duty towards our neighbour. Such points as Chinese labour, fiscal policy, education, and peace and war, must be looked upon from the point of view, not of what will pay best, not of what is for the interest of England only or of the Empire only, but what are for the interests, both temporal and eternal, of mankind as a whole.

Some things are, and others are not, within the functions of our own Government. It is obviously no part of our business to deal with the internal affairs of France, Germany and Russia. It is sometimes difficult to lay down a rule how far we ought to interfere with other countries when they are doing things we disapprove of, but in the same way it seems to me exactly as difficult, neither more nor less, to know when we ought to interfere with our neighbours when they are doing things we disapprove of or know to be wrong.

In a country with such far-reaching interests as England, and such world-wide influence, it is above all things necessary that we should strive to ensure all our doings being carried out in the highest, broadest, and most unselfish manner. As an illustration,

I would point out a fault which we sometimes see: when we make an arrangement, such as a treaty with a foreign power, some thoughtless statesmen talk as if they thought England was humiliated unless we have got the best of the bargain, often perhaps without looking to see how scrupulously that result has been obtained. Now, while those who are making a national arrangement must of course remember that they are simply the trustees for an enormous number of individuals, all of whose interests may be affected, still a trustee ought not to do anything unfair, harsh, or dishonourable, even in the interests of his client; and I should always be sorry if I thought that England, as a strong country, had taken advantage of her strength to make an unfair bargain with one who was weaker than herself.

A point which I think will perhaps help us in some of our difficulties is this: no man can very well be held responsible for what was done before he was born. People often raise such questions as this: What right have we to be in India? Now, the simple citizen may find that a difficult question to answer, but why should it be answered at all? There we are. The practical question is, whether we had better try to govern India as well as possible in the interests of its inhabitants, or whether it would be better, in their interests, for us to clear out altogether. I am quite prepared to say that the question ought to be settled primarily in the interests of the people of India, but we are only one out of a number of conflicting peoples in that country. Before we went there, first one and then another of those peoples conquered and more or less enslaved the other and weaker nations, and before we left I think we should have to see that we were leaving behind us a well-organized, happy and united family, who would be able to get on peaceably and prosperously without us.

Personally, I always feel as if it was more difficult to justify our action towards some of the more obscure races, such as the natives of Australia, than it is towards the more powerful and complicated community of India.

Speaking of India leads one by natural stages to consider the whole question of peace and war, which is one of the most responsible and painful questions with which a Government can have to deal. War is terrible in every aspect: killing, destroying, not only undoing everything that ordinarily we try to accomplish, but awakening all the worst and bitterest passions of our nature. We keep an army and a navy prepared for war, and we train men up to war as the business of their lives. People often say it is horrible; and in speaking of our building ships and doing other things for the defence of the country, they say we are spending so many millions simply for the purpose of destroying our fellow-creatures. Now, with all deference to these people, I think the majority of us will agree that this view is perfectly untrue. You might just as well say thas you keep policemen in order to make burglars. The use of an army and a navy is to prevent violence and to secure peace. There is an expression that Mr. Haldane constantly uses which I think an exceptionally happy one, when he says that the first use of our Army is to police the Empire, and I think we have always considered that the use of our Navy is to police the seas.

I will speak of the Navy first. For a hundred years we have enjoyed an unquestioned supremacy, and the consequence is not only that since Trafalgar no hostile fleet has ever deliberately faced our fleet, but piracy has been abolished all over the seas. My own belief is that if our Navy had been weaker there would probably have been far more war and bloodshed, and I think this will come out more clearly if we consider the position of the Army.

I suppose it would not be possible for us to have an army of such dominating strength as our Navy, but a little reflection will show that our wars, especially the larger ones, are generally caused by the other side thinking either that we cannot, or that we will not, fight, and I think we must all agree that no course can be more fraught with evil than for a country like England first to give the idea that it will not fight and then to do it.

To consider our recent wars, I believe there is very strong reason to think that the Tsar would not have entered on the Crimean war if he had thought that England was really in earnest and would put forth her whole strength, as she ultimately did, to oppose him. The Tsar apparently very much over-estimated the influence of the peace party in England; and that, coupled with the state of unpreparedness of our Army, probably made him think that we should only protest and not take stronger action. But we know that he was mistaken, and I think the younger generation do not realize the intense feeling on this question among the mass of the people in England, who I believe really carried the Ministry off their feet and forced them into the war.

Again, in the case of the Indian Mutiny, I think we may take it for granted, knowing the facts from history, that the Mutiny would never have broken out if the leaders had not believed that we were very much weaker than we were, that our troops in India were few and unprepared, and that there would be time to annihilate our forces before they could be supported. There again it was a case of counting their strength against ours. Had we had more troops on the spot, every extra regiment would have made the Mutiny so much less likely.

Our only other first-class war of recent times was, of course, the war in South Africa, and I can hardly believe that President Kruger would have embarked on the war had he known that we should send out considerably over 200,000 men, first and last, in order to fight the Boers. Had we sent out half the number at once, probably there would have been no war at all. And if you like to go further back in history, you will observe how often the position of England has been to slide into a war in an unprepared and apparently half-hearted manner: when once in the war she has become more and more obstinate, and ultimately has come out victorious, after great sacrifices both of her own and the enemy's forces, which would have been prevented had her Army been stronger to begin with.

It is also interesting to examine the cause of our smaller wars. If you take the case of the hill tribes in India, it would be a fair sample of almost all our little wars, whether in India, Africa, or elsewhere. There are perhaps industrious farmers and peasants cultivating the plains; they have warlike neighbours in the mountains, who hate work and love fighting and plunder. These men, like the old Highlanders, would constantly plunder the plains if there was no stronger hand to keep them in order. That stronger hand is created by our stationing a few troops here and there to keep the peace, just as a few policemen scattered over a town will maintain quiet at home. The fact of the soldiers being there keeps the people in the hills quiet.

People often think that a man who goes into the Army and never sees a shot fired has had an unsuccessful career and perhaps a useless one, but this is altogether untrue. If a young man, by spending his life doing nothing in an unhealthy climate, thereby enables a large number of peaceable folk to earn their living and bring up their families in peace and plenty, can it be said that he has spent his life in vain? Had he and his comrades not been there, nothing would have stood in the way of rapine and murder. It is often said that the world knows nothing of its greatest heroes, and I think those people who by their action hinder fighting from taking place are perhaps among our greatest heroes and most useful citizens.

To think that the reduction of our forces would conduce to peace is the same as to think that by reducing the number of police we should lessen crime and make our streets more quiet and orderly. We know how a crowd of disorderly boys and men, whom we now call "hooligans," can be kept quiet by the presence of one policeman, and were it not for the good sense and training of our constabulary, it would very likely be impossible for people to walk alone in the streets of a large town without danger of being annoyed or insulted—possibly robbed.

People complain of the extravagance of a Government spending money on armaments, but they forget that immeasurably the most expensive thing a Government can do is to get the country into war, and no expenditure in time of peace is comparable to the appalling cost of a year of real war such as those to which I have alluded.

Let us turn to our home policy. We have in our midst crime, poverty, ignorance, and disease. We would grapple with these with a view to conquest, and we are anxious not only to raise the community as a whole, but to give to each individual the best chance of raising himself and making himself useful to the community at large. But let us also look at the same question from a brighter point; we are part of a country very powerful, and on the whole prosperous, notwithstanding the distress that is going on at this moment, and we may fairly say the standard of living is higher than it probably ever was before in this country, and higher than it is in almost any other country; but we still want to improve this, and to pick up and take care of all those who fall below the average. Probably what we hope for is to make the lives of the succeeding generation brighter, happier, safer from misfortune, and to make the people themselves better educated, more useful, and above all, more virtuous.

I think we shall all agree that whenever we legislate for the benefit of the community in general, we should take very great care to consider those, possibly not a very large minority, who instead of gaining by the change will be the worse for it, and we ought to do all we can to guard their interests; and if the country as a whole gains largely in prosperity, it should out of those gains do something to compensate those people whose interests happen to lie in an opposite direction, and who are being sacrificed for the benefit of the larger number.

Now, to face the actual question of government and legislation. The party system is, for Parliament and the nation to pretend to be divided into two hostile camps which are, more or less, at war with each other; and too often, instead of putting their heads together to try and do the best they can for the country as a whole, they appear to do all they can to thwart and discredit each other.

They keep saying what they know is not the case: that the other side is unpatriotic, foolish, and altogether wrong; whereas there is always an enormous amount on which we are all agreed; there is an equal amount on which the moderate men of a party disagree with extreme men of that party; while we probably know that a great number of the men on the opposite side are just as honest, conscientious and patriotic as we are ourselves. If the party system is to stand—and for the moment we see nothing else—we ought to look upon it from a somewhat different point of view. The one party proposes some piece of legislation: the Opposition may say, in the first instance, that they think it will do more harm than good, and this is practically decided at the second reading of the bill in Parliament. But after that, when the bill goes into committee, the Opposition must accept it as inevitable, and then their business is to point out the difficulties so that they may be mitigated, met and alleviated as far as possible. This the Government ought, in all common sense, to take in a perfectly friendly spirit. Nothing is perfect, few things are easy, and no people are more their true friends than those who point out the dangers which loom ahead, so that we may all of us on both sides think of the best means to meet and avert them.

I should like here to suggest a point which is far too much overlooked, which is, that the party in power, whether we have chosen it or not, for the moment represents that great principle which we call the monarchy, or in other words the executive; that the whole burden and responsibility of carrying on every branch of government rests upon it; and that it is to this Ministry that we have to look to meet every emergency that may arise. If, to take a most serious case, the country went to war, it is behind these men as our leaders that we ought to rally, and just like soldiers with their officers, we must obey and do our best to support those who are in power in carrying out what they have to do. Of course this in no way keeps us from either criticizing or recommending alterations, or, if an opportunity arises, from changing our leaders; but though you and

I may hope that to-morrow we may see a change of government, I maintain that in all cases of emergency it is our duty, until the change actually has come, to obey them faithfully, and not to throw unfair obstructions in their way—just as an army must obey its general, and just as a boat's crew or football team must obey their captain. The fact that the head is not of our choosing is no justification whatever for insubordination or disobedience. But above all, and this I would say most seriously, we never ought to forget that if we attribute bad motives to men who are acting in good faith, if we exaggerate their faults and misrepresent their intentions or actions, we are doing that which is absolutely unworthy of a Christian gentleman, which is disloyal to our King, injurious to our country, and degrading to ourselves.

But now, as a Church, as the followers of Christ, are we satisfied with our present social system? What are our ideals, and can we, by political means or by legislation, bring them about, or usefully modify the existing state of things? On this point, of course, there is an enormous divergence of opinion. Some of the great democratic leaders of the last century considered that though law was necessary to control violence and hinder people from inflicting actual injury upon each other, legislation could do little towards making people better or happier—not that they were less keen than the most enthusiastic about carrying out these reforms, but they considered that these should be effected by other influences and not by the mere making of laws. These people would point out that legislation is to the ordinary work of the world only what the printed rules of cricket are to the game, and they would say that no alteration of the rules of cricket could ever make a bad eleven into a good one, or teach a man to defend his own wicket, or take his opponent's, who could not do so under the old rules. On the other hand, some of our friends seem to think that if you can show that a reform is desirable, you have at once made out a case for fresh legislation. The truth may perhaps lie between the two, but the fact that men calling themselves by the same party name have held such opposite views, is quite sufficient to make us careful in dealing with these questions.

Probably no question has exercised our minds more than the general question of riches and poverty, luxury and misery. A sympathetic body like the clergy find it very difficult to see with patience the extremes of bitter poverty side by side with the most reckless and lavish squandering of money. Indeed it is most unsatisfactory, and we must all wish to see it otherwise, but, alas, theory and practice combine to show that many people, in their impatience of what seems to them a great wrong, advocate measures which, far from alleviating the evil, would only intensify it. Of course the first thing to be done is the work, not of Parliament, but of the Church: it is, to teach those who have money that they are stewards and not owners, that they will some day have to render an account of all that has passed through their hands, and that it is both their duty and privilege to use it, not for their own luxury and indulgence, but as a talent which they are responsible for employing, with the best discretion in their power, for the good of the community as a whole.

But I claim that it is the duty of every man who has anything to spare, after providing for the reasonable needs of himself and his children, to do what he can to save money, because in that way, and that way only, can the general position of the people ever be improved. This means that nearly every mechanic, at any rate, ought to have saved a certain amount of money before he marries, even if he cannot continue to do so afterwards.

One point as to capital. It seems to me that those who now agitate so violently for legislation against wealth forget that by no means all, and probably only a small part of the profits of wealth goes to the nominal owner; generally speaking, a far larger proportion goes to the general community as a whole. For example, if the North Eastern Railway ceased to pay dividends it would be very disagreeable for the shareholders, but probably the trade of the community, as long as the railway continued to work, would go on pretty much as it is now; but if the shareholders, seeing no hope of dividends, decided to close the railway altogether, the whole of the northern counties would be absolutely ruined, which means that the public as a whole make an indirect profit out of the railway compared to which the amount paid in dividends is absolutely paltry. I find in the world numbers of cases of railways which have never paid any dividends at all, and yet which have been the means of opening up districts and making them prosperous and comfortable for thousands of inhabitants.

It may interest you to be told (and if you will take trouble and spend an afternoon with the Stock Exchange Year Book—which is available at any library and at most offices—you can see for yourselves) that in the manufacturing concerns of this country, roughly speaking, for every £1 that is paid in dividends £10 are paid in wages.

But almost all efforts, both past and present, to deal with these questions by legislation have been unsuccessful. The first effect of it generally is to make people nervous, suspicious and anxious, and besides that, in a time of difficulty all history shows that nothing is so great an advantage as the present possession of ready money. If there comes a panic, the rich man can quietly wait until it is over; the struggling man is ruined. It seems to me that the tendency of every disturbance is to make rich men richer and poor men poorer, and the most suicidal action of which the working classes can be guilty is to frighten capital, because that more than anything else diminishes their own employment, and throws greater power into the hands of the capitalists who remain.

These social changes ought to be made, but I certainly believe they cannot be made by agitation, and very little by legislation. The Bible proposes to bring them about by changing the hearts of the selfish men, and this is not only the best but probably the quickest way in the long run.

I feel that I have now come to a point where, if I were to go further, rules would have to be laid down, and precise principles advocated; therefore also I feel I have come to the point where my self-imposed task is ended. I would ask you to remember that power and wealth are both trusts given you by God to be used absolutely unselfishly and entirely in His service, and that each one of us must now seek for the guidance of the Holy Spirit, so that in the full light of truth and justice—of truth however unpalatable and of justice even to the worst—we may strive earnestly for the attainment of universal peace and happiness, for so, and so only, can religion and piety be established among us for all generations.

XXI

Insurance against Unemployment

[THE ENGINEER, MARCH 19TH, 1910]

YOU ask me for my views on the Government Bill for Insurance against Unemployment, which is, we understand, to be presented before Easter. Of course we have not seen the details of the Bill, and I have not had an opportunity of discussing the matter with other employers, so I can only speak for myself.

I understand that the idea is that a fund is to be collected from the workman himself, from his employer and from the Government, out of which he will be insured against unemployment. Assuming this view to be correct, I must say the Bill seems to me to be full of danger, and unless more precautions can be taken than appear possible at first sight, it will be likely to do more harm than good. Hitherto, among mechanics, this work has been done by the trades unions, and done extremely well, although I fear that during the last few years they have found that no funds that they could subscribe were equal to the strain caused by the large number of unemployed, and this of course must be borne in mind.

But, irrespective of political economy and of strict justice, when we know how much the unskilled labourers have suffered during the last few years, I think we must feel that we would all stretch a great point in order to help them, and, provided that some safeguards could be found to give this money to those only who were genuinely willing to work, and who were out of employment through no fault of their own, I think we would all gladly pay the money and try very hard to make the principle succeed in some shape or form. The unskilled labourer cannot support a union strong enough to provide funds for this purpose.

But as regards mechanics, the case is somewhat different. No doubt the man with a large family is also very much to be pitied, and if he is out of work so long that his union cannot continue to support him, one is inclined to take a lenient view of his case and to think that, after all, one ought to be exceedingly tolerant towards anything that will relieve his difficulties. But even with him we are getting rather near the edge of what is wise and prudent, and when you come to the young man, possibly unmarried, the case is wholly different; and, to my mind, to allow such a man as that to be insured out of money which is not contributed by himself or his colleagues would be extremely unwise and unjust. In the union, the whole of the money is subscribed by the members, and they may be trusted to do their best to see that no man is idle who can be at work; but young men like holidays, and I am afraid there is no doubt that sometimes, especially in summer, they are inclined to go out on strike very much for the sake of enjoying a whole holiday with partial support from a subsidy.

No doubt there is a strong feeling, both in and out of Parliament, that the poorer classes ought to be helped by drawing money from the wealthier, but as the taxes are paid by everybody, it is quite clear that, averaged under this theory, no person is entitled to help from the Government whose income is above the average income of the community. Now, according to the opinion of the best economists, the total income of the United Kingdom is supposed to be about £1,700,000,000. If we divide that by the number of the population—43,000,000—it gives something under £40 a year for each person, so that a young unmarried skilled mechanic gets about double what is, strictly speaking, his share, and though I am not aware that anybody proposes a redistribution of property, yet it is obvious that if he gets helped by the Government, a great deal of the money must be contributed by people who are very much poorer than he is himself.

Then there comes the question of employers contributing to this fund, and this may be looked at from two points of view. I believe

some thoughtless people have an idea that the employers like to
have a large body of unemployed labour, but I can only say that,
if they do, such employers must be very blind to their own interest,
because it is quite clear that the unemployed, in the long run, have
to be a burden upon the trades at which they ought to work; and
just as people who are thrown out of work by winter or bad weather
have to be paid a higher rate when they are at work, so, if in any
trade there is a great risk of long periods of unemployment, the
wages must be higher in average times to make up for it, or good
men would very soon cease to try and live by the trade. We, as
employers, should certainly be better off in the long run if the
number of unemployed was enormously less than it is at present.

Then, some people think the employers can compensate out of
their profits. This is equally illusory. After spending a lifetime in
engine works, I should say that no engineering business can be
called unsuccessful which has paid dividends equal to a tenth
part of the amount that is paid in wages; this would probably mean
5 per cent. dividend permanently, and if people were sure they
would get this the shares would stand at par. If the profits fall
below this, capital cannot be got, and the consequence would be
that the employers would have to refuse work unless they could
get higher prices, or, which is the same thing, they would contract
their operations, and instead of increasing their works to meet the
ever-increasing trade and population, they would diminish their
works and so employ fewer and fewer men.

Everybody really knows, if they would only think it out, that in
any trade or investment this rule holds good, that *the higher the
possible profits the lower the average profits*; and where you see a few
millionaires, or a few large fortunes made, the public are dazzled,
and quite forget that the fact of these large fortunes is very strong
proof that a great number of people have put their money into the
business, and either made no profits or lost their capital altogether.
As an illustration, I had occasion, in 1872, to make a list of the
engineering works in and close to Newcastle and Gateshead. Of

these there were fifteen, of which the subsequent history has been as follows: between then and now, ten of them have ceased to exist—some absolutely ruined, and others closed because they could not be made to pay. I think I may say that none of these ten had a profitable time before they closed. Five only still remain, one of course being Elswick, which has grown very large and of which the shares stand at a high price, and of which people talk a great deal, while they are perfectly silent about the ten firms that have gone down. I should say that in London things are still worse. If anybody goes back in memory for a generation, and thinks of the world-wide and brilliant engineering firms that existed in London at that time, supposed to be making money, earning high reputations, and managed by men of world-wide celebrity, and thinks what an enormous proportion of these works have now been closed, mostly ruined, I think it will be seen that the employers have no fund in their possession out of which, even in the interests of the working classes, any supplies can wisely or fairly be drawn.

So I should say that if the Bill is confined to those who are really poor, and who may be trusted to work whenever it is possible, we may look on it with a considerable amount of sympathy, but if it is to be applied to the well-to-do mechanic, it would certainly do a great deal more harm than good, be very unjust to whoever finds the money, and would, practically speaking, be one of those numerous measures that, in a back-handed way, inflict an amount of misery upon the working classes which is enormously greater than the direct benefits that they appear to give.

XXII

Gambling in Relation to Business

[READ AT THE NEWCASTLE DIOCESAN CONFERENCE, OCT. 18TH, 1910]

MANY people speak as if they considered that business was one form of gambling, and as if business, which is necessary to civilization, threw a sort of sanction over ordinary gambling; and, at the same time, that a business man, as a gambler, was morally somewhat inferior to those people who have no connection with trade and commerce. I think there is also a further idea that trade and commerce are apt to lower people's standards of honour. There is no doubt that every occupation and every environment has its own risks and dangers, but personally I doubt if, on the whole, trade and commerce are any worse in this respect than any other conceivable calling by which a man can earn his living.

Business really consists in the creation and supply of every article of use, convenience or luxury, although conventionally people make a distinction between it and such a thing as agriculture. The distinction in principle is quite unreal, although the surroundings appear to be different.

Now, as I understand it, there are two principles in which business may be very materially distinguished from gambling, though no doubt, in practice, matters may shade into each other by gradual degrees, which makes it rather difficult to draw hard and fast lines, especially when one has not exact information as to the particular transaction in question. As far as I understand gambling, though I have had no practical experience of people who gamble, the main principle is that what one man wins another man loses, so that, on the whole, the world is made no richer but rather is it poorer by whatever cost is involved in carrying on the practice.

On the other hand, the underlying principle of business is that everybody ought to be a gainer: for example, a tailor is a man in trade; if you order a suit of clothes, it is because you think the suit of clothes is a more profitable possession to you than the money which it costs. As the tailor devotes himself entirely to this work he can make it cheaper than you, and you will be glad to pay him something more for the suit of clothes than it costs him to make it. This is his profit, and in doing this he finds employment for men and women who would otherwise be out of work, so that everybody is better off all round.

The second principle, which I think is quite as real, though not so universally visible, is that in gambling the element of risk is essential: no risk, no gambling. In fact, I believe that if a man bets on a matter where there is *no risk at all*, those who are learned in these things will say that it is a "bubble" bet, and refuse to enforce payment. But a careful business man will try to reduce his risk to a minimum. For example, a man thinks he can make his living by bringing goods from America and selling them in England. This involves a great many risks, but he insures his steamer and his cargo, gets the best ships and the most experienced officers and crew that he can find, and very probably tries to secure a market for his goods in England before he brings them from America. In this way he makes the element of risk as small as possible. Again, suppose a man tenders for the supply of a ship, a railway, or any other large article, he will probably try and get other men to tender to him for all the material that he requires, subject to his getting the order, so that he guards himself against any rise or fall in the cost of material. As a rule, he cannot contract beforehand for his supply of labour, but where he can do so, I think he will generally embrace the opportunity. Of course there are other risks, such as that of a man who owes him money failing to pay him; but caution is a very strong element in business, and there remains the fact referred to: that there is a margin of profit which ought to be fairly allotted between the manufacturer, the consumer, and the workpeople, whereas, in gambling, there is a margin of loss which somebody has to face. So, on the whole, if a group of men engage in gambling, the sum total of their transactions would be that they got up the poorer; if they engage in business, the sum total of their transactions would be that they were the richer.

Of course there are many transactions in business in which the element of gambling may not only come in but be deliberately imported. Men may gamble on the Stock Exchange just as much as they gamble on the Derby or at bridge, but so, equally, they may bet upon the weather, the death rate, or any other possible subject if they choose to do so; and I should say that while I believe nothing is easier than for any man to know in his own heart and his own conscience whether he is gambling or not, it is absolutely impossible for any of us in this respect to judge our neighbour; it is not our business, and we cannot do so. Supposing a man buys certain shares when they are very much depressed in price, and they afterwards rise, people will say, "He made his money by gambling on the Stock Exchange." It may be so, but also it may not be so, and I will put the same transaction from a different point of view. I have known a man see perhaps a certain small company under a cloud. There is a panic, and the shares are being pushed on to the market, falling in price; the more they fall the more nervous the holders become, and the evil increases till the shares go down to almost nothing, and the whole business is likely to be ruined. But a man, strong in purse and in character, says, "This is all nonsense, this affair is only a small temporary cloud, and there is nothing seriously wrong with the Company"; and he says to his broker, "Go in and buy all the shares you can for me." If he is a really chivalrous man he will often add the words, "and let everybody know it is for me that you are buying." The result of his transaction is that from that moment the shares fall no further; probably those who are on the verge of selling, feeling that the market is getting stronger, will cease to be in such a hurry and will pause, which will instantly cause a slight rise. If he goes on buying at the slight rise, the shares will very soon cease to fall, and I have sometimes seen that the firm and open buying of a very small number of shares indeed will entirely stop a panic.

I remember when the greatest failure of my time happened in London, there was a provincial bank which was very seriously shaken by the mere belief that it was connected directly with one of the concerns which had fallen in London. There was a run on it, which, in itself, caused a difficulty, for, of course, it is never easy for a bank to find the whole of its resources at a moment's notice. But a certain peer of the realm, who was a large land-owner in those parts, put up a notice that if any of his tenants lost money owing to the failure of this bank, he would refund the whole of it. This showed that he believed in the bank and was pre-pared to back his convictions, and the run was stopped at once.

But having pointed out what is *not* gambling, I must, as I have already said, admit that business is often used as a means of gambling, and those who are impatient to get rich will combine gambling with industry in the hope of securing a larger total gain.

Now, we have already agreed that the sum total of gambling is a loss, so if a number of men add the risks of gambling to the un-certainties of business, they must and will, on the whole, lose more than they gain by doing so. But any one man may be a winner, and it is the hope of being this so-called happy man that induces speculation. On an average, it makes business profits less and not more, besides demoralizing those who engage in it and lowering the whole commercial tone of the country.

Rings or combinations to keep up prices are, perhaps, not exactly gambling, but they have much in common with it, and though occasionally right and proper, if not pressed too far, they are, as a general rule, an effort to get richer by making someone else poorer, and, as such, are selfish and degrading.

Perhaps I may digress a little to point out some of the special features in the case of successful wealthy men. There are, especially in London, a large number of enormously wealthy men and women, many of whom appear to waste their money very recklessly, and the world naturally compares these millionaires with the great mass of grinding poverty, and feels very bitterly that things ought to be more equal. Yes, but how to carry this out? Let us see how this money has been made. England is possibly the greatest financial centre in the world, and numbers of rich men crowd here who have made their money elsewhere. The foreigners, rich Colonials and Americans who swarm in our great hotels have made their money in other countries. A very large proportion of the richest Englishmen have also made their money abroad; say, in Argentine, South Africa or elsewhere. Now, if this wealth could be so redistributed as to go more to the labour that produced it and less to the capital, it would go to enrich the workers in other continents, but none of it would help the English working classes, and, indeed, why should it?

Again, richer capitalists often succeed, especially where speculation and gambling come in, in drawing to themselves the profits which have gone to, and ought to remain with, smaller and poorer capitalists.

All that could go to the working classes really would be the profits that are made on English manufactures and agriculture.

As regards this, although some few men make enormous fortunes, it is a question whether the average profits on this class of investment are not too small to induce the necessary number of people to employ British labour. A manufacturing business does very fairly which pays in dividends one-tenth of what it pays in wages. And if we could imagine the whole of the profits of our English manufacturing trade going to enrich the working classes, they would only get about a 10 per cent. rise of wages, and capital would get nothing, which means that no capital would be forthcoming and our trade would cease to exist.

Now, what is the moral of all this? I do not say it would be *wrong* to try and improve the present position by legislation, by organization, or by arbitrary interference. I will not discuss the question of the right or wrong, for the simple reason that all arbitrary interference with other people always has ended, and always will end, in making rich men richer and poor men poorer. You perhaps legislate against the employer and for the workmen. What happens? The extra burden kills the poor and most struggling employers, their workmen are thrown out of work, and the business is absorbed by the wealthier employers. In any disturbance or upheaval, the man who suffers least is the richest man.

I fall back on the only remedy—the teaching of the Church, and especially of the Catechism, in which I was brought up. I was thoroughly taught my duties, both to God and to my neighbour: I was told nothing about my own "rights." I was not only taught that I ought to love my neighbour as myself, but I was taught that money was simply a talent which God entrusted to me; to be used, not for my own pleasure, nor as an owner, but as a steward. I must consider that I hold it in trust, to use as God would have me to use it, and that I shall one day have to give a full account of every sovereign. This view is a great discouragement to gambling, to hard bargaining, or to any desire to become very rich, and I have very little faith in any reform except that which the Bible teaches and the Church formulates, namely, for every man to reform himself.

XXIII

Strikes

[THE TIMES ENGINEERING SUPPLEMENT, DEC. 22ND, 1910]

THE shipbuilding strike is over at last, and we hope the terms are such as will make it unlikely that trouble will recur from the same causes.

One point that ought to be mentioned at the outset is our admiration for the excellent conduct of the men who were out of work, both on the east and west coast; for not only were the mechanics on strike, who were more or less supported by their respective unions, but large numbers of labourers were thrown out of work, who had no unions, and whose means are such that they have little or no power of saving money at ordinary times, so that to them and their families the suffering must have been very severe indeed, and all the harder to bear because it was through no fault of their own, and they had no voice in the settlement. That these men should all behave so well and steadily under such trying circumstances is indeed very much to their honour, and would seem more remarkable if it were not, as we are proud to feel, a very general state of things in England and Scotland, though, alas! we see something terribly different in another part of the United Kingdom.

One naturally asks, was the strike necessary? It seems hard to an employer to think that anybody can justify the action of the men in constantly throwing down their tools at a moment's notice, in defiance of the distinct agreement which forbade them doing anything of the sort, and there is no doubt that for men to disregard the agreements that have been made by unions, and the arrangements and orders of their leaders, is a very severe blow, not only to the whole system of trades unions, but to that peace and order without which industries cannot be carried on with any profit to either the employers or the workmen. On the other hand, the men no doubt say that the employers, or rather their representatives, were often so slow in agreeing on the price at which work should be done, that they could not or would not go on working, and so run the risk of finishing a job before they were sure they would get a fair price for doing it. We must hope that the settlement now made will be loyally adhered to on both sides.

It is not so uncommon a thing as the world fancies for workmen to repudiate the acts of their leaders; for example, it will be easily remembered that at the beginning of the great engineers' strike of 1908, on the north-east coast, Mr. Lloyd George, who was at that time President of the Board of Trade, arranged a settlement with the employers and with the leaders of the workmen, which would have been carried out had not the general body of the men, by their vote, refused to agree to it; and other instances might easily be recalled.

But every succeeding strike shows us what an appalling price both sides have to pay. Probably such a stoppage, even if ending in an absolute victory, would cost the winners incomparably more than they would gain, by the amount of trade alienated and by the irritation and loss caused to customers. It is not difficult to point out how at least two very large and important branches of engineering were for a long time almost entirely lost to England by the great strike of 1897, and have only been recovered very slowly and partially.

The men seldom seem really to get the best in a large strike now, notwithstanding their higher organization and the greater rates of pay allowed to men on strike. This is obviously because, owing to the altered conditions of trade, employers necessarily have to carry on their business with a very much larger amount of capital than heretofore. The men have probably never sufficiently appreciated this point, but of course, when it comes to the works standing idle, the richer a man is, the longer he can live without an income, and the better able he is, directly or indirectly, to keep on terms with his disappointed customers and to minimize their losses.

It always seems very strange, considering how in every other kind of warfare—physical, commercial or verbal—people have studied deeply and written many books on the science of the battle, and the strategy and tactics to be observed, that so few people, even of those who are frequently engaged, have ever really studied the management of a strike or lock-out with a view to getting the best possible results out of any given conditions. I believe we may fairly say that the large majority of men, employers as well as workmen, lose their temper and get irritable to a degree that makes them neglect that calm study and calculation which is necessary equally in a first-class military campaign or in a game of chess. It was often said that if a man who was fencing or boxing lost his temper, he lost half his chance of victory, and there is good reason for supposing that the same thing applies to anyone engaged in these strifes, and perhaps it tells most of all in inducing people to hurry into extreme measures, when patience and tact might possibly have averted a strike and brought about an equally good settlement without involving so much loss and misfortune.

It was mentioned in the papers at one time, for example, that some of the railwaymen proposed to go out on strike to show their sympathy with the boilermakers. Had they done so, they would, by enormously increasing the difficulty of bringing food and milk into the towns, have added to the sufferings of the working classes, but it is hard to see that they would have brought the slightest pressure to bear on the employers. When a shipbuilder has already lost all his men, it is a matter of almost complete indifference whether he can get deliveries of his material or not; and as regards his personal comfort or loss, he need only, if he chooses, take his motor-car and go to the first town outside the district, and he will be perfectly comfortable, no matter how much the misery may be increased in his own neighbourhood.

One would think that the sound policy of the workmen would be to see that the number of men who had to be supported when out of work was as small as possible, while the number of people to subscribe to their funds was as large as possible. But in considering the employers' tactics there is a further complication, for while it is to the advantage of the employer that there should be as many men as possible receiving pay and as few as possible to subscribe actively, the employer's weakness lies in the amount of work in progress which is lying idle and cannot be proceeded with. Not only is this absolutely unprofitable to him, but, what is infinitely more serious, his customers are very often suffering tremendous losses, which they may either visit upon him directly or which may make them very much less willing to give him orders in the future.

I do not work out these questions exhaustively, but I merely suggest them as some of the considerations which have to be borne in mind in such a struggle.

It used to be said that if an employer could keep right with his bankers and his customers, his men could never get the better of him. For reasons above stated, most employers are in a far stronger financial position as regards their bankers than they used to be, but as machinery becomes more costly, and all commercial arrangements much larger and more complicated, the question of the customer probably gets increasingly difficult.

One tremendous element in a strike is public opinion. This means not only the sentimental view of those who are in no way concerned, but, to the workmen, it means their chance of getting subscriptions outside. To a great extent it means the opinion of all those of their members who are not actively in the forefront of the battle. In the case of the employer, it very probably influences the amount of pressure that may be brought to bear upon him by shareholders, and also by his customers, who, if they do not sympathize with his actions, will be far less patient in their endurance of losses. It may probably be considered that workmen are also very much more sensitive as to what the newspapers may say than the employers are. Human nature is the same among all sorts and conditions of men, but an employer is probably, in the first instance, a man with a considerable amount of self-reliance, without which he would hardly have earned his position, and all his training goes to make him more and more prepared to rely on his own opinion, and to disregard that of other people. One way of proving this is by observing how many of the men who make large fortunes have done so by buying or selling at some time something of which their opinion as to its future was at variance with the general opinion of all the rest of the world, so that they bought a thing cheap because nobody else valued it, and then reaped a rich reward.

As regards this last point, I think most old employers will say that those small strikes which do not get into the newspapers are very much more easily settled than those where the men feel that the eye of the public is upon them, urging them to fight hard and stand out. The Engineers' Nine Hours Strike of 1871 and the celebrated Dockers' Strike in London are cases where the men probably won chiefly because they had such a very large amount of public sympathy, which took the form both of substantial subscriptions and also of a great deal of side pressure brought to bear on the employers by those whose interests suffered from the continuance of the strike.

I have only touched on the fringe of this question, with a view of showing how much more consideration and study it deserves than it usually gets, but a far more important question is the prevention of strikes, and it is much to be regretted that more definite efforts have not been made by either party in Parliament to this effect. The present Government organized the system of Board of Trade arbitration, which, as far as it goes, was all to the good, but it did not go very far. On the other hand, when they passed the Trades Union Disputes Bill, which made the union funds not liable for the acts of their leaders and legalized what Parliament was pleased to call "peaceful picketing," they tied their own hands in some measure as to disapproving of strikes; because, if you pass laws to regulate anything, you thereby show that you expect it to continue, and probably approve of its doing so under the terms you lay down. Of course, as regards the liability of union funds, and what was called the Taff Vale decision, it was a very great hardship for a workman who was dependent on these funds for his support in sickness and old age, to have the money squandered without his consent by the union officials; so, although it was not perhaps exactly just, there is good enough reason for sympathizing with the effort to make the position of the ordinary trades union member as secure as possible. But as regards peaceful picketing, it is hard to see what justification there was for it, or that it has worked anything except unmixed evil. As things were before, there was no difficulty whatever in letting every man know that a strike was in existence, and peaceful picketing only brought about a state of affairs which enormously facilitated the use of intimidation and brute force.

Compulsory arbitration has certain very obvious evils connected with it, but, on the whole, are these anything to be compared with the evils of a strike or lock-out? Strikes are only one form of private warfare. Sixty years ago we had hardly seen the last of duelling and boxing, which were other forms of prize-fighting. Our grandfathers said these could never be abolished: that the world would be unendurable: that there would be no restraint on insolent and overbearing people; and they propounded theoretical cases which were exceedingly difficult to answer. But these have gone, and the world, on the whole, probably behaves a great deal better, and not worse; and my own belief is that if we could once get out of the habit of strikes and lock-outs the relations between employers and their men would be more easily adjusted, and would be, on the whole, more satisfactory to both sides.

XXIV

Industrial Peace

[INAUGURAL ADDRESS TO THE ECONOMIC SOCIETY, NEWCASTLE, OCT. 18TH, 1911]

I HAVE been asked to read a paper on this subject, and, considering the times in which we are living, and recent events and disturbances—political, industrial, and national,—I think we may feel there is probably no topic which is more deserving of the careful consideration of an Economic Society.

Before proceeding to discuss the question, I will, however, give a hasty review of what appears to me to be the present industrial position of the community, and I hope I may be pardoned if I lay special stress on the engineering trade as a representative of all industries, for two reasons—first of all, because it is probably better known to the majority of the people in Newcastle than any other, but still more because there is no industry of any importance which is not involved, more or less, with machinery or other engineering work, so that it really participates in the good and bad fortune of every class of the community.

Trade is of course very much better, and employment as a whole is far more plentiful than it was three or four years ago. Engineers' and most other wages are, on the whole, probably higher than they have ever been before in this country, or than they are in any other country in Europe. Hours are also considerably shorter than they were fifty years ago. Labourers' wages have not, during that time, risen so much as mechanics', but they have risen a certain amount. The cost of living is higher than it was a short time ago, but probably considerably less than it was during the greater part of the last century. I would add that skilled workmen are more highly trained, and they have very much better opportunities than they had formerly of rising to positions of trust. The salaries of foremen, managers, and other higher officials have increased in proportion far more than the rate of wages, and numbers of these positions are held by men who, had they not taken advantage of their opportunities, might have been to-day working as ordinary mechanics. At the same time, for reasons that I have often mentioned elsewhere, a workman has less hope of being an employer, or of owning the shop where he works.

On the other hand, the question of unemployment is a very serious one. I do not think the numbers of unemployed during the last ten years have been at any time nearly so great as they were in 1877 to 1879, but there is this difference: in those days, all the unemployed had hope of employment whenever trade revived, and I should say, as a rule, their hopes were realized; but there are now —especially in London, but more or less in other places—large numbers of men belonging to the working class, whose position is almost hopeless. The old man, the inferior workman who may be a very steady and deserving individual, the one-eyed man, and all those, in fact, who do not rank as being of a high class, have unfortunately much less chance of being employed than they had heretofore, and their condition is one of the saddest and ugliest blots on our present civilization.

In fact, as regards the working class, I should say that the majority are better off, but the minority are far worse off; and we cannot admit that the additional comfort of the majority is a sufficient set-off for the misery of the minority.

So much for the environment; now for ourselves who are living and working.

The feature of these times which I ask you to consider this evening, is the great unrest—especially in the relations between capital and labour—and we naturally ask ourselves what are the causes of this. Possibly something may be due to a much wider state of unrest, of which this is only one part. As regards labour, the dissatisfaction with present conditions seems to exist in most other countries as well as in England. The nations also seem to be in a highly excitable state, and to be much disposed towards war, and in our own country we are going through a time of great political excitement, but this perhaps is nearly the same as the agitation by labour for improved conditions.

In a widespread movement, few things are more difficult than to define the exact views or states of feeling which are behind the agitation. One careful trades union leader may think that the improvement in trade warrants his seeking for a moderate advance of wages, while an agitator of extreme views may preach that all society is on an utterly false basis and the least we want is an absolute redistribution of property. At the moment, both men are moving in the same direction, but by to-morrow the cautious man may have been satisfied and refuse to move any further.

As some of our papers pointed out, in the recent Trades Union congress, the enthusiasm of the younger men contrasted very remarkably with the apathy of the older and more experienced delegates; and, no doubt, not only among the average younger and more ardent workmen but also among a very large number of the general community—notably, in the universities and among the clergy of all denominations—there is an intense feeling of dissatisfaction with the present distribution of wealth, and a great wish to bring about an entirely different state of affairs.

One development of this is a wish for all sources of wealth to be in the hands of the State. Another development is a violent feeling of hostility to employers as a class. The first of these, I fear, we cannot discuss this evening; the second, that is the hostile feeling to employers, we must study more closely.

As I understand, there is a general feeling in the country, not only among trades unionists and socialists, but in the whole community, that the contrast between great wealth and extreme poverty is very terrible, and ought not to exist in a Christian country. This opinion probably would be admitted by all sorts

and conditions of men. I doubt if even the largest capitalists would
say that the present state of things is satisfactory; almost anybody
would say it would be better for the world at large if, instead of one
man with a million, there were ten men with £100,000 apiece, and
probably many people would say that it would be still better if it
were one hundred men with £10,000 apiece, though few people ask
themselves where this process ought to stop. My own feeling is
that the point at which ideally it ought to stop would be the point
at which men cease to save. No workman can produce anything
without suitable tools, workshops, and material to work upon: in
other words, without capital. This capital must be saved up by
somebody, and what people save is the surplus income after they
have spent what they consider proper; but as long as sufficient
capital can be found to make work for all the unemployed, and
then for the ever-increasing population, that would be all we should
have to consider; and clearly this would be perfectly practicable if
wealth were more widely diffused than it is, but if no money was
saved there could be no increase in the number of men employed.
Whether poverty is on the whole more widespread than it was
before, is perhaps open to discussion, and I have already tried to
depict what I believe to be the present position, for good and for
bad, of the working classes at the present time.

But I think the world generally follows up the last proposition
by another, which is, that all wealth is a product of labour. This
is not altogether true; but, supposing it were so, we should be
brought to the next point. Many consider that, if not all wealth, at
any rate a much larger share of it, ought to go to labour as the
producers. But now comes, for practical purposes, the first great
fallacy which we have to point out, as it is the bed-rock of the
whole question. Such seem to assume that employers and rich
men are an identical class: that all the rich people you see in
London have probably made their wealth out of the employment
of English labour, and that therefore you have only got to take the
money from them and give it to our own working classes. Now,

I should like to point out that an enormous majority of the employers of the country are poor men, and not rich ones. There are no statistics, but I think the evidence is quite irresistible that certainly two-thirds, and probably three-quarters, of the working classes work for men whose income and social position are not much above that of a farmer or shopkeeper. The large works, of course, are very conspicuous, but they are mostly confined to a few parts of England—chiefly those where coal is found. These small employers, as a rule, have a hard time. To my mind they are one of the most valuable classes of the community, and it is a very great calamity that, as a body, they are getting weaker both in strength and in numbers. The tendency of the world to gravitate to large works is very serious indeed, and a great misfortune. The poor employer is not popular with anybody, but he knows his workmen; he probably began as a workman, and his position is often a stepping-stone by which the journeyman may himself become an employer, and after that gradually develop his position to something much better and more permanent.

But even in large works many of the shareholders are poor men. The employer or the capitalist is not necessarily a man who has a great deal of money; he is a man who *finds* a great deal of money, but very often it belongs to other people, who are not strong, and are very easily frightened and made to divert their savings into other channels. Besides which, it is by no means all large works that make large profits. But of that I will speak further on.

Another most important point is this. People look at the great wealth and extravagance that they see, for example, in London. But London is probably the chief financial centre of the world. Enormous numbers of rich people come there from other countries, and even of the Englishmen there, a very large proportion have made their wealth out of England. A large West-end mansion may probably belong to some man who, beginning with nothing, made an enormous fortune in, say, South Africa, and probably most of these men have a great part of their investments in other countries. In places like South America, most of the capital belongs to Englishmen, and many of the Englishmen have made enormous fortunes. Now, if we accept the doctrine unconditionally that the money that is made ought all to go to labour, not one penny of this money would go to the relief of the English working class, but the whole of it ought to go to such people as negroes in South Africa, or natives in the Argentine Republic and elsewhere.

There is an old story, which you have very likely heard, told about Baron Rothschild, in Paris, perhaps sixty years ago. A Socialist called on him and pointed out the injustice of the great inequality in wealth, and told him that he ought to allow him, as a poorer brother, a share of his money. Rothschild thought the matter over, and is reported to have given this answer: "I quite admit the inequality, and, for the sake of argument, I will admit the injustice. I have an enormous fortune, but I and my family have made it by dealing in practically every part of the world, and, therefore, it ought to be divided among all the people in the world. I am willing therefore to give you your full share. Suppose I am worth a couple of millions, your share will come to something under one halfpenny, and here it is." This story may sound unreasonable, but London is the gathering ground of the wealth of the world, and while, on the one hand, every right-thinking man must wish to see poor people a great deal better off, that is quite different from putting in a claim on the grounds suggested, because people cannot first demand a thing as a right, and, when they find the ground untenable, beg it as a favour. So we had better consider what are the profits that really are made by employers in England out of their works.

Now, as I pointed out, the small employers have very little to give. When I came to Newcastle as an employer, forty-two years ago, I had occasion to meet all the engineering employers in Newcastle and Gateshead, about matters that concerned us all. I have kept an account of all the businesses that were represented, and I find that two-thirds of them perished disastrously. Thinking

Newcastle might be exceptionally unfortunate, I tried to examine similarly into the case of London, and I should say that was distinctly worse. Where people run so great a risk of ruin, those who succeed ought to have a compensating advantage. Now, the question is, do they? I do not observe that the public are very fond of putting their money into what are called industrial investments. I observe that when a man like Lord Furness offers to give his workmen a share of the profits, they do not seem in the least inclined to accept it. This does not look as if the profits were so enormous. If I look at the profits as advertised in stockbrokers' lists every day, which I suppose contain only the most attractive businesses, I should form an impression that an average of 5 per cent. on the capital would be as much as successful businesses commonly make. One of our largest coalowners recently published some figures in which he showed that existing collieries were making, on an average, something like 6 per cent., but, so far as I can see, he took no account of those collieries which had been closed as failures, and the loss of their capital would be to cause a serious deduction from the 6 per cent., and might reduce it to 5, or even 4. People often talk as if the capital accounts of works were very much exaggerated and were fictitious figures. Sometimes, no doubt, people float companies, as it is called, upon nominal capitals, which are more than it costs to produce the works, but unless they can justify these figures by paying proportionate dividends, the public very soon assesses these at their true value, and the shares stand correspondingly below par.

But the real thing we want to arrive at is this. If people say that a larger portion of the profits ought to go to labour and less to capital, they must to be practical answer two questions. Firstly, how much capital is there for each workman employed? and secondly, what proportion do the dividends on that capital bear to the amount paid in wages? Let us try to solve this. Take any moderate-sized works belonging to a public company. It is not difficult for any workman to find out the number of men employed in the factory. Now, go to the public library, if there is no place more convenient, and ask for the "Stock Exchange Year Book." You can there find out exactly what is the capital account of the company—ordinary shares, preference shares, and debentures, and everything else. Confining ourselves, to save trouble, to engine works, which are however a very fair sample of other industries, you will find the average capital comes to something like £150 per man employed. If the works pay 5 per cent. per annum, we have 5 per cent. on £150, or £7. 10s. 0d., as the amount that is paid in dividends for every workman employed. Now, if you take the pay-bill of skilled workmen, labourers and apprentices, you will generally find it comes to something like 30s. per man per week. Taking fifty working weeks in the year, it means that the men and boys, on an average, draw £75 a year; in other words, labour gets about £10 for every £1 that is paid in dividends to capital. I do not say that capital gets too little, but that that is what it does get. I believe I have been reckoned among the rather more fortunate employers, and, taking over twenty-five years, I find that the affairs in which I am interested have paid rather more than £10 in wages for every £1 that has gone in dividends to capital.

It is also often overlooked that, of the profits that are made, by no means the whole is retained by the employer. An employer may be under heavy liabilities to bankers or other money-lenders, or, what is far more serious, he may be obliged to sell what he makes for ready money, to some middleman, who himself again makes a much larger profit by holding it or selling it to some other person.

The only point I wish to emphasize is that, while I hope we may live to see the working classes a great deal better off than they are, this cannot come by merely taking the money out of the pockets of the employers, for if they got the whole amount it would not do very much to improve their position, and then why should any-body put money into any manufacturing business at all?

I would just remark that even if the Government took over the industries, things would not be much better, for the Government has no money except what it borrows, in the form of loans, consols, or funds of some sort from private individuals, and on this it has to pay interest, and this interest would pretty nearly amount to as much as the profits that are, on an average, obtained by the private manufacturer.

We have now to take an entirely new view of the case. The subject of my paper is "Industrial Peace," and I must therefore speak about strikes, and to those of you who are not very familiar with works, I want to point out exactly what a strike is, and what it is not. If one man leaves his work because he is dissatisfied with his wages or other conditions, that is not a strike; if all the men leave their work because they are dissatisfied, that is not a strike; but if they not only leave but also try to prevent other people taking their places, that is a strike. Similarly, if an employer discharges all his workmen, that is not a lock-out; but if he tries to hinder those men being employed by other employers, that is what we do exactly mean by a lock-out. In other words, in both a strike and a lock-out, the aggressor tries to keep possession of something which he has really renounced, whether in one case it be the position in the works, or, in the other case, the services of the man who has left. It is very important to bear this in mind.

One can hardly think it would be just or practicable to hinder any man, or any number of men, leaving their work, provided they give (as, till very recently, they nearly always did) due notice, and do not violate any agreement or understanding; so the essence of the contention is not in the men leaving, but in their hindering other men from taking their places.

What hope have we of the present unrest lessening, and of a more peaceful era taking its place? My own impression is that, at present, we are going through a period of great political and industrial excitement, which, as far as I can see, is due to the fact that the public do not demand any standard of knowledge or experience from those who usurp the position of leaders, and therefore the more cautious advice of their old leaders is discarded in favour of the more violent counsel of men who have had little practical experience and who do not look below the surface.

I think it may clear our way if, as an illustration of most points of discussion between employers and workmen, we consider the case of an advance of wages. By what rule ought advances to be given? Is there any limit, from the workman's point of view, as to how much he would take, or does a point come when he would refuse any further advance and perhaps insist on a reduction?

Compare his case with the employer's. As a simple case we will assume that of the coalowner. Now, if all the coalowners agreed to put up the price of coal 5s. per ton, would that enrich the owners, and would it be wise? A great deal of coal is sold in keen competition with other countries; when the price of English coal is less than that of other countries, it makes its way further afield; every rise of a penny makes it draw back a little, and a serious rise in selling price will oust it altogether from many important countries. Of course, if the English coalowners can sell all they have to sell, it is no use pushing any further, so what we may call the natural price is the highest price at which we can sell all we have to sell.

So with labour, which is what the working man has to sell. His interest is to keep wages at the highest point he can, consistently with men not being paid off; but higher wages probably mean higher costs, and if the higher costs hinder the employer selling his products, it is quite inevitable that men must be thrown out of work. And so we come to the self-evident point that what matters to a workman is not the nominal rate of wages, but rather the actual amount of his income. Personally, when I have to consider the question of an advance or reduction of wages, I put the problem in this form. It is to the interest of the working classes that we should pay the largest total amount in wages that is possible. But every increase in wages must, in some degree, affect the selling

14—2

price of the finished article and so reduce the sale, and thereby diminish employment. If a 2 per cent. advance in wages throws 1 per cent. of the men out of work, the gain is, on the whole, greater to the men than the loss, but if a 1 per cent. advance throws 2 per cent. out of work, it would be more loss than gain. To take an extreme case, if any manufacturer doubled his rate of wages, his costs would be so much increased that he could probably sell nothing and employ nobody, and his men would get nothing and lose everything.

I would remind you that I have already shown that nothing can be got out of the margin of the average employer's profit.

This brings us very near to the most important point, which is, that the interests of the employer and workmen are far more identical than appears to be commonly supposed. Let us assume that the employer sells what is made for a certain price, from that deduct, first, the cost of material which he buys, and, second, the cost of carrying on the works, such as rent, rates, coals, repairs, and charges of all sorts, which are indispensable in a factory. The balance is the fund out of which come wages and the employer's profit, which fund is, as I have shown, generally divided in the proportion of wages £9, and profit, or interest on capital, £1. Now, the obvious interest of both workmen and employer is to make this fund as large as possible, and anything they can gain by snatching at each other's margin is very small compared to what they may gain if they pull together loyally to make the total amount as large, and the work as good and as cheap as possible. But, alas! we do not always agree, and then, if neither side will give way, the tension becomes extreme and ends in a strike.

Now, I must ask you to compare a strike in a factory with a strike on a railway. Suppose we consider a strike of a number of works in some large trade. The men believe that some benefit is withheld from them to which they are justly entitled; they stop work, and would strongly object to anyone taking their places. The employers, probably thinking that it would be impossible to get new bodies of really efficient men to take the places of those on strike, especially as the new men would have no inducement to mix themselves up with someone else's quarrel, usually just remain quiet, and it becomes a question of which can hold out longest. The loss to both sides is very great, but generally there is no disorder, little excitement, and the questions of picketing, etc., do not generally arise. The men get help from their unions, and perhaps from subscriptions, but as all this money has been subscribed by working men and will probably have to be replaced, or in some form repaid, we may say that the cost to the men is really just about equal to the amount of wages they would have received had they been at work. So, if mechanics are earning 35s. a week and are on strike for an advance of a shilling a week extra, it will, if they win, take thirty-five weeks of the advance to make up for each week that the strike lasts. The employer's losses, though much less of course than the men's, are also very great. But the object of the two sides is, presumably, to hurt each other, and we may nearly always congratulate them on their dismal success; and, as in the case of a boxing match, we will hope that each of the combatants considers that the punishment he has received is compensated by what he has inflicted on his opponent.

The case of a railway is very different. When the men on a railway strike, the amount of loss they inflict on the directors and shareholders is comparatively small, but they inflict an enormous and appalling amount of suffering, loss and misery on the general public. As Mr. Churchill recently pointed out, the rich suffer very little, but on the poor the blow falls with terrible force. Numbers of poor people are left homeless and penniless at all sorts of places, possibly at the end of an excursion with children; shop girls are unable to go home at the end of their day's work; mothers are unable to get food for their children, and there is other suffering of the severest description. Here the loss falls almost entirely on the poor and the innocent, and the whole position is incredibly more painful. This has further results. The railway authorities feel that the state of things is too bad to be tolerated, so they use every means to induce other labour to take the place of the strikers. If this is too much opposed, the police have to intervene, then the soldiers. Incidentally, we here see picketing, intimidation, and rioting in their ugliest forms; and when public opinion has time to assert itself I hope the verdict will be that public services, like railways, tramways, gas and water works, should not be allowed to be suspended on any consideration whatever. The largest gains the strikers hope to secure are as a drop in a bucket compared to the misery they cause to the poorest, weakest, and most inoffensive members of the community.

To be brief, I would say that as the public have given the railways valuable privileges and monopolies, which equally benefit shareholders and workmen, so both one and the other should be prohibited, under the severest penalties, from causing the service to be interfered with. Special privileges ought to carry corresponding liabilities.

Observe, I advocate Government interference in the case of railway strikes, because I think the protection of the weak and helpless is exactly what Government is for; but of course this applies far less to manufacturing strikes. And how do I hope for industrial peace as regards these? Not, I think, so much in legislation or Government action as in mutual good-will and a better understanding.

Still keeping to the engineering trade, I have good opportunities of seeing and knowing what goes on all over England and Scotland, and I believe I am right in saying that, in spite of the stormy times in which we live, there is a real amount of good feeling both among the leaders of the trade, as a whole, and also in a very large number of individual works. Personally, notwithstanding strikes, I have always experienced the greatest courtesy and friendliness from my men, and I think very few on either side feel much bitterness or ill-will after a strike is over, but it is the conventional way of dealing with a disagreement, so we do as we have always done.

I feel bound to state that, having studied the matter very closely and carefully, I cannot see that strikes, on the whole, have done anything to benefit the working classes, or to improve their condition. You may point to an occasional victory, but how often does anyone refer to the failures? and, where an object is gained, the cost at which it is gained is rarely calculated.

I do not think public opinion is ripe to consider this question thoroughly, but I will suggest a few points which you may think out at your leisure.

There is an element of the unreal about a strike. We know that all the men expect to come back to their old places, and the employers expect them. If, instead of a whole shop going out on strike, 10 or 20 per cent. really left and took employment elsewhere, it would do far more to alarm an employer and make him realize either that his wages were too low or that his employment was in some other way unsatisfactory, and he would see that if he did not want to lose his men he must act liberally. This is what happens with draughtsmen, domestic servants, and many others.

Then there are powerful employers' federations which, but for strikes, would not exist, and competition between employers to secure labour, which ought to be one of the workmen's most profitable assets, is almost non-existent; but probably much the worst evil is the amount of trade a strike drives away, or, still worse, annihilates.

Employers actually suffer much less than formerly, but that involves costly precautions.

In short, is a state of war ideally the most prosperous condition for human well-being and happiness? for that is simply what it amounts to. No, there are plenty of employers and employed who go on year after year with no quarrelling, and if we could only get a fair start, and a little mutual forbearance, things might go on peaceably. I believe what we want is not legislation but sympathy.

If they say that we employers are paid out of the labour of our workmen, well, so are the trades union leaders and the labour members. We prosper on our men's prosperity, they might almost be said to live by their adversity; or, to put it more kindly, their business is to rectify the misfortunes of the workmen, and our business is to prevent these misfortunes.

These are times of violent forces and violent reactions. Let me close by comparing strikes with other forms of private warfare Duelling was an institution in the forties, and dead in the fifties; boxing died more slowly, but as certainly; and possibly our grandchildren may feel ashamed to think that we, their ancestors, were mixed up with such strange and unsatisfactory methods of settling our differences.

XXV

The Duties of Employer and Employed

[A Paper read at the Church Congress at Middlesbrough, Oct. 1912]

THERE is, unquestionably, a great deal of sympathy in the Church with the present restless feeling which exists in the country—first, as to the distribution of wealth between rich and poor; and, secondly, as to the relations of employers and workmen.

As regards the great contrast of wealth and poverty, everybody would be glad to see these differences much less than they are; but it is apparently not so easy to alter, or even alleviate, this state of things, for I think there is no doubt that recent legislation has made things worse and not better.

There seems to be a general and earnest wish to do something definite towards the greater equalization of wealth, but this feeling often hastily takes the form of a complaint that workmen ought to get a much larger share, and employers a much smaller share, of that which is produced by manufacturing. This, however, implies that the employer class is identical with the wealthy class, which is a very inaccurate view indeed.

Some go still further, and say that the employer ought to be abolished altogether, and that other arrangements could be made which would be far more beneficial not only to the working classes, but to the public generally. But no practicable alternative policy has been proposed.

Speaking generally, all proposals fall under two heads—government ownership of the means of production, and co-operation.

As regards government ownership, if the Government took over either manufactories, railways, mines, or anything else, it would have to borrow its capital and pay interest on it, and also pay appropriate salaries to its managing staff. The salaries would be quite as high as they are at present, and the interest on borrowed capital would be, at the very least, as much as the average amount now made in the form of profits by private owners; and as all experience shows that the Government cannot usually work as cheaply as private owners, there would be no margin for higher wages, but quite the reverse.

Co-operation, speaking generally, seems to be very unpopular among the workmen. Any number of employers are willing to adopt it, but workmen never seem to care to accept it, and I think they are quite right from their own point of view. As things are at present, no share of profits that they could get would be worth any material alteration in their position, unless we could put the question on a much broader footing, as to which I will say more hereafter.

Of course, each of these subjects would be worthy of a paper to itself, but I will simply say further, as regards government ownership, that there is no reason in the world why it should not be tried at once. By all means let the Government try their hands at it. If they succeed, well and good; if not, let them leave it alone for the future.

As regards co-operation, the immediate results are extremely discouraging, because, even in a prosperous manufacturing business, the amount of money divided in profits is so small compared to the large amount paid in wages, that no percentage that could be reasonably taken off the profits would be a strong inducement, when it was turned into a percentage on the much larger amount of the wages. In engineering and shipbuilding, for example, if the shareholders can divide as profits one-tenth part of what they pay in wages, they are doing above the average, in these cases the amount of capital being about £150, or two years' wages per workman employed.

But if the workmen were shareholders, and took a keen interest in the success of the business, trying to understand it and to further its interests by every means in their power, they, being owners, might be given a far greater insight into the business than they have at present; and among those men there must be several who, if they had the training, would develop into first-rate scientific men, managers, and even financiers; and it would be an enormous gain to have the brain-power of all the workmen steadily trained in the direction of helping the business forward.

We will next consider what the employer class, as it stands, really is. It distinctly is *not* a limited number of rich men simply making large fortunes by the employment of workmen, for the number of large or rich employers is comparatively very small indeed. The whole number of workers in the country is variously estimated at from ten to fifteen millions, according to what is included, but probably not more than one quarter of those, at the outside, are employed in what may be considered large works. The number of employers is enormous. In agriculture alone there must be well over half a million. In every village there are some small employers; more and more in every town according to its size; and in London alone the small employers could probably be reckoned by hundreds of thousands. Of course you may say that this does not interest you; that you only wish to consider the rich employer. But Parliament, within the last few years, in such Acts as the Workmen's Compensation Act, the Insurance Act, etc., has deliberately included *all* employers, small as well as large, and thrown upon them the burdens which, while quite reasonable in the case of large works and rich men, are very heavy indeed upon the small employer, who perhaps only has a limited amount of capital which is the hard-earned savings out of a life's wages. The harm was first done when the Workmen's Compensation Act was applied to agriculture in 1900; and when the present Government revised the Workmen's Compensation Acts, they deliberately, instead of confining the Act to well-to-do employers, extended it so as to include every employer of every kind, even the lodging-house keeper with one domestic servant, and many others who are quite unable to face the risks. This was done in defiance of the advice of their own Home Office.

I hope I have said enough to show that the idea of getting rid of the small employer, which is so often advocated by a certain school of modern politicians, is quite mistaken. Even if the Government could take over our large cotton mills, engine works, and blast furnaces, they could not take over the village blacksmith, the local builder, and the small market gardener, let alone the question of domestic servants, and I must candidly say that I think the fairly prosperous small employer is a very useful man.

I have given you an idea as to the average profits of the employer. A little study of the Stock Exchange Year Book and the daily papers will prove what I say. A very few employers make really large fortunes by manufacturing, but those who do generally own either valuable patents or monopolies.

I am aware that Mr. Chiozza Money (*Riches and Poverty*, 1910, p. 95, etc.) makes the ratio of profits to wages very much higher, but I cannot see where he gets his evidence. I have investigated the figures for many years over a very wide area, and I am satisfied that to put the average profits of engine works and the like at 5 per cent. is really putting it rather too high. Five per cent. on the capital in such works is on an average about 10 per cent. on the wages.

The most obvious apparent exception is in the coal trade, but this is because opening a colliery is a lottery. When a new colliery is opened out, the value of the coal is very much guesswork. If the seam turns out much thicker or better than was expected, the owner makes a fortune; if it turns out much worse, very likely he is ruined.

But now, as to a remedy. Nothing in the world would add so much to the greater profit of British manufacturing, mining, and employment generally, and do so much to improve the position

and incomes of the working classes, as a cordial and friendly understanding between employers and their workmen. I know that ill-
informed people habitually talk as if employers and workmen were
natural enemies. But why? Is it because we employers live out of
the workmen's earnings? So do the labour members and the
trades union leaders, and we employers can only get the full value
out of our men when they are happy and contented.

It is very difficult to carry on the complicated and delicate
arrangements of a large business under the present conditions of
unrest, which make the public more than ever unwilling to invest
capital in manufacturing, to the great loss of the working classes.
It makes customers unwilling to order, and the manufacturer cannot give proper attention either to getting orders or to turning out
first-class work, if he is liable at any moment to have all his arrangements paralyzed by a labour dispute, or by reckless legislation.

The first step towards improving the incomes of the working
classes is to make the amount to be divided between them and the
employers as large as possible. To this end, it is absolutely self-
evident that nothing is more injurious to the interests of the working classes than to worry, frighten or interrupt the only man who
finds the capital, organizes the industry, and gets the orders—the
only man in fact who can give employment.

I do not for a moment say that the employers are free from
blame in the present unrest. They must take their share of blame,
but the object is not to apportion blame but to bring about a
better state of things. There are to-day literally millions of working
men and women working cordially with those who employ them,
very much to the profit of both.

I must again emphasize the distinction between the employer
class, taken as a whole, and the wealthy class. Of course they over-
lap, but not to a very great extent.

Let us now consider the effect of bringing a strong pressure to
bear on a body of employers. At first they all suffer, but not
equally; gradually some, and then more and more, are crushed out

of existence. Now see how this works. Those that are poorest will be ruined; all their workmen will be thrown out of work, and will have to seek employment at the gates of the employers who survive. The customers of those who are gone must also seek to get their orders 'executed from these same survivors. So, while the poor employer is ruined, the rich employer gets more and therefore cheaper labour, and more orders, and therefore higher prices.

Nothing enables a man to face the unexpected, or to survive long periods of trouble, like a long purse. The poor man is ruined; the rich man waits patiently and then emerges to face reduced competition. Drastic changes in the law, unexpected strikes, and all other sudden and violent measures, have this effect; and whatever may be the intention of the ardent reformer, the practical effect of his action generally is to make rich men richer and poor men poorer.

If it was gone about in the right way, I believe that very great improvements might be expected in the condition of the working classes, unemployment might be minimized, and even the excessive accumulation of wealth might be checked. But Parliament, the Labour party, and the newer leaders of the men will have to change their policy entirely. Above all, the small employer ought to be encouraged; he simply is a workman who is himself securing the profits which would otherwise go to the larger employer—and rightly, because he is doing the work and taking the risk.

But now, as regards the duty of the Church in this matter. Let her more and more teach employers and workmen to sympathize with each other's difficulties and to smooth each other's path. Can any good be done by stirring up bitterness, by misrepresentation and exaggeration? If the employer says that trade is in danger, is it wise for any man to ignore his warnings when he is the only man who is on the look-out? The co-operator and small employer will take pains to see for themselves; the ordinary workman should be encouraged to do the same.

To conclude, I agree that the wealth of the country has increased very much in recent years, and yet the working classes are worse off. But this I hold to be simply due to the lamentable policy which has been pursued in their supposed interests. No policy could be easily devised more calculated permanently to increase the cost of living than the gigantic strikes which have done so much to paralyze our whole social machinery. Would any man take the risk of supplying food or other perishable goods to London, without a far greater margin than he would have thought sufficient ten years ago? It is important to observe that both Mr. Snowden and Mr. Barnes have recently spoken against the general strike policy, and most of the older trades union leaders notoriously dislike it. What we want is to see two employers running after every workman. Increase the total production of wealth, and the greater part must go to the workmen, the demand for labour must increase, wages must rise, and the price of living must fall.

I have already alluded to the millions of men and women who are working steadily and happily and are on friendly terms with their employers. I have had responsible charge of workmen for more than fifty years, and, notwithstanding occasional differences, my relations with them are among the happiest memories of a long life.

XXVI

The Church and Labour Questions

[LETTER TO THE EDITOR OF 'THE GUARDIAN,' APRIL 28TH, 1913]

THERE is often a great deal said and written as to what line the Church ought to take about social and labour questions, and I think we often overlook the work that the Church has done in the past, which has, I believe, been of the greatest possible benefit to the country.

As for my own experience, I was brought up on strict Church lines, and what the Church did for me as a boy, she has continued to remind me of ever since.

What I wish to lay before you is that the work of the Church is to teach us really Christian principles by which all our actions may be guided, and that she can only do harm by taking sides on special questions. As an illustration, I will speak of wages. It is very easy to say that men ought to have a living wage, but the question is how to get it. There are still numbers of workpeople who fix their own rates of remuneration, and experience shows that they are no better off than the rest. Increasing the wage merely means increasing the selling price of the article made, and then probably much fewer are sold.

If, for example, the wages of watchmakers were materially increased, the number of people who bought watches would be very much diminished, and many men would be thrown out of work and starved. This is not in the least an argument against all increases of wages; our—the employers'—tendency is steadily to raise wages higher and higher, but it must be done with care and knowledge, and with a full view of the circumstances. From about 1870 to 1900 wages increased from 25 to 50 per cent., and the cost of living was materially reduced. During the last ten years things have not gone nearly so well for the workpeople.

Some people say that the employers ought to give a much larger share of their profits to the workpeople, but, taking average manufacturing profits, if the whole were given to the workpeople it would not do very much to improve their position. An enormous majority of workmen are employed by really poor employers, and at any given time a great number of employers are working for very small profits, or none at all. The wealthy class is one thing; the employer class is a wholly different one. Of course a few very rich men are employers, but they are in a small minority.

I am only a layman, and I simply regard the teaching of the Church from the impressions it left on my mind. I understood that the work of the Church, as voiced by the clergy, was to instil into our minds certain principles which each of us were to apply to our own work and duties in that state of life to which it should please God to call us, these principles being that we ought to love God and His law above everything and our neighbours as ourselves, and in everything endeavour to follow the blessed steps of our Lord's most holy life. This is of course more fully set out in the Church Catechism, which we learn not only to qualify us for Confirmation, but as a hand-book to help us in all our subsequent life; and I believe the value of the Catechism to the whole standard of right and wrong in England has been something marvellous.

My contemporaries, as they grew up, went into the Army, the Navy, the Law, to the land, business, and other things, and it fell to my lot to become a manufacturing engineer, and I would try to show how the teaching of the Church appeared to me to apply to my new life. It taught me, for instance, that I ought to treat customers and workmen as I would like to be treated myself, not only with strict justice but with love and loyalty: that I ought to be disposed to give everyone credit for truth, honesty and good motives, till he is shown to be unworthy of confidence: that sound business emphatically does not consist in getting rich at other people's expense (that is gambling), but that in each transaction everybody engaged in it ought to benefit—purchaser, manufacturer and workmen: that we decidedly ought not to be eager to accumulate great wealth, but should remember that every increase in our income is a trust from God of which we must hereafter render account, and further, that much wealth adds neither to our usefulness nor to our happiness. This particular view was, I think, especially impressed in those days by the teachers of the Church of England.

I might enlarge further, but the above may be taken as examples.

To conclude, I believe that employers, as a class, are desirous to do their duty by their workmen. By all means keep before us our responsibilities, but no direct good can come from blaming us for not doing the impossible.

On one point I fear the teaching of the Church is not so good as it used to be. I think both the clergy and laity of sixty years ago not only taught, but convinced us, that we might easily place far too high a value on money as a source of happiness or of power, and I think the average public-school boy of those days did not grow up at all especially eager for wealth. I wish our Bishops and clergy would consider this point very seriously.

XXVII

The Ownership of Capital

[WRITTEN FOR 'THE ECONOMIC REVIEW,' OCT. 15TH, 1913]

IT has been suggested that I should write a paper setting forth the interests and point of view of the employers, but I would rather investigate the use and position of the employer from the point of view of the workmen's welfare; for unless the present system is the best in the general interests of society it had better be altered, and unless we employers are indispensable to the well-being of the working classes, we had better be abolished altogether.

In a leaflet published by your Society, No. 64, III, paragraph 4, you say that "the most that labour can obtain in any industry is the total product minus the minimum which is necessary to induce landlords, capitalists and employers to take part in the industry or to find the means of production." Now it seems to me that this point has been reached and passed, and that so far from employers, on an average, getting too large a share of the profits, numbers of them get so small a share that, as a class, they are diminishing, and a certain reluctance is felt in starting new industries—hence too much unemployment.

If any of us want to sell anything, we wish to find as large a number of customers as possible, and for those to be as wealthy as possible. For the number of our customers to be diminished, or for them to get very much poorer, would be for us the road to ruin.

Now, the only thing a working man has to live by is the sale of his labour, and the only man to buy that is the employer. The working classes dislike co-operation, though nearly every employer would be content to adopt it with very slight encouragement.

Neither the labour party nor any other party is seriously in earnest about any extensive form of State employment, as you can find from conversing with them, and in any case it would be a very slow process to introduce such a reform without a tremendous dislocation of industry and widespread distress.

There are many industries that may be carried on tolerably well by either the State or private enterprise, such as supplying gas, water, and electricity. In poor countries, railways must be made by the State, or not at all. So far, governments have done very little towards manufacturing for the general market, and most people who study the question come to the conclusion that it would pay very badly. But I am not aware that employers, as a class, have ever opposed the movement very much.

Co-operation is a subject on which a great deal has been written, but the present position is apparently as stated above. At any rate, in large works, the men do not like it, and personally I quite see that where the amount of capital per man employed is small, they are very likely right.

I think most employers believe that the best movements in the interests of the workmen are those that are based on the workman becoming a real shareholder, owner, or capitalist, and at last, if possible, the sole owner. So far from this being imaginary, the greater number of employers have come from the working classes, and, furthermore, probably most of the wages-paid men in the kingdom are employed either by ex-workmen or by men whose social and financial position is not above that of the farmer or small shopkeeper.

But the present labour leaders appear to take a very hostile view of the position of the small employer, and I have constantly been told by them that they wish he could be abolished. Now, as I have already said, of the wage-earning population probably at least three-fourths are employed by what can only be called poor men. The large employers probably do not employ more than the other quarter, and the crushing out of these small employers would throw an enormous number of men out of work. Besides, the small employer not only employs labour, but he is a centre of education to all his working-class relations and neighbours, not only teaching them how to rise in the world, but teaching them how to understand the employers' business so that they can protect their own interests much more easily.

I believe the real fallacy lies in the confusion of the wealthy class with the employers of labour. There are a few wealthy employers of labour, some millionaires, but they form a very small fraction of the whole, and the bulk of the large fortunes of this country are not made by direct employment of labour.

In justice to my brother employers, I must also say that I cannot think it fair to assume, as people do, that employers are either the enemies of the working classes or that they are hard in taking advantage of them. I believe the employers, as a class, are at least as unselfish, and quite as anxious to improve the conditions of those they employ, as either the trades union leaders, Members of Parliament, or even the clergy.

Now, whether capital is defined as "Accumulated Labour," as "Wealth applied to Production," as "Labour-saving Appliances," or anything else of the sort, it is evident that capital—the thing (apart from the ownership)—is as necessary to the working classes as the air they breathe or as the food they eat. Without it there would be no employment, for without it a workman can practically produce nothing. He wants appliances and material, and he wants to be fed and supported till the produce of his labour can be sold and paid for. The more capital there is the more demand there will be for labour, for the most wicked and selfish millionaire cannot get any return on his money except by employing labour, and even if he lends it as a usurer, it is only in order that the borrower may use it for productive purposes. So that workmen not only ought to encourage the growth and accumulation of capital by every means in their power, but they ought also to remember that the larger and safer the profits are in any business, the more capital will flow into that business, and the more demand there will be for labour.

There are two qualifications mentioned—large and safe. Now if the profits can be made safer the capitalists will be satisfied with less, and the difference will probably find its way into the pockets of the workmen. On the other hand, if capital is frightened and the owners of it are nervous, the capital can only be induced to come forward by the hope of larger profits, which will probably mean slightly lower wages. Frightening the capitalist may be great fun for the working classes, but it is a terribly expensive amusement for them. It does not much affect the old manufacturer or managing director whom they see every day; past experience has taught him where to look for safety and for danger; but in these days of large works a great part of the capital has to be found by a timid shareholding public, and the action either of Parliament or of the unions has a very appreciable effect on investors.

If the working classes realized their own interests, they would try to make the investment of capital as attractive as possible, and for the workman the cheapest attraction he can hold out to the investing public is security—both security of capital and regular and reliable dividends; and the more regular the dividends are the smaller they need be.

Nor do even our great statesmen, alas, always realize the heavy loss it is to the public at large if capital is destroyed or lies unproductive. And the public mainly consists of the working classes. Only a fraction of the profit on useful capital goes as a rule to the owner, the bulk goes to the general public. Let us look at a few examples. Take any inland town—nearly all its wealth and well-being depend on the provision of railway communication with London and elsewhere. Were the railway put out of existence, the flourishing town would become a very uncomfortable village, with impoverished property owners, bankrupt tradesmen, and starving workpeople. The amount that the capitalists who run the railway take in the form of dividends is absolutely paltry, compared to the indirect benefit that the public get in the way of trade and convenience.

Again, take the case of a town like Crewe or Swindon, which is practically dependent on one large railway factory for employment and prosperity. Suppose this factory were suddenly burnt, and was not insured. The railway company would lose the value of the works, *plus* some inconvenience in getting its wants supplied till the place was rebuilt. This is what the owners of the capital would lose. But the workpeople, deprived of employment, would forfeit the whole of their income, and the shopkeepers would lose all their trade. The public would suffer more than the railway company; and so not only is every investment of capital a public benefit, but capital cannot be locked up or laid idle without the public as a whole suffering a loss probably far greater than that of the owners of the capital.

When we talk of the unemployed, that is of men who would work if work could be found for them, we know that the cause of their being unemployed is that there is insufficient capital in the industries to which they belong. Find more capital, and, to make it productive, men must be taken from the ranks of the unemployed.

We must now consider the man who finds and manages the capital, whom we call the capitalist. Now, what is he? He is not, as a general rule, a man who has inherited a large fortune from his ancestors; he is seldom a man of blue blood or ancient lineage; more often he is a self-made man whose father or grandfather was very likely of humble position. That being so, how did he get into this favoured position, and earn the distinction of being so much hated and abused?

The way, in most cases, was very simple. He was just a man who worked when others played, saved when others spent, and learned how to do what he did not like. If industry, thrift, and self-denial are vices, he is a bad man. If he has another special quality it usually is that he has stuck to his own opinion in defiance of the judgement of the rest of the world, has bought what nobody else would look at, and so got it cheap. If a man does this and is ruined, nobody pities him; so, if he succeeds, need he be grudged his success? But whatever he is, good or bad, hard or gentle, he is the man who makes employment where there was none before, and is the best friend the working classes have.

But he is the man who *finds* the capital; it is not all his own; he has to gather much of it from the public.

I have said that it is a mistake to confuse the wealthy class with the employers of labour, and that there are a few wealthy employers—some millionaires, but these are a very small fraction of the whole—and that an enormous majority of employers are men in a comparatively humble position. People ask, where then do the millionaires come from? On this subject I will try to say something.

Probably most very large fortunes that are made quickly are made by speculation, which really means that what one man gains other men have lost. For example, a man may buy shares in a thoroughly discredited company. These may rise very rapidly in value and he may make an enormous profit. Again, I was told the other day of a shipowner who had made a great many thousands of pounds out of the recent boom in shipping; he had, in fact, contracted for a number of ships before the boom began, and when things rose, certain unhappy shipbuilders had to build these ships for him, with increased price of material and enormously increased price of labour, and only be paid at the lower price. Their balance sheet shows that up to this moment they have suffered a heavy loss. Another case I recently knew was that of a man who bought the debris of an old mine. When this mine was worked, the processes of extracting the ore from the rock were very imperfectly understood, and a great deal of admirable material was left behind. By smelting the spoil-heap over again, this man (a German) made a vast deal of money. But none of these fortunes had anything to say to the employment of labour. I should say that the employers who have made fortunes rapidly, come generally, though not always, under one of two heads—either they are men of great ability who have patents and specialities for which they get fancy prices, or else they are men who have bought the works at a very low price in the first instance, simply because nobody else would buy them at all, and who are therefore working on a comparatively small capital. Now, in these cases, the men might say, " If the employers make so much money we ought to have a share "; but, by universal consent, the wages of any trade in any district are more or less uniform, and as it is no excuse for an employer to want to pay lower wages because he has had great losses, so the men can hardly claim a rise in one particular works, either because one employer owns patents for which he gets an extra price, or because he bought the works in the first instance very much below their value.

But it will be observed, in most of the cases I speak of, that the money which the millionaire has got is not because more wealth has been created, but because it has changed hands. This is really on the same principle as gambling, though in a somewhat different form, and if you look on the lucky men you must also look on the unlucky ones. Nothing would pay better than horse-racing if you could be perfectly sure that your first and only horse would be a Derby winner, but yet we all know that if a man goes on the turf we look on it more as the road to ruin than anything else. Suppose a politician, a university man, or a trades union leader, were to point to the man whose horse won the Derby, and say, "What enormous profits people make by horse-racing," he would be looked upon as perfectly silly; and the man who points out the very occasional millionaire as a fair example of what people in business are likely to become, is not very much wiser. If you put £2 into a foreign government lottery you may win enough money to be independent for life, but if you took all the shares in that lottery and so won all the prizes, you would find that it would be a loss of something like a quarter or a third part of all the money you had invested; and so the man who makes money by sudden speculations must be averaged with a number of other men who have risked what they had, and perhaps lost everything. It is a great maxim, universally recognized by those who study political economy, or by those who calmly look at the world as everybody can see it, that wherever you find the greatest *possible* profits you find the lowest *average* profits, and workmen would have far more to hope from a state of society where there were several employers with moderate means, than from one where a number fail, leaving one millionaire here and there.

I have had a tolerably wide view of the engineering and ship-building trades for about half a century, and I observe that at least two-thirds of the works perish miserably, leaving their owners worse off than when they began. I have enlarged on this very fully in other places.

I may further add that in these trades an employer will do fairly well, will not make a fortune, but will make his living and keep his capital intact, if he can pay in dividends a tenth part of what he pays in wages. But obviously this leaves no margin for the workmen materially to improve their position by forcing an employer to abandon part of his profit.

I should further add that a great many of the rich men in England make their money outside England, say, in Africa, South America, and elsewhere. Obviously, if labour has a right to claim a larger share of the profits, none of this money would go to English workmen, but to negroes and South Americans.

Do I then say that the position of the working classes is hopeless, or that they cannot expect to be any better off than they are? if salvation is not to be found by fighting the employers, where will it come from? These questions I will now try to answer, but I must first point out two more matters which are often overlooked.

Firstly, Parliament especially, and to a certain extent the work-ing classes, are apt to look with light hearts upon throwing burdens on to what they call "the public"—be it taxation, supervision, or anything else. This may be right or wrong, but practically speaking, "the public" is another name for the working classes. Rich people can, to a very great extent, avoid burdens they do not like, but poor people cannot.

I would further point out the effect of bringing pressure to bear upon a body of employers. Suppose a state of things is brought about which makes trade unprofitable, the poorest employers are ruined; the others can hold out longer according to their means; when a certain number have gone, their workmen are out of work, and their only chance of getting employment is among the minority of employers who are left. This means that they compete with their fellow-workmen for a reduced number of situations. The rich employer, therefore, has a greater choice of men and he finds the labour market easier, and the men are lucky if wages are not reduced. But, furthermore, those customers who used to be supplied with what they wanted by the poor employers who have failed, now have to go to the minority who still survive; these then have a greater selection of orders and can naturally charge higher prices: so the rich employer gets higher prices and cheaper labour, and the poor employer is ruined. When will people learn that the tendency of all interference and all upheaval is to make rich men richer and poor men poorer?

The next question we must consider is, what can we hope from advancing wages? I believe I speak the mind of most experienced employers if I put the following down as what we believe to be the sound basis for a rate of wages: namely, that the total amount of wages paid either by a district, by a trade, or by an individual employer, should be as large as possible; that is to say, one must look at the total actual income of the working classes, not at the nominal rate which happens to be paid to individuals. In nearly all cases, if a manufacturer were to double the rate of wages he pays his men, he could get no orders at all; he would pay no wages, and all his men would starve, because he could only sell his goods at such a price that nobody would buy them. This is not only on account of competition, and work going elsewhere, but on account of the tremendous power the world has of going without what it does not think worth paying for. We must remember that the greater proportion of the working classes of this country are engaged in making things which nobody had, and nobody wanted, a hundred years ago, and it is extraordinary how quickly even a slight increase in price will reduce the demand. Savages will only buy clothing as a luxury if it is cheap enough; if the price goes up, they do without the clothing, as their forefathers did before them. Almost everything that is made by engineers and shipbuilders is bought by somebody as an investment out of which they hope to make a profit, and if the cost of a ship or a railway is too great and you cannot make a satisfactory profit upon it, people don't make the investment at all.

One other point before I pass on is this: the comfort of the working classes depends not only on the rate of wages, but on how hard they have to work. Now, as an illustration of this difficulty, riveting in iron shipbuilding has become much harder than it used to be. Owing to the increased size of ships, rivets have to be larger, and we use steel instead of iron, so the strain on the human frame is very severe indeed. The employers' remedy for this is to do the work more and more by machinery, but unhappily neither the unions nor the workmen give us the encouragement that we should like to have. They possibly think that to introduce machinery would throw men out of work, but this is not the case. Every step we take in the way of making work cheaper enables us to get more work, and the whole history of civilization shows that the cheaper you can work, the more men you can employ, and the higher wages you can pay; and let it never be forgotten that low wages do not necessarily mean cheap labour cost, and high wages therefore do not necessarily mean dear labour cost. To take one instance only, the navvy gets a much higher rate of pay than an ordinary labourer, but he can dig a hole for half the money.

We now come near the end of our investigation. Another point to be borne in mind is that managing a business is a very difficult thing indeed. It is not too much to say that, whereas it takes years of laborious study to make a man a good mechanic, an artist, or an accountant, it takes far greater study, and far more labour, and probably far greater natural gifts, to give a man the experience, the nerve, and the moral qualities which are necessary to make him able to manage a large business. That is where the Government almost always fail; they get admirable officials and faithful servants, but they never have succeeded yet in getting the general controlling power.

Occasionally people speak of the employers or capitalists as the idle class. This is sheer nonsense and hardly worth contradicting. Anybody who associates with employers, business men in the City, or men who have made money, knows that they are among the hardest working of the whole human race.

Where we believe the position of the workman could really be improved very much indeed is, first of all, by the old old story of thrift. If even only a proportion of the workmen could save a little money, it would help the whole class. Every bit of capital must make work for somebody, and the workman who owns money is not only stronger himself, but he is an educational object lesson to his fellow-workmen. It may be said with truth that the working man with a family has enough to do without saving, but nearly all workmen could save between the time they are out of their apprenticeship and the time that they marry. Taking this period at five years, if a man was really serious he could often save an average of 10s. a week, or say £25 a year. This will mean £125, which is very nearly as much capital as the world has to find to keep him in employment.

Working men frequently rise to positions of foremen, managers and directors. This should be encouraged by the general body of workmen as much as possible, since every workman who rises makes it easier for other men to follow him.

In conclusion, I may quote the words of one of our greatest ironmasters in the north of England. He used to say to us,

"Gentlemen, please remember that only a tenth part of the human race really uses iron and steel and machinery. If a second tenth part suddenly wanted to buy in the same proportion, all the output of the world could not supply them." As we opened out more and more trade, we could work more economically; we should select, instinctively, those parts which paid best, and there would be an ever-increasing demand for labour, higher and higher wages, and more and more promotion. The numbers of the wealthier classes can only be increased by drawing recruits from the working classes, and if this is coupled with an advance of wages, you will get very much what you want.

As it is, I believe what now keeps the world right is that the large majority of the working classes take an interest in and are proud of their work. These are not the ones that make a noise, but they are the ones that keep the world going. As I have often said before, speaking as an old manufacturer, the pleasantest memories of my life are the thoroughly cordial terms on which, notwithstanding an occasional dispute, I have lived with my workmen.

XXVIII

Apprenticeship

[REMARKS ON A PAPER BY PRINCIPAL MUNDELLA, FEB. 1916]

WE ought all to be very much indebted to Principal Mundella
for his most interesting paper on the education of our young
people, and, like all these papers, we may look on it either as an
ideal to be approached gradually, or as a standard which ought to
be adopted at once. I hope Principal Mundella will allow us to take
it in the first light.

I cannot say that I should like to see the Government take such
a leading part in the business as Principal Mundella would like it
to do. I think the Government has as much right to say to parents
that they ought to educate their children as to say that they ought
to feed them, but I doubt if the Government is by any means the
best qualified body to take the initiative in saying what the education ought to be. I think we may all agree that it has not shown
itself so in the past. Until the national schools and other such
bodies had made considerable progress, the Government took very
little trouble about education. The numbers of technical schools
and universities which exist in our great manufacturing towns
have been nearly all produced by voluntary enterprise—chiefly,
I think, by the contributions of employers of labour, from whom
so many of them take their names. Principal Mundella refers to
the technical schools established by Sir W. G. Armstrong, Whit-
worth and Co. at their Walker shipyard, and I may perhaps remind
the audience that the same firm started technical schools for their
engine works at Elswick, prior to 1850, and that these were an
enormous success not only for the work they did but as forerunners
of many other efforts of the same kind.

As regards general education, I should certainly like to see Government insist on it being carried on compulsorily, somehow or somewhere, for at least three years more than the present limit. Of course, a boy might be released if he went to be apprenticed in a suitable manner.

One evil in Government initiative is that it almost of necessity tries to measure all progress by examinations and marks. Now numbers of the most important subjects cannot be so measured; tact, good sense and strong nerves, which are some of the most important qualifications for a young engineer, are very much helped by wise training, but the extent to which they have been acquired can hardly be proved until we come to later life, and if the Government makes mistakes in the origin, as has certainly been the case in both Germany and the United States, there is no power on earth to put them right; whereas, if there are many governing bodies—be they those of religious denominations or of different technical universities—they will not all make the same mistakes, and if any one goes wrong, the others can probably be relied upon to rectify the error.

Now, a most important point on which the Principal dwells is the boy's choice of a calling, and here we must remember that many boys have not the knowledge which enables them to choose rightly in the first instance. A boy, after getting so far in one calling, feels instinctively that he might do better work at something else, but perhaps he does not find out what the something else is for some time; and some of our most distinguished men were trained in one profession and then took up something quite different. Let us not forget that Lord Armstrong had an influential practice as a solicitor, and that Sir Andrew Noble was a captain in the Artillery. I would then point out that a boy must not choose his calling with a view entirely to his own taste or his own advantage. I remember a German telling me that what struck him as the difference between German boys and English boys was that the German boy always said, "What shall I be?" while the English boy always said, "What shall I do?" As he rather sadly put it, the German boy looked on all his knowledge as something to put himself into a high position; the English boy looked on his own personality as something that ought to be sacrificed in carrying out the most useful work possible. This is the unselfishness that we expect in the sailor and the soldier, and we ought to try, as far as possible, to get it in every civilian also—duty before self-interest, and patriotism before selfishness.

To come to details, our present system is that the ordinary apprentice has to do the best he can with evening classes, and people point out how tiring it is to go to evening classes after a day's work. This is quite true, but of course he does not go every evening—very likely if he goes one or two evenings a week at the outside it is quite sufficient, and then he can do a good deal of work at home. I think the objection to sandwiching college and workshop together is that this disturbs the continuity of the boy's workshop experience, and that is a very serious matter. To take an extreme case—suppose, instead of going into a workshop, a boy goes to sea, it is obvious that he cannot get out of the ship to attend classes, but must stick to his floating home for better or for worse; the necessity of sticking to a workshop is not so obvious superficially, but I believe it is quite as real; the boy ought to live the life and see the big job through from the start to the finish.

I should like to hear a good deal more about employers having classes of their own, which they could dovetail in with the work of the shops better than a college could. Obviously, a young plumber ought to be taught the theory of his trade, and every young mechanic should learn something of the nature of steel, the foundry, crystallization, and many other things of which he vividly feels a need when he has been a little time in the workshop.

I am glad that Principal Mundella speaks favourably of the study of economics and history. I myself have no hesitation in saying, after a long lifetime, that viewed merely as money-making subjects, I have found them more valuable than anything else.

Hard study of social and economic questions often enables one to get a foresight of priceless value, which people who have not studied these things believe to be merely a matter of guesswork.

The question is often raised by different societies, "What is the best training for a young engineer?" Now, I have no hesitation whatever in saying what would be the *worst* training, and that would be any system which was uniformly the same for everybody. Engineering includes an enormous variety of spheres of action: to begin with, the highly scientific draughtsman and the practical pushing foreman require entirely different qualifications; then there comes the question of getting on with the workmen, and, perhaps still more difficult, of getting on with the customer and exactly realizing what he wants; and, besides all this, there is the endless variety of works which are included under the name "Engineering."

There is no doubt that while we may be thankful for what has been done in the past, we must always be taking one step further forward; but, when all is said and done, the young man must work out his own life, his father must help him, the trade will do all it can, and Government only comes in fourth.

XXIX
Scientific Training of Young Workmen

THERE is a general idea which comes to the surface in certain quarters that apprenticeship, as a means of learning trades, has become obsolete. Speaking of engineering, in the principal manufacturing centres this is certainly not the case, and perhaps I might give the experience of a very old-established works as to how the apprentice system is carried out now.

We consider that it is perfectly impossible for a lad to become a skilled mechanic except by doing real work in a tolerably large factory; because an engineer must not only know how to use his hands and his head, but he must learn that he is part of a large and carefully balanced organization of human beings, in which the work of each is related to, and is influenced by, the work of every other, and that all parts of a machine ought to be made independently and then go together perfectly as a matter of course.

But besides the workshop training, we consider that for modern work it is necessary that a young man should have sound theoretical knowledge, and we try to give apprentices every facility for securing this.

To save trouble, I will confine my remarks to engineers pure and simple, and the more so because, while they are as a rule exceedingly keen about attending classes and getting theoretical knowledge, we find, unfortunately, other trades are by no means their equals in this respect. We may occasionally find a young boilermaker or blacksmith who takes advantage of his opportunities, but, on the whole, his eagerness to rise in the world cannot be compared with that of the engineer.

The training therefore is something of this kind: suppose a lad who has done well at school comes into the works at sixteen. (We name this age because a mechanic is not merely a man who has learnt to perform certain processes with his hands, but he is a man who, having commenced his training in boyhood, has had his whole nature modified and certain faculties very much developed in accordance with the special trade. This can only be done while the body as well as the mind is unformed and highly susceptible.) He goes into a workshop where the proportion of apprentices to workmen is larger or smaller according to the class of work, but never so large but that the high standard set by the best mechanics may influence the whole body. He works fifty-three hours a week and his pay may probably range from 6s. to 12s. a week[1]. According to what line he may take up, he is put through a regular course, beginning with the easiest and ending with the highest class of work. For example: a young turner would very soon be put to a small slotting machine, then to planing machines, first to simpler and then to more complex lathes, finishing up perhaps with a first-class screw-cutting lathe. Young fitters and erectors in the same way are brought on from the simplest work till they can do whatever is most difficult, complicated and accurate.

Sometimes we hear complaints in other places of boys being kept too long at one class of work under the idea that this is profitable to the employer. Of course, this is neither fair nor wise, and if one considers that, as soon as a lad is able to do a simple job without any supervision whatever, he is ready to take up something rather more difficult and costly with a very small amount of supervision, it may well be that even the money interest of the employer will be compatible with the lad making constant progress.

I believe that if a father is looking out for a shop in which to apprentice his son, the point at which he ought to aim, if he has any choice, is that he should go to a shop where the work done is really first-class of its kind. I believe this is more important than

[1] All apprentices are legally bound.

to choose any particular branch of engineering. If a lad can recognize the highest class of work when he sees it, as his ideal, and can carry it out in practice, he will always be an exceedingly valuable member of society, go where he will; but if once he gets used to slovenly and ill-fitting work, it is very hard indeed for him to recover a high standard afterwards.

When Messrs. R. and W. Hawthorn's works changed hands in 1870, the management of the shops devolved on the late Mr. F. C. Marshall, and the question was what to do for the theoretical training of apprentices. He decided that whereas there were plenty of schools and classes, what was wanted was to induce the largest possible number of apprentices to attend them; and that what was needed was not so much a few brilliant men such as would be secured by offering high prizes and scholarships, but that the whole body of mechanics, as far as possible, should be raised to a higher level. He therefore began by announcing that he would pay the whole of the fees of every apprentice who would attend any evening classes whatever. At that time some of them had to go to common night-schools to learn reading and writing, but of course those days are happily long gone by. Very soon the classes that were in demand were for such things as mathematics, machine and boiler construction, mechanical drawing, applied mechanics, metallurgy, chemistry, etc.

In 1895, Mr. Marshall made a further advance. He gave a silver cup to be held as a trophy and to be competed for annually by the apprentices. To this was added a scholarship of £10, to be expended on educational purposes, the winner having also the privilege of being taken into the drawing office. This of course involved an annual competitive examination, for which all apprentices were eligible, the examination being carried out by Mr. Weighton, the Professor of Engineering at the Armstrong College in Newcastle. The arrangements are controlled by a committee consisting of two managers, ten foremen and a treasurer. Any apprentice who gets 10 per cent. of the possible marks receives

1*s.* a week extra as good conduct money for the ensuing year, and this he may earn again in succeeding years.

In 1906, of the engineering apprentices, 101 entered for the examination, and no doubt there were others who had benefited more or less by the free education, though they might not feel qualified to enter for the prize. The six highest all got prizes.

Looking back over past years, beginning in 1896, we find that from four to six lads were generally taken into either the drawing office or some other special department, and out of the first eight years a number of lads, owing to their success, are working as draughtsmen at Hawthorn's or elsewhere; about thirteen have already risen to really good positions of more or less responsibility, and it may reasonably be expected that the more recent years will show results equally good. There can be no question that the general effect of this system has been to make the lads altogether keener and more interested in their work. If it were to be made universal, and if other trades would take it up as keenly as the engineers have done, the result on the productive capacity of the country would be enormous, and the men would probably benefit to an untold extent by having more employment and earning very much larger incomes. Nobody who knows anything of the trade can doubt that the demand for engineering and shipbuilding products could be increased to an absolutely unlimited extent if they could be produced cheaper, and everything that adds to the productiveness of the individual workman increases his own income and improves his position; and also, by making the whole world better and more comfortable to live in, improves his position further as a consumer.

XXX

The Unpopular Employer

[WRITTEN FOR 'THE NATIONAL REVIEW,' JAN. 1916]

THIS paper is, I believe, the result of a letter I wrote to *The Times*, calling attention to the contrast between the kind feeling and brotherhood that exist between our soldiers and their officers, as compared with the unpopularity and hostility that exist in so many cases between employers and their workmen at home. This contrast was formerly not nearly so strong as it is now; a generation ago, army officers were by no means generally popular, nor were employers anything like so generally unpopular as they are at present. This may, of course, in part be due to social considerations. In old times nearly all the officers were from the public-school boy class, and nearly all the soldiers were recruited from the ordinary unskilled labourers; comparatively few men of the highly-paid, skilled mechanic class enlisted, and the shop-keeping class used to be conspicuous by its absence both among officers and men. This is different now, and whereas the social gulf was too great to be easily bridged over in old times, now it is not so at all. The public-school boy and the skilled mechanic have quite sufficient in common to converse and make friends on comparatively equal terms, and to understand and sympathize with each other's points of view. The same applies to the squire's son and the gamekeeper. This is all to the good, but it does not of course in the slightest degree account for the worse feeling between capital and labour at home. It is difficult, if not impossible, to go into all the causes of this feeling—they are so much mixed up with social, political, and other questions—but we might try and stand at one side and look at the state of things as it exists, and then see what we can suggest for its remedy or improvement.

Now, it must always be borne in mind that the bad feeling is by no means universal, or even dominant. There are an enormous number of workmen who are proud of their work, who take an interest in it, and who get on very well with their employers; they may be drawn into disputes, but they would rather go on peacefully if they could. Correspondingly, there are a large number of employers who care as much about their workmen as ever any employers did, and who really have their interests at heart, and probably these form the majority; for if it were not so, how would it be possible for the trade of England to take the magnificent position that it does, and for the quality of the work turned out to be perhaps the most perfect in the whole world? If anyone doubts this, let him look at one fact out of many. Nearly all the large manufacturing towns, such as Glasgow, Manchester, Newcastle and the others, now have universities, or, at any rate, exceedingly good colleges. These are mainly for lads who cannot go to Oxford or Cambridge, but, directly or indirectly, they are chiefly used by young men connected with the large works, or who propose to earn their living therein. Now, the bulk of the money for building these colleges, and for carrying them on, has been found by employers, who also have given probably the greater part of the care and attention required for initiating them. The whole object of this is to improve the position of the working classes, and raise up high-class men, because we know perfectly well that, for the trade of England to prosper as it ought to do, we want far more first-rate scientific men, and also a far higher average amount of scientific knowledge among the rank and file. The more knowledge, the more the country will prosper as a whole; and the more the country prospers as a whole, the more we shall prosper with it. Besides that, in probably most large works in England a good deal of trouble and money is spent on providing classes for the apprentices, and every encouragement is given to them to attend these classes, and in other ways to improve themselves. In fact, for the whole movement in favour of technical training, the country is mainly indebted to the large employers of labour. But, in speaking of the large towns, I may say that we must exclude from our consideration the largest town of all; no doubt the aggregate amount of manufacturing in London is very great, but, owing to the entire absence of large works, and the wholly different social conditions under which the people live, London experience is of little or no use as applied elsewhere, and as a guide to legislation or Government action it is very misleading. But there is quite enough bad feeling and bitterness in the country seriously to hamper our trade, for a disloyal minority on either side may fearfully cripple the work of a loyal majority; besides, it is very much easier to stir up difficulties and bad feeling than it is to allay them. Probably a large majority of our trades union leaders are really anxious for reasonable and peaceable settlements, especially those men who have filled their posts for a long time and who occupy leading positions in the world. It would be easy to name half-a-dozen of our leading labour Members of Parliament who have won, and retain, not only the implicit confidence but the respect and sincere regard of all the employers in the kingdom, and there are many more such men coming on.

But we are here to look at the ugly side, which causes the strikes and makes the difficulties, and I am afraid we see before us more and more that trade is dominated by conditions which are very unsound. There are employers who seem to think that if the workman gets his exact wages for what he does, with no credit for good work, no information as to what is expected by the customer, no sympathy or friendship, and no appreciation either of effort or attainment, the employer's side of the bargain is fulfilled. Now, would anybody trust his stables to a coachman or groom who hated horses and had no sympathy with them? and yet, to put one's fellow-men under the control of a hostile or unsympathetic manager or director is quite as certain to be disastrous.

Conversely, there are those who teach the men that the less a workman can do for his day's work the better for his class; they ignore the interests of the trade, and rather revel in being injurious to the employer: in other words, they try to teach the workman that the less work he turns out, the better off he and his fellow-men will be, which is the same thing as saying that the less valuable he makes his labour, the more valuable it will be! These foolish and false views have not only injured the trade of the country, but when we first found out that our armies were in danger, and that our brave soldiers were being killed for want of a sufficient supply of ammunition, these detestable views were a serious danger to our very existence as a nation. Since that, nearly all the trades union leaders have done their utmost to urge the men to turn out as much work as possible, but I fear very much mischief had been done first.

To revert to the employer's position. I believe it is an absolute fallacy that you can ever get really good results out of men by mere money payments, without confidence, sympathy and friendship, and I believe I might advantageously pause at this moment and try to describe a few of the various types of employers, so that we may realize more what we are discussing.

To my mind, the interest of the individual always will, and always must, give way to the interest of the community as a whole, and the use of employers is to be officers of the industrial army; and unless we are useful, and unless we do the work better than any other organization that could be put in our places, the sooner we are abolished the better.

There are various classes of employers, but the great change of modern times is that in so many cases the large company has taken the place of the old master, and, not only that, but there is an increasing tendency to choose the directors, who are the final appeal, from among financial men who have never lived amongst, and are not really in touch with, their workmen. For a very large number of workmen there may be one technical director, who has an increasing

staff of managers, foremen and superintendents of different kinds;
but probably the number of men under his charge is far too large
for him to know them personally. However good very large works
may be from a purely industrial point of view, there is no doubt
that they tend to keep the employer and the employed separate
from each other; the men, finding their individual voices are not
heard, combine in unions (and, dealing with very large numbers,
it would probably be impossible to arrange their affairs unless they
did so), and when these get too powerful the employers also
associate. Thus we come to the large federations, and very often to
fixed agreements drawn up by lawyers, which, though they may
be just, are generally very inelastic and sadly weaken the sympathetic and human footing which ought to exist.

At the other extreme of the scale is the small employer. He still
exists in enormous numbers in many trades in many parts of the
country, but it is very much the fashion to run him down and say
that he had better be abolished. This I think is wrong altogether.
For one thing, probably a very large majority indeed of the working classes work for employers who only have a small number of
men. It is by becoming a small employer that the workman has
his best chance of rising in the world, and I believe that nothing is
more important for the capitalist class than to be recruited constantly and in large numbers by men rising up from below. There
is an idea that the small employer is very hard. I think that is
scarcely a fair view; everyone is hard when he first gets into a
position of authority, but that is not due to harshness but to
nervousness. The first time a young man sees his orders deliberately disobeyed, he feels as if he would be humiliated for ever
unless he took some violent step to get his authority justified then
and there. When he gets older he finds that he is strong enough to
support his own authority, and therefore he can be more patient
with the impulsive stupidity or impertinence of some thoughtless
individual; and possibly the disobedience may be purely a case of
misunderstanding or forgetfulness. If workmen would only believe

it, a very short time will often make a young manager or employer who seems to be very harsh, into a peaceable quiet man like other people.

But not only is the small employer valuable as a step by which men may rise in the world. All his relations and friends being of the working class he has a tremendous educational influence; he gradually tells his friends and people all his difficulties and troubles, and they learn to see more of the employer's side of the case, and what a very uphill life he often has to lead.

I will just touch on one other type, the one which most resembles the army officer. The type to which I propose to refer may be taken as the average public-school boy whose parents give him a good professional training, and could probably give him some little capital, say, for the sake of argument, £5000. But this, as a rule, is not enough to start him in business, unless he has attained a position of some eminence beforehand. He probably has to borrow a considerable amount of money before any business will take him in, and, after that, he is very likely a good deal indebted to the bank from time to time for the extra money that he may require to carry on his business. Here again, numbers of these young men lose all they put in, and retire unsuccessful. In most cases where they are successful, it takes them many years to pay off their borrowed capital, and until that is done they cannot be considered to have succeeded or to be in a position of safety. In a case with which I am most familiar, it took the man thirty years before he finally paid off the last shilling of his borrowed capital; after that, of course, his income was considerably larger, and he was looked upon as a very successful man. But the thirty years were a very severe ordeal, and a long illness, or any other serious or unexpected disaster, might have led to his ruin.

Having sketched two or three types of employer or capitalist, I will now face the question of whether the working men get a fair share of the results of the trade. This question may be considered from two points of view:

First, whether any different arrangement could be made that would improve the position of the workmen.

Secondly, whether they could do better under existing arrangements.

As regards the first alternative, I may say that I think it a very great pity that such a large proportion of the population are paid simply by weekly wages, in such a way as to give them a very small interest in the success of the business or in the excellence of the work. I am very sorry that the sub-contractor has been to so great an extent abolished; if the workmen contract to supply the labour in any given trade, it gives them a training in organization and self-reliance which they cannot get by working for weekly wages. It is no doubt attractive to get your money at the end of every week, but it is a very serious thing to think that an enormous majority of the voters of this country know nothing at all, and have no means of learning anything, about the trades on which their very existence depends.

Let us assume that two brothers go to work, either as joiners or as blacksmiths; one of them goes into a large factory, at a weekly wage; the other starts business on his own account, in his native village. As long as all goes well, probably the factory man will feel far more comfortable, far better off, and have far less responsibility, besides which he will see a very high class of work, and associate with a number of other men of his own sort—which is all pleasing. On the other hand, the man in the village has to get his own orders, make his own connection, and satisfy his customers, be they reasonable or the reverse; he has to buy his own material, and have the money to pay for it. But he runs the risk of his customers being behind in their payments, or not paying him at all; if he makes any mistakes in his estimates, he has to bear the consequences; if by any mischance he turns out bad work, he has to replace it at his own expense. From all these things the factory man is free; but the village man is a complete self-contained organization, and when he has learned to stand on his feet in that capacity, his business may grow and grow, till he becomes one complete section of the trade of the country. He is better trained, more self-reliant, and more able to take care of himself and others.

If all the engineers or shipbuilders in England were left without employers, they would have no idea where to get orders or how to buy material. They have probably never thought about what it costs to find the buildings or machinery on which they work. Some of them, I think, believe that these things require very little thought and experience, but they are quite mistaken; it is far harder to find a man who can organize a business than it is to find a man who can turn out first-rate scientific work. A good illustration of this may be got from agriculture. The small farmer or peasant proprietor is often a very successful man, and produces more from an acre of land than a large farmer would do; set him down in a colony, or elsewhere, and simply give him a little seed corn and enough to live upon till that corn ripens, and he will command success; and the same ought to apply to a man starting business on a small scale, as the small employer does.

But now, as regards the present employer, the proper way to look upon him is simply as an officer of the industrial army. The question is, can the world get him any cheaper? It compels him to find the capital, and both the commercial and the scientific brains; he may do some of this work by deputy, but if so, he has to find the deputies and pay them. It is the foolish fashion to think of him as a man of great wealth, some of which might be very advantageously taken from him. Of course there are a few very rich employers—probably a larger proportion than there used to be—but the average profits are lower, and when a young man goes into business, he runs a very great risk of failure and has a very remote chance of making a fortune; and thus we come to the old maxim in political economy that everybody knows, that wherever you find the greatest possible profits you find the lowest average profits. If you were to take the men of the various classes of employers that I have instanced, and offer them the alternative of a reasonable salary, you would probably find any number of them eager to jump at the offer; and if it comes to a question of risking capital, they are, very wisely, increasingly suspicious. It is by no means easy to find young men now who will buy shares in businesses, nor are their fathers very fond of their doing so. Suppose you could fancy the Government taking over some of our large works, and offering such salaries as they give in the dockyards or arsenals, or even at the Local Government Board and such other offices, I believe such a move would be hailed with the very greatest delight by the employer class. Most men would infinitely rather have a moderate salary with a retiring pension in their old age, such as the Government commonly gives, than have the remote chance of making a large fortune by the time they are, perhaps, sixty. I have watched men of this class all my life, and when you talk to young men or their fathers you find that their ambitions very seldom indeed lie in the direction of spending all their lives in running great risks, with the remote chance of making a large fortune at the far end of it. What a man really wants is a comfortable income according to his bringing up, and anything he gets beyond that, more especially if it comes late in life, is a very insufficient reward for the risks he runs. As a consequence of this, we do not find a large and increasing number of employers; the number of small employers is diminishing; and I think the large ones feel the competition from below less than they used to do, and less than they ought to do in the interests of the country. I myself worked for some years for the Government, and if I could have been reasonably sure of a good position at a moderate salary, I would not have been attracted away from that for any profits that a private business would be likely to offer me.

This leads at once to the question of other forms of employment. A great deal has been said about profit-sharing, but few people ask themselves what this really involves. In a district we have a number of firms, and, to keep to the trade I understand best,

I will assume that these are the owners of engineering establishments. Some of these are rich, some are poor; some are making money, some are losing; but they are all expected, and compelled, to pay a uniform rate of wages. This is not unsound: the workman says, "My services are worth so much; if a poor man wants them he must pay the same for them as a rich man, just as he must pay the same price for food and clothing if he wants them." But this, though perfectly true, is the death-blow to the question of profit-sharing, because in some works which are doing very well the men might get a very large share of the profits, while in other works which are doing badly, there would be nothing for the men to share. The workmen would then all want to go and work at the well-paid places, and the poor employer would probably have to pay very much higher wages to keep his men, which sounds all very nice, but conversely the rich employer would find that he could get his men at a much lower wage. If we are to have collective action of employers and workmen, it seems to me that profit-sharing is impracticable. Another thing about it is that, taking the trade as a whole, nobody can make out that the profits thereof average more than 5 per cent. at the very outside, and probably they are considerably less. If people will think of the number of works that die down and fail in the course of any given ten years, or if they think of all the works that were at the very head of the trade in London a generation ago, and of their subsequent history, they will see the force of what I say; because, of course, unless the employer can save enough money, while his works live, to replace his capital when they cease to exist, he simply will not go into business.

But I sometimes think more might be done in the way of workmen really and truly owning their own works. For example, while I see great difficulty in workmen owning works where they have to find large sums of money and embark on costly undertakings, it has always seemed to me that repair work is exactly the sort of thing that workmen might undertake without any expensive employers;

the amount of capital required is small, payments come in quickly, there is every inducement to the individual workman to exercise initiative and originality, and, as all experienced men know, repair work and new work get on far better separate than together. It would be, I think, a step in the right direction if workmen would try to combine a little to do repair work, and leave the question of new contracts to further consideration: in fact, the young men would all be trained on the new work, and as they saved a little money and got a little experience, they might drift into the other, where they would become real owners. There are several other lines which might easily be carried on without the capitalist employers, and doubtless many more would disclose themselves if the matter were studied. Fishing, I believe, is almost always managed by the men who do the work, but I think that, as a general rule, the fish are bought and paid for *en masse* by certain special buyers, which saves the fishermen all the worry and anxiety of looking out for orders and finding markets. It used to be common in my young days for a gang of navvies to take a railway cutting or the excavation of a dock, and very likely one of their number would take a contract for making a road, in which case it always seemed to me that he picked his men very carefully, and paid them higher wages than they would get in ordinary employment.

Another alternative is Government work. I have seen a good deal of this in my time, and it seems to me that people are too much inclined altogether to approve of it or altogether to condemn it. Some things, I think, are quite suitable for Government work, and, by gradually pressing the point, we might find that this principle could be carried further. Most small local bodies own their own water supplies; it is not uncommon for corporations to own tramways and gas works; and I should say that these, one with another, are just about as successful—neither more nor less —as the work done by companies; but if, in course of years, the town or district grows and there is a large unearned improvement, this of course would go to the public instead of to a company. What

I cannot see that any Government has ever succeeded in, is in travelling for orders and pushing sales; it may have been attempted, but only, I think, in a very few cases, and generally not successfully. But I think we might say that wherever the products sell themselves, or are a universal need, as in the cases mentioned above, the work is of a kind that the Government might suitably undertake. Then comes of course the question of railways. In this country all railways hitherto have belonged to private companies, but probably in the greater part of the world, especially in colonies and in poor countries, the railways must be made by the Government or not at all; and though they may not usually, in these places, show much in the way of dividends, they show an enormous deal in the way of increased prosperity to the district where they are. In some countries no doubt Government ownership has failed, largely owing to the difficulty of getting really honest officials, but one would hope that in England this could not possibly apply, because there is no doubt that, as a rule, our Government servants are a very upright and honest class of men. Nobody would wish to see the dockyards and arsenals put into private hands; the work might, in some cases, be done equally well and rather cheaper, but probably the advantage of the Government having them in its own hands is very great.

As regards the question whether the workmen could do better under existing arrangements, I must revert to the subject of profit-sharing which is the panacea so often quoted. As I have pointed out, even when some firms are making enormous profits, many others are making none at all, or are losing money; and this, coupled with the fact that we have a more or less uniform rate of wages for each trade in each district, makes profit-sharing intensely difficult, if not impossible. But, more than that, it is all very well to share profits where the capital per man employed is very large indeed, as in the Metropolitan Gas Works, where, thanks to Sir George Livesey, it has been perfectly successful; but it is quite a different thing in those industries where the amount of capital per man is compara-

tively small. Now in engine works and shipyards, during the last
four or five years, things have been in a very excited state; but if
we go back to the previous years, and for a long time before that,
we come to those figures which have been so very often published,
that for every man employed there is about £150 of capital, and
that the weekly wage, taking mechanics of all sorts, labourers and
apprentices, averaged much about 30s. per head, equal to £75 a
year; so that we might very fairly say that an employer paid away
in wages per year an amount equal to about half his capital. Then,
if you take any of the lists published by stockbrokers, or sometimes picked out of special newspapers, you cannot shut your eyes
to the fact that, taken as a whole, these businesses do not, on an
average, pay more than 5 per cent. per annum on the capital;
and out of this the employer has to pay interest on any borrowed
capital. If he paid 5 per cent. dividend on his capital, he divided
£7. 10s. 0d. per man employed per annum, or a tenth part of
what he pays in wages. He ought to be able to save up something in case his business comes to an end or his works become
obsolete, so this leaves practically nothing to give the workmen.
Taking a wholly different trade, I may say that after the Franco-
German War, say from about 1871 to 1875, in some places the
coal trade made profits that were simply enormous; but, going
on from that time to pretty nearly 1890, there were years and
years in which numbers of collieries literally never paid a shilling;
and, on the whole, if you took these collieries over the twenty
years from 1870 to 1890, you would see that the total profits were
nil, though you might pick out one colliery here and there that had
made a good deal—just like the winner of the Derby compared to
all the losers. I myself believe that the uncertain profits of the
trade cause the workmen a great deal of their suffering, for the
simple reason that people are not so willing as they might be to
invest their money in manufacturing businesses. Now, they all talk
about the large profits made on account of the present war, but yet,
in the two largest and most prosperous works in the kingdom, the

shares are standing distinctly lower than the average, which shows that the public do not think the chance of these very high profits is sufficient inducement to them to buy the shares; the obvious reason being that when the war is over it may be found that many people have spent an enormous amount of money in increasing their powers of producing war material, and as there may be an almost complete cessation of demand for such things, a vast amount of machinery which has been bought will be no longer useful. That is what happened after Waterloo.

I should like to mention one point which, I think, causes great dissatisfaction among the workmen, though it hardly ever gets into the papers, and that is the very high rate of wages which similar men earn in America. A workman sees a Ford motor-car imported from America and being sold cheaper than English cars, and he is told that the men who actually made this car earn something like £1 a day. Now, why is this? I believe one reason is that among the men who make the car there is no such thing as restriction of output; a great deal of the work is done by sub-contractors, who do not care what rate of wages they pay, provided the workmen can only turn out a corresponding amount of work cheaply enough; and if workmen go on year after year working with their brains as well as with their hands to see how much they can do, the brains of a thousand workmen in one establishment all co-operating with each other will increase the output by an amount which is almost incredible. Let us consider a case that is not uncommon in piece-work. A man works at a new lathe which turns out, say, four times as much work as the old one, but under existing conditions of unions and associations we cannot pay that man four times, or even twice as much wages as we pay all the other men surrounding him; and if, in the course of years, almost all our tools are superseded by tools which do a great deal more work, the general effect of it is not so much to raise wages as to lower the selling price of the article. I question if this is as it ought to be: in some shape or form the workman ought to get a greater and more prompt share of the benefits of labour-saving appliances, and I also think he ought to get more definite encouragement for any savings that he himself can originate. If our men earned more money, more men would want to come into the trade; but they would have vastly happier and more interesting lives if they simply let themselves loose to do as much work as possible, and it is a great fallacy to suppose that doing more work means taking more out of the men or tiring them more, or employing fewer people. Generally speaking, the highly-skilled man takes less out of himself than the inexperienced clumsy one, and certainly when you come to the adoption of improved methods, one cannot compare the man who works a planing machine with the man who used to chip up a bed-plate by hand, taking ten times as long and using very hard physical force the whole time he was at work. But I fear these things can only be carried out either by sub-contracting or by piece-work, unless the workmen choose to become thrifty and buy the works themselves; then of course they can do whatever they please. But there is no doubt that employers ought to take a far more bold and sympathetic view of the workmen's aims and difficulties. I believe every small point ought to be decided in favour of the workmen; just as I think, between the rich and the poor man, the rich man ought almost always to concede a small point; the reverse process only causes irritation and bitterness, while one sees what a very large amount of grateful return a small concession will often bring. This is on the same principle that I believe coursing often kills poaching, by giving the working classes an interest in game-preserving and in sport generally. I believe the same principle applied to everything else has a very great effect, and a workman ought to feel that if he makes any suggestion it will be listened to respectfully even if it is not adopted. I have known a workman told that if he was going to suggest improvements he might go and seek a job elsewhere. Now this is no way to treat him; the mere fact of trying to make improvements educates a man, and, among them all, a certain number will succeed. But restricting the output is simply a means of keeping the working classes down in a position which will always get lower and lower the longer that sort of thing goes on.

I think some relief may come in the future from the large increase in what may be called the intermediate class, such as foremen, draughtsmen, superintendents, and special workers. The increasing requirements of higher and more complicated products as well as organizations, will probably cause a great demand for such people, and that will have the effect of making any young workman feel that his chance of promotion is very much greater than heretofore; and we, the employers, ought to bring these men on and encourage them to come to our various scientific organizations to hear papers read and discussed, and, generally speaking, use them as much as possible to bridge over the gulf which exists between employers and workmen.

I suppose I ought now to say something of that panacea which is often recommended as a cure for all the ills of the working classes, namely, the strike. During the last year or two, causes which I need not specify have given the men a considerable advantage, because employers were most unwilling to close their works even for a very short period. But if we take the years from, say, 1890 to 1910, it will be found that the proportion of strikes which the men won was exceedingly small, while the cost of their fighting was very great. The cost of a strike to the workmen is really a very simple affair. Every man who strikes for a week loses his week's wages; he may get some of it from the union funds, but those are his own savings; other men may subscribe to the strike, but, if so, that is a liability which will probably have to be repaid in kind sooner or later, and, on the whole, the men on strike lose exactly the amount of wages that they would have earned had they been at work. So, if men go on strike for 1s. a week advance, and get it, and their wages were £1 a week, it would take twenty weeks of work at the advanced rate to pay for every week that they have been on strike, before they began to reap any advantage. Recent legislation has given the men some advantage: for example, in the great national coal strike, which ended in April 1912 after lasting six weeks, the men were on their last legs; the employers could have held out a great deal longer, but Parliament intervened and gave the men what they wanted, by legislation. This might, at first sight, look as if legislation were the key to the whole position and the solution of the workmen's problem, but that is not quite so. The employers have one weapon, sometimes visible and sometimes invisible, which, if they choose to use it, is absolutely irresistible, and the whole forces of the working classes, and the Government behind them, are perfectly powerless to meet it—that is, permanently closing their works. I do not allude to a lock-out—that is only a temporary expedient—but if employers find that their business is not paying they close their works. In the above case, I do not know that any collieries were closed, as prices rose considerably, but I fancy that many of the worst places and less profitable seams had to be abandoned. Every thoughtful man who knows any large town must see that the closing of works is by no means so infrequent as people might fancy. The invisible and more irresistible form is that they do not start new factories or extend the old ones, so that gradually the men find their trade is not what it ought to be. I fancy few people really ask themselves what is the effect of putting pressure on a body of employers, and I will try and deal with it briefly. Suppose a number of employers, some richer and some poorer, are subjected to pressure from a strike or anything else, what happens? Presently the poorest ones are ruined; the customers who used to get work from them now have to go to the wealthier remainder, who therefore get more orders to pick and choose from than they had before, and can get higher prices; but, further, the workmen who were employed by the poorer, and now ruined, employers have to go to the doors of the richer ones to seek work, so these same employers also get a greater selection of workmen, which probably means cheaper labour. In other words, like almost all arbitrary interference with the state of trade, and like almost all violent legislation, it simply means that rich men become richer and poor men become poorer; in fact, the impatience of people to make reforms by short cuts which can only really be made by industry and intelligence, tends to bring about exactly the results they do not want. This accounts a good deal for the existence of the millionaires, who are, of course, simply the survival of the fittest, *i.e.* of the strongest and most powerful, but not necessarily the most virtuous.

But I believe we may hope for better things if we take a broad view of the question. First of all, as regards the financial aspect: there would be an absolutely unlimited demand for our manufactures—for example, for engineering products—if we could reduce the price a little. It is extraordinary how even a very small reduction in price increases the demand very largely, and, emphatically, cheap work does not at all necessarily mean low wages —note the American motor-car—or, again, a navvy gets a much higher wage than an ordinary labourer, but he can dig a hole for less money and is not nearly so tired when the work is done.

It is probably not much use for us, as employers, to spend our time in the very easy occupation of pointing out the faults of the men and giving them good advice. The only suggestion I will make to both sides equally is that a compromise is better than a victory; it leaves no bitterness and brings about no reaction. And then let us as employers try to see our own faults, and think what we can do towards bringing about a better state of things. It seems to me that, as a class, we have very much overlooked some of the first principles of government which are perfectly well known not only to the army and navy officer but to every colonial and Indian official; such as, that to govern well you ought thoroughly to understand and sympathize with the character and position of the governed; that an unpopular government has very great difficulty in bringing about any measure of prosperity; and that, in fact, you want mutual co-operation and sympathy. This by no means implies a weakening of the government, or indicates that we ought in any way to give up the responsibility of controlling our own works. A father, in every transaction of his life, from morn till night, is always considering and working for the good of his children, but he very likely does not even consult them as to what he does, because he knows all the circumstances and has all the experience and training, and knows too what is best for their interests; and, what is more, a happy family is one in which the children know this and trust their parents. In the same way, in a well-ordered works, though all guidance and decision must be done by highly-trained people who have seen the correspondence, understand the finance, and know all the circumstances, still, if the workmen knew and believed that their interests were really cared for, I believe they would trust us.

A manufacturer and his workmen ought to honour and trust each other. The first thing a young soldier is taught is that he must live for the credit of his regiment and not of himself; the oldest general never loses sight of this; and we ought to have the same spirit in the factory. I fear the wrong spirit comes very much from an undue wish to make money, or, which is still worse, from jealousy lest others should make money. If we could only forget our own self-interest and try how much work we could turn out, we should all be very much better and happier, and the country would be free from those really serious dangers which we have felt for many years past, and which all the world realized so vividly when there came the question of increasing the output of munitions of war.

Position, influence, money and property are not given to us for our own pleasure and profit; they are talents to be used for the glory of God and the help of our fellow-men; and be our income dividends or wages, when we die let it be said that we made that income honourably and dealt with it unselfishly.

XXXI

The Return to Work

[LETTER TO THE EDITOR OF 'THE TIMES,' SEPT. 9TH, 1916]

I CANNOT help thinking that the public generally are taking too gloomy a view of the question of getting men back to work when the war is over. I believe in the end there will be more stalls than horses to put in them.

Before going into this, I should like to clear out of the way two points that perhaps a little confuse the case. First, of course, we want to develop each of our colonies in the best way for its own interests, and we thus hope to increase their surplus production. But probably they will increase as consumers to about the same extent, and any surplus will be probably either food or raw material. Also, we find that we were without certain things that were necessary for our existence. It was very easy to buy them, and it was nobody's business to think what would happen if there was a war. I fear Government are the only people who can see to this sort of thing, and their case is complicated as follows:

I do not think it has ever been sufficiently recognized that this country is getting dangerously short of the class of men who are on the look out for new fields of enterprise either as employers or as capitalists. The public will never be able to buy what they want as cheaply as they ought, and the working classes will never (in normal times) have such plentiful employment or such good wages as they wish, until we can increase the number of those younger men who want to become manufacturers or employers of labour; and I think when foreigners (say Germans) have been blamed for stepping into the breach, it has been because no Englishman took the trouble to do so. I have long thought it was increasingly hard to get new enterprises taken up in this country.

Then to face the simple problem. To restore millions of men and women to their old occupations is, of course, a gigantic task, but I think more interesting than disheartening. When the trades unions agreed to waive their customs, their employers promised to find work for all their members as they came back, and of course the new jobs must be at least as good as the old ones. I suppose this actually bound only those employers who were federated or associated. This would be a large majority, but not all. But for those who were not associated there would be Government pressure, and, beyond that, public opinion, which is perhaps the strongest of forces. Above all there is a great safeguard in this fact. These people were living somehow before the war, and what they really claim is to be put back into the same positions that they left. Now alas! those coming home will be considerably fewer than those who went out, and besides this, owing to the war, there are two years' arrears of the world's requirements to make up, as well as such an amount of repair work as the world never saw before. My own impression is that if every man and woman in Europe worked like a slave, it would be many years before we caught up the arrears.

No doubt to put every peg into its proper hole will be very difficult, but if people work together and Government co-operates, I do not think the problem will be at all hopeless. I should think every coal miner could go straight from his regiment to the coal-pit, and the same applies to numbers of other men. When we have got the first million to work I think we shall see our way pretty clearly. If only employers and workmen will work together like officers and soldiers the problem will not be formidable, and I shall be very much disappointed if the working classes are not decidedly better off than they have ever been before.

XXXII

Industrial Conditions after the War

[LETTER TO THE EDITOR OF 'THE SHIPBUILDER,' JAN. 1ST, 1917]

YOU have raised the question of discussing the industrial conditions after the war, and you have done me the honour of asking me to give my views on the subject. Frankly, I may say that, as a general rule, I think these discussions do a good deal more harm than good. At the present moment we all of us have our nerves more or less strained by the war; a large majority of people are overworked; we have to deal with a future which we cannot foretell; and, on the whole, I should say that the country could hardly be in a state of mind less suitable for the calm and well-balanced consideration of these various subjects. Whenever the time comes that we see peace looming in the early future, it will take us a very short time indeed to think out all possible contingencies and to decide which is the best line to take.

These subjects are mostly ranged under three heads:

1. The possible terms of peace.
2. Trade arrangements.
3. Labour questions.

Now, as regards the possible terms of peace, we must, of course, first put before ourselves what were the causes of the war. Whatever the views our enemies may have upon the subject, the line that England took was an intensely simple one; the preparations we had made were very slight; our army was a small one compared with that of other countries; we had a strong navy, but that we always have had for many, many years past, simply as a defensive and protective measure. Then how did we get into the war? We took exactly the same line as Mr. Gladstone took at the beginning of the Franco-German War in 1870. We, with France, Prussia, Austria and Russia, had guaranteed the neutrality of Belgium, and, whatever other people did, we felt it our duty to keep our promise. In 1870, the moment war broke out between Prussia and France, Mr. Gladstone made a treaty to the effect that, if either side infringed the neutrality of Belgium, we should join the other side. Bismarck at once said we were quite right, and that they, as well as we, were responsible for the independence of Belgium; and he signed the treaty with great cordiality. The Emperor Napoleon also signed the treaty at once on behalf of France; and every soldier who passed between Germany and France went right round, south of Luxemburg, in order to avoid trespassing upon the territory of the neutral.

I suppose we may also say, in this way, that we should probably have gone into the war in any case sooner than see our old ally France invaded, despoiled and ruined; but, whatever was the reason, our action was absolutely unselfish, and we simply did what we felt to be our duty. I believe that, if you were to poll the men of England, you would find that nine-tenths of them, and probably far more, felt that we had promised to defend Belgium, and that, whatever happened, we were bound to fight.

Had peace been under consideration within a very short time, the question would have been simple; but the line the Germans took with Belgium and France, to say nothing of the Eastern countries, made the whole question far more difficult. We then had to call in the help of our colonies; and, in making peace, these who have fought for us so devotedly will have to have their say in the matter as well as England.

But now, whenever peace has to be discussed, it will be a question for France, Belgium, Russia, Japan, Roumania, Serbia, Montenegro, Italy and Portugal, besides, as I have said, our own colonies; and it is of no use for one party to say what they will, or will not insist upon until they know what all the others think, and also until we see what condition we are all in when the war ends. Many people are now saying that we must insist on having all sorts of trade arrangements. The people who hold opposite views on tariff reform abuse each other and say strong things, quite forgetting that these other countries may not care to keep up this tremendous war simply for the benefit of English trade. We shall get a certain amount of our own way, but not all of it; and, furthermore, if the war is costing England, as we are told, £5,000,000 a day, I very much doubt if any benefit we can get for our trade by any special terms of peace would be worth paying anything like that price for. It always seems to me that, when England really exerts herself, she can fill up with trade very fairly; and certainly whenever other countries get a monopoly of some particular product, it is very generally because we have not troubled with it. For example, during the last seventy years or so, the greater part of the zinc trade in the world has been in the hands of Belgium, though latterly Germany has gone a good deal into it; but other parts of the world have had their specialities, and the amount of trade that could be executed by our average number of unemployed is comparatively small, and certainly not worth talking about in connection with a war of this unheard-of magnitude.

Looking at past wars, England has generally, I should say, been very successful in her peace negotiations—usually very liberal and tolerant, and the arrangements therefore have been very permanent. To take two examples only: people talk very fiercely about making Germany incapable of doing this sort of thing again, which is exactly what Napoleon Bonaparte said after the defeat of Prussia at the battle of Jena. He reduced her army to, I think, 32,000 men, compelled her to declare war on all his enemies, and to ally herself with him in all his wars, besides paying very heavily in other ways; and what was the consequence? Within the next eleven years the Prussians twice invaded Paris successfully! After Waterloo, the Duke of Wellington would only allow us to take two very small islands from France, neither of which did she care about and which were very important to us. We did all we could to lighten her burden as regarded other Powers, we took no payment for expenses, and we succeeded in getting France clear of the enemy's troops quicker even than was arranged under the terms of peace. Other people wanted to take territory from France, but the Duke said: "No, taking territory simply means laying the seed of future wars." If anyone is curious enough to read the life of Napoleon, he will see how astonished Napoleon was at our action. He considered that "England had acted most foolishly in her own interests; she had everything at her feet and she had taken nothing[1]." But mark the consequences: notwithstanding that there have been any number of burning questions between France and us, we have now gone through a hundred years since that time without any war, and have ended by being the most thoroughly loyal and sincere friends.

And, finally, to threaten what you are going to do after a war, when you have conquered, is encouraging the war party of that country, and discouraging those who would be glad to seek for peace.

The third point is the question of capital and labour. It seems to me that some employers are afraid that the men are organizing in order to crush them; on the other hand, there are those among the labour party who seem to think the employers are organizing to crush them. I must frankly say that I believe both these are bogies caused by nervousness rather than by well-defined dangers. All the trades union leaders seem to me to be most anxious to arrive at some settlement to avoid the tedious and expensive strikes that have been such a trouble in the past, and I believe a large majority of the employers feel the same way; and I am very much inclined to think that, now the Government have got such a strong control of our works, they will not take their hands off until they feel that they have capital and labour on a fairly satisfactory working footing.

[1] See Sir Walter Scott's *Life of Napoleon*, Appendix IV.

May I first say how I believe the question will really work out? Of course, if peace came at all suddenly and the armies were disbanded, it would be a work of very great difficulty—confining ourselves to our own country—to get four or five millions of men back into civil life without a great deal of confusion and waste; but I do not believe the task would be insuperable. If the Government would discharge some of the soldiers as quickly as possible, taking care always to send away those who had work to go to at once, I believe the matter would become easier and easier every month. They must be prepared to keep on some of the soldiers perhaps rather longer than they are absolutely wanted, until the others get shaken into their places; but, if we consider that for three years all ordinary industries have been paralyzed; that hardly anything has been produced except munitions of war; that, alas! a large number of the men who have gone have lost their lives and will not come back; that, in other words, we have three years' arrears to make up; that everything is in disorder and that there is not a railway, nor a road, nor a factory, hardly a dwelling house, we might say hardly a suit of clothes, in the whole of Europe that does not need repair badly, it stands to reason that the demand for labour as soon as we can get the men into their places will be something far greater than anybody has ever seen before. Repair work, as probably every workman knows, takes more labour in proportion to the amount of capital involved than almost anything else, and when we come to replace all the things that have been neglected, I think there is no doubt whatever that we shall have the ideal state of things of two employers running after every workman.

There is another point which I have never seen sufficiently emphasized, and that is the extraordinary way in which, owing to the war, the working classes especially are learning to save money. If they do this, all their savings help to make work. You cannot invest money without making employment for somebody, and there is no limit to what the world could buy if only there were capital enough to keep the industries going while it was being produced. The Government have told us how important it is, on account of the war, that we should be thrifty, and they teach us that every atom of capital, no matter to whom it belongs, is an absolute strength to the country. This is true in time of peace as well as in time of war, and if only working men can continue to save a certain proportion of their wages it will enormously increase not only the stability of the country but their own daily wages, by making a much greater demand for their services; besides enabling them to meet their employers on far more equal terms.

But I should like to appeal to all your readers as to whether they are not intensely proud of the people of England under the present condition of things? Could anything be more unselfish and more chivalrous than the acts of our soldiers? Only second to them is the way in which the enormous majority of those who have been obliged to stay at home have stuck to their work, and overworked themselves in order to produce that which was wanted. Of course there are exceptions: there are bad people and idle people everywhere, but they form a very small minority. As far as we know, only a very small fraction of our men had ever wished to be soldiers; they went because they saw it to be their duty for the sake of their country. And see also how the women of England, from the highest to the lowest, have turned to work of any kind in order to keep the country going, and to supply it with what it wanted. It is horrible to think of being on bitter terms again after this. The officers and men in the trenches work together like brothers, and are intensely loyal to each other; that is the feeling we ought to have between employers and workmen in this country. When I first became an engineer, my feeling was to look upon every man in the same works with myself as a comrade and a friend, and I have always succeeded in having that feeling towards a good many of them. There have been exceptions—like the rest of us, I have been mixed up with trade disputes and strikes—but still there is a large amount of good feeling; and that is what has really pulled the country through, notwithstanding the quarrels, and that is what we want to encourage. It seems to me that the feeling of capital towards labour ought to be very much the feeling that parents have towards their children. I will take the words of an old cavalry colonel. The commissariat officer had complained that some new arrangement about feeding, which the colonel thought would be better for the men, would give him more trouble. The colonel took the commissariat officer to the window and showed him the soldiers sweeping the yard. "Look here, sir," he said, "those are the men who fight the Queen's battles. I have to lead them; you have to feed them; but you and I are of no use except in so far as we make these men more efficient than they would otherwise be; and so I am afraid both your convenience and mine must give way to theirs." Soldiers cannot fight without being led and without being fed; workmen cannot produce anything without both capital and organization; but the organization ought to be thoroughly loyal and sympathetic. My own impression is that, if employers will do what they can towards meeting the men on a friendly footing, they will find the men fully prepared to meet them half-way; but they should never drive hard bargains, and should always treat the men with sympathy.

BIBLIOGRAPHY

*List of further papers not included
in this volume.*

1866. On the indigenous Mammalia of the British Islands.
(*unprinted*)
1874. Charity organization. (*unprinted*)
1874. Self-help and Poor Relief. (*unprinted*)
1877. The legislative aspect of the Temperance question. Read
at Church Temperance Congress, Newcastle (printed at
Daily Journal Office, Newcastle; reprinted 1878 at
County Prison Press, Gloucester).
1883. The attitude of the Church with reference to infidelity.
Read at Newcastle Diocesan Church Conference.
(*unprinted*)
1884. The Rights of Property. Read at Church Institute, Newcastle. (*printed*)
1885. Church Defence, the duty of Churchmen at the present
time. Read at Newcastle Diocesan Conference. (*printed*)
1885. Work of the Bishop of Newcastle's fund. (*unprinted*)
1886. Presidential address to Y.M.C.A. (printed by A. Dickson,
High Bridge, Newcastle).
1886. Outdoor Relief. Read at Gilsland Poor Law Conference
(printed by A. Dickson, High Bridge, Newcastle).
1889. Apprenticeship in Engineering and Shipbuilding trades.
Read to British Association. (*printed*)
1889. The Crimean War. (*unprinted*)
1890. Duty of the clergy in strikes and labour-questions.
(*unprinted*)
1891. Productive Co-operation as applied to local industries.
Read at Auckland Castle Conference (printed for private
circulation).
1894. The fight for profits (printed in *Newcastle Daily Leader*).
1897. The Engineering Dispute. Presidential address to Economic
Society, Newcastle. (*unprinted*)

1898. Our foreign and colonial policy. Read to St. Philip's Debating Society, Newcastle. (*unprinted*)

1899. Three papers on Standardization (published in *The Engineering Magazine*).

1900. Notes on result of the Eight-hours' Strike. (*unfinished and unprinted*)

1906. Christian politics. (*unprinted*)

1907. The regulation of output (printed in *The Shipbuilder*).

1908. The question of unemployment (printed in *The Iron and Steel Times*).

1909. Capital and Labour (printed in *The Iron and Steel Times*).

1909. The cause of unemployment (printed in *Newcastle Daily Journal*).

1913. Letter on the finances of Benwell Parish. (*unprinted*)

1913. The Employer and the Employed. (*incomplete, unprinted*)

1913. Labour disputes in the Engineering trades on the North-East Coast. (*unprinted*)

1914. History of R. and W. Hawthorn's from 1870 to 1885 (printed by B. Robinson and Co., Clavering Place, Newcastle).

1915. Output of war-work (printed in the *Times*).

1915. Profits in war-time (printed in *Co-partnership*).

1915. Early development of marine Engineering on the Tyne and elsewhere (printed in *Syren and Shipping*).

1916. The relations between Capital and Labour; the standpoint of Capital (published in *After-war Problems* by Geo. Allen and Unwin, Ltd., Ruskin House, Museum St., W.C., June 1917).

INDEX

Index 285

Index
287

For EU product safety concerns, contact us at Calle de José Abascal, 56–1°, 28003 Madrid, Spain or eugpsr@cambridge.org.

www.ingramcontent.com/pod-product-compliance
Ingram Content Group UK Ltd.
Pitfield, Milton Keynes, MK11 3LW, UK
UKHW012329130625
459647UK00009B/171